S0-AXQ-894

WHY I FIGHT

WHY I FIGHT

THE BELT IS JUST AN ACCESSORY

BJ PENN

WITH DAVID WEINTRAUB

*it*books

AN IMPRINT OF HARPERCOLLINS PUBLISHERS

*it*books

A hardcover edition of this book was published in 2010 by William Morrow, an imprint of HarperCollins Publishers.

WHY I FIGHT. Copyright © 2010 by B.J. Penn. All rights reserved. Printed in the United States of America. No part of this book may be used or reproduced in any manner whatsoever without written permission except in the case of brief quotations embodied in critical articles and reviews. For information address HarperCollins Publishers, 10 East 53rd Street, New York, NY 10022.

HarperCollins books may be purchased for educational, business, or sales promotional use. For information please write: Special Markets Department, HarperCollins Publishers, 10 East 53rd Street, New York, NY 10022.

FIRST IT BOOKS PAPERBACK PUBLISHED 2011.

Designed by Jamie Kerner

Library of Congress Cataloging-in-Publication Data has been applied for.

ISBN 978-0-06-180366-6

11 12 13 14 15   OV/RRD   10 9 8 7 6 5 4 3 2 1

I dedicate my book to my daughter,

to my family,

and to the future of MMA

CONTENTS

PREFACE

THINKING BACK TEN YEARS AGO, if someone told me I was going to write a book about myself, I could think of a handful of people who would read it, and all of them would probably have the name Penn. In fact, I don't even really know if they would read it, let alone a lot of people I don't know! I would bet my mom would, but I am not sure how much I would wager. Even recently, when I was first approached about writing a book, it was not something I was overly excited about. A TV show? Yeah, sure, that's easy. They just point the camera at you, then you kind of do your thing, whatever that thing is. A magazine article? That can be done in one day, maybe with a flight. A book written by someone else, about me, taking guesses about who I am? That would probably leave me with another fight on my hands. A book about fighting? Easy. But to write a book about me, by me, to talk about my life? I have to be honest and say I was not that excited.

Then I sat back and realized that if only one person I do not know actually picks this book up and decides to read it, that is such a huge compliment, I cannot even explain. So while I write this book, assuming people are going to read it, if only one person I do not know chooses to, that makes me really happy. I want to say thank you to that person, and any person who has taken enough interest in me to allow me to have the time in my life to actually do this. Even if you decide to read it because you do not like me, you too have taken enough interest in me, which has given me so much in return.

I never ever thought I would be in this position in my life, and here I am. I am responsible for things, and to other people, and to places I never even considered, or ever thought about. For a kid from Hawaii, all of what has happened to me means a lot more than you could possibly realize.

ACKNOWLEDGMENTS

BJ Penn

I dedicate this page to those who had a profound impact on my life and who enabled me to be the person I am today and will be tomorrow:

The most obvious, to my parents who gave me life, inspiration, and the opportunity to be who I am. They taught me the virtues of love, family, and friendship, and how to pursue my dreams without fear and how to overcome it.

To my brothers and my sisters for their support, and especially my brothers Jay Dee and Reagan who are by my side at all times as my sparring partners, teaching me my next move before I submit them. They have been and are my right and left hands, whom I thank and dedicate my life to.

To Tom Callos who had a vision as to who I could become and ran with it; and to the Gracies who created modern BJJ and with whom I began my studies as a BJJ practitioner.

To all my teachers and training partners from the beginning to the present who most notably include Andre Pederneiras, Charuto Verissimo, Dave Camarillo, Jason Parillo, the Marinovich team, and Rudy Valentino.

To my legal team and close friends Gary Levitt and Raffi

Nahabedian who look at everything I do to make sure I should do it (even if my dad disagrees with them). And, no matter when I call, they are always there with answers and solutions, and ready to take on anyone—even the UFC.

To Pat Tenore, the RVCA team, and all my sponsors who have supported me over the years and will into the future.

To the Fertittas and Dana White for their vision, dedication, and commitment to the sport of Mixed Martial Arts and the advancement of its cause.

To David Weintraub who had the tolerance to write the book and did a fantastic job (although I did want to choke him out on a few occasions).

To all the men and women in the Armed Forces and their families who sacrifice so much to provide us with the life we live.

To Shea who has been understanding of my demanding schedule and our daughter, Aeva Lili'u, who has given me a greater purpose in my life, a purpose greater than my own.

And, finally, to my fans and the fans of MMA throughout the world, without whom I would still be wondering *Why I Fight!*

David Weintraub

I'd like to thank my parents, Martin and Linda, for their continued love and support, as well as my sisters, Jennifer and Michelle, and Michelle's husband, Sheldon, who have always been there for me. My niece, Drew, and nephew, Jack, who make me realize what's really important. Aunt Rosanna and Uncle Al who told me "you can do it!" P.M. "Pat" Tenore, Pat Towersey, and everyone at RVCA for making my time spent there so enjoyable. Janet Keating and her children for providing me with a place to do so much of my work. The people who were involved at HarperCollins, namely Matt Harper and Adam Korn, for their pateince and guidance. The Penn family for being gracious hosts while I was in Hilo. Jeff

Gonyo, Charles Sorrentino, Spencer Parker, Steve Leavy, Chris Mazzuchetti, Russ Goldstein, and Dan Haklim for being great friends. Brian Davidson for getting me involved in any of this in the first place (and putting up with me). BJ Penn for being a good, willing, and honest person. Everyone who has known BJ and has contributed to this book in any way. And Erin Ness who was loving, caring, patient, sturdy, and steady throughout this entire process, which was probably harder on her than it was on me, or anyone else. Again, thank you.

WHY I FIGHT

THE FIRST PART

MY NAME IS JAY DEE PENN, but most people know me by my family-given nickname of "BJ," or BJ Penn. It stands for "Baby Jay," as in "Baby Jay Dee Penn." The reason they call me BJ instead of, say, Junior, Trey, the second, or the third is that there are more Jay Dee Penns than just me. There's my father, and a brother, another brother, and now a nephew—who all have the same given legal name: Jay Dee. It might get confusing to some, but it's pretty straightforward for those who know us.

Some people say having so many Jay Dees in a family could possibly take away from our individual identities. I disagree. In fact, I look at it from the opposite view, in that having the same name, or just being a Penn, means we all have something we must strive to uphold. For one of us to tarnish or trash the name would make us all look bad. In a family like mine, that's a risky thing, tarnishing the name. But if you did this, whether by mistake or intention, the first people to help and support you would be those whose name you tarnished. It binds us together, and in a way that ensures each of us that the other will work hard to do great things, not just for themselves, but on behalf of everyone in our family. For what happens to one Penn happens to us all, and while it may not be perfect for everyone in the world, it's what makes us who we are.

This is true whether the name is Jay Dee Penn or something else Penn. In total, my parents ended up having six children, five of them boys. I have other siblings, like my little brother Reagan, who is littler only in age. My three oldest half siblings are my brother Kalani from my mom's first marriage, and my brother Jay and sister, Christina, from my dad's first marriage. At the end of the day, we all tend to look after each other simultaneously. My parents have given us the ability to be on our own, think on our own, act on our own, but also made us responsible to everyone else.

Ultimately I am just one of many "Jay Dee Penns." It's the name BJ Penn that has come to represent everything about the world I was born into and the choices I have made.

I WAS BORN IN HONOLULU, OAHU, Hawaii, on December 13, 1978, to my parents, Jay Dee Penn and Loraine Shin, who to this day remain together nearly every waking minute. According to my parents, I was not a difficult baby once I entered the world. Getting there was slightly more of a problem, at least it was for my mom. While eight pounds and two ounces does not compare with my nephew LJ, who came in at nearly ten pounds, my birth was difficult for my mother. As the doctors and my mom were bringing me into the world, my umbilical cord was wrapped around my neck, choking me. My mom had to stop pushing so the doctors could make sure I arrived healthy. Once she started pushing again and they finally got me out, my face was all bruised up. From the beginning, I guess I was making my mom nervous with my chokes, bumps, and bruises.

My parents met when they were both pretty young, but by the standards of their time, I guess it was normal. My mother was twenty-two, of Korean and Hawaiian descent, and was born and raised in Hawaii. My father, twenty-three, of Irish roots. He was a guy from Kansas who had left home at a young age, only to join the military and eventually find himself in Hawaii. Not exactly two people from the same place, but in many ways of the same mind, which was what mattered most.

Oddly enough, what brought my dad to Hawaii was not the military, but a visit to a friend of his who was living there. His buddy told him how beautiful it was, and that he had to come see it for himself, but by the time my father arrived, his friend was nowhere to be found. I guess in a time of no cell phones, and when you're a few thousands miles from the mainland, if someone doesn't show up where they're supposed to be, you just have to make do. And my father definitely did that. He ended up living on the beach in Waianae and hitchhiking to town to find work. As one of the few haoles living on the beach in Waianae, he encountered racism from the locals and had many fistfights during those early days.

My dad was always one to make do with what he was given. He had a very difficult childhood, and most everything he did as a youth, he did alone. Throughout my life he has been very reluctant to discuss his upbringing, and given the way he is, I've always known it best not to dig for answers. What I do know is that he grew up without the type of love and support he has given us, and for much of his life he was left to take care of himself. At the age of thirteen, Pop, as we call him, was already working hard. He sold newspapers to people in Kansas, made candles to be sold on holidays like Christmas, cleaned people's yards, and worked as a laborer on farms in the Midwest. Eventually the military helped him see the world a bit more than he had the means to do.

My mother also worked very hard—only instead of Kansas, she was on the island of Oahu. Her family owned one of the first businesses to sell fresh flower leis on the Royal Hawaiian Hotel grounds. Leis, you may or may not know, are fresh flowers strung together like long necklaces that people wear around their necks when they are welcomed to Hawaii, and since the early 1900s my mother's family sold them—from her grandma to her mother all the way down to her and her six sisters. To this day, one of her family members operates the lei stand my mother worked at for many years.

When they first met, my father was the branch manager of an outlet in Waikiki selling and renting motorcycles. My mother was in between jobs and applied for a cashier position. My dad hired her immediately. How he convinced my mom that he was a real catch is still a mystery. I guess that's the benefit of being young and in love. I can only imagine how taken my dad was with my mother when they met because he still treats her today as if they were on a honeymoon.

My parents didn't have much money when they met, but they had the dream and vision to be young entrepreneurs. They worked hard buying and managing several different businesses, from a restaurant to a health food store to service stations and real estate, among other things. My parents were determined to build a solid foundation for our family and to prepare us the best way they could to work together as a family.

On the day I was born, my parents brought me home to a three-bedroom house in Kailua, Oahu, with a separate little cottage and a swimming pool in the back. The house was located on the eastern side of the island, about forty minutes from Pearl Harbor, though I was so young when I was living there that I don't remember much about it. From early on, I was pretty active and alert. I began walking by the time I was eight months old and used to go everywhere that I could. That got trickier when I was two and my brother Reagan Keone Penn was born, but no matter what was going on with my other siblings, my parents always encouraged me to be energetic.

Though my parents were devoted to us, the endless routine they needed to keep up so they could provide for the family came with a price. I didn't recognize it much as a kid, but my parents were working and looking for opportunities to make money and build a successful future for our family. My mom enrolled in the University of Hawaii for five straight years to obtain her BBA degree. They found a babysitter for Reagan, Jay Dee, and me, one who was willing to watch over us when they could not, and he became like a third parent. His name was Emmanuel Chen, but we called him Uncle Manny. He was Jay Dee's kindergarten teacher, and Jay Dee was very fond of him. My parents could see how much Jay Dee liked him, so they asked him if he would be willing to babysit when they were working, going to school, or out of town.

At first Uncle Manny watched us once or twice a week, but more and more my parents found themselves out of town, especially Pop, who was often away for long stretches working on business deals over on the Big Island. We spent most weekends at Manny's house, which was not so bad since he had a pool, but at the same time he was something of a hard-ass, always whipping us into shape. Whether it was about how we acted at the dinner table or out in public, we had to be on our best behavior. He would demand that we eat our food over our plates, and not chew with our mouths open. When it came to manners and respect, Manny required us to be at our best all the time. In a lot of ways, my parents were lucky to have found him, because he didn't see his job as simply a paycheck. He cared about what we did and believed how we acted was a reflection of how well he was doing his job. Manny treated the three of us like we were his own.

OUR CONNECTION TO MANNY WENT ON for some time, even after my parents decided to move the whole lot of us to Hilo, Hawaii, in August of 1983, when I was four. In a lot of ways this move marked the beginning of my life, since my first real vivid memories go back to this new house in Hilo, a house that my parents live in to this day.

The house sits high up on a beautiful piece of land on the corner of two streets just above Highway 1, the road that circles all of the Big Island. From the back, you can see the ocean, and the property is surrounded by trees. But back when we moved in, it was in a much sorrier state. The large Victorian-style house with its veranda overlooking the bay was built in the early 1900s. Much of it was run-down and not in livable shape. It was a house that made creaking noises and needed a lot of work. I later learned before we took the place over, it was known around Wainaku as a party house. Wainaku is the side of town I live on, just over one of the rivers that come down from the mountains. And a party, you know what that is. So this was the party house of Wainaku back in the day. It was now home to the Penns.

My parents approached the house as they did most everything else, seeing it for what it could be not for what it was; however, until their vision could become reality we all had to make sacrifices. They continued to travel frequently, and they even flew Uncle Manny over from Oahu to watch us on the weekends. Even though the new house in Hilo was big, the entire family lived in the one main living room, which had damaged hardwood floors and walls and ceilings that were falling apart. Hawaii was probably one of the only places in the world where we could have lived comfortably in a house that was so messed up. Although it does rain in Hilo, thankfully it was summertime when we first arrived, and the weather was not a real problem.

For a while it was pretty much all of us crowded on top of each other whenever we went to sleep. While this was difficult on my parents, it brought us together and gave us a closeness that most families didn't have. When you're forced to live a certain way, your tolerance for dealing with certain things, like sleeping right next to all your brothers every night, grows. Though the situation was not ideal, it was a fun way for a little kid to live. After all, being four and having sleepovers with your family every night is probably the most fun a kid can have. It really defines what it means to grow up together. At the time it was both my parents, Jay, Jay Dee, Reagan, and me. My half siblings, Kalani and Christina, were older, but they were around a lot of the times as well.

But it wasn't just the inside of the house which needed work. The place was a disaster in every sense of the word. There were four acres of land around the house, and a decent amount of trash, broken glass, and other things that had to be removed. Not exactly the best of playgrounds. Luckily, my dad, with his carpenter background and building experience, knew what he was doing.

Over the years it slowly went from being a place with broken glass everywhere to one covered with beautiful windows. What was once a ramshackle collection of rooms became an actual home— an inviting place where my family could spend time together and others could spend time with us too.

Because my family was always very welcoming, having a home with a warm atmosphere was important. The doors to our home were never locked, which was probably an indication of what was to come. To this day there always seems to be someone there— maybe hanging out for a day, visiting for a week, or living there for longer—you never know with us. While it is not the party house it once was, the invitation to come visit and stay with us has always been open.

The house became a playground for my brothers and me. We would spend hours playing there. One of the coolest things about the house was the secret passages you could enter through the closets; these extended around the attic and allowed us to sneak into other rooms. Jay Dee was certainly on the receiving end of this since we were small enough to crawl through them, and mischievous enough to bother him whenever we could.

By the time the house was completed, there were three rooms upstairs where my family slept. Reagan and I lived together in one small room, while Jay Dee had a gigantic room, which was about twice the size of ours all to himself. Reagan and I shared that room for a long time, and it's one of the main reasons we are so close today. Because I was his big brother, Reagan put a lot of trust in me—almost too much. One time we were playing in our room, and we decided to lock Reagan in the suitcase and have me pick the lock. At that time Reagan loved to play lock doctor and had several different small pick-lock sets that he practiced with. So that's what we did: Reagan got into the case, and once in there I closed it up and locked it. Once he was inside, I proceeded to unlock the lock with Reagan's pick-lock set. The only problem was I got nervous and couldn't open the lock, and had no way to get him out. I remember sitting there on the floor, Reagan couldn't have been more than four or five years old, and I was trying so hard to pick the lock with my hands. I was yanking on all sides of it, pulling at the fabric, picking at the lock, but I just could not get it to budge. This was probably the most stressed I had been up until this point of my life. I mean, what does a little kid really have to be stressed about? Suffocating your little brother—that would definitely count.

There was this tiny little hole he could barely see out of, and he was looking at me, instructing me how to pick the lock and saying "You can do it, BJ. I know you can do it . . ." Meanwhile, I was really nervous. What if I couldn't do it? What if I couldn't save my own little brother, my best friend? What would everyone think? I was working so hard with this little piece of metal to pick the lock, but I could not do it. It was so hot out, and it had to be so much hotter inside that case.

At some point my mom heard us struggling in the room, and she came in to see what was going on. I had not seen her walk in. For all I knew we were totally alone, trapped in this situation. She ran downstairs to get a knife so she could just cut away the fabric, sacrificing the bag to save her youngest son. By the time my mom returned with the knife, Reagan had emerged from the suitcase, soaking wet with sweat. After all that, I had picked the lock open with a piece of metal. He wrapped his arms around me and said, "I knew you could do it! I knew you would get me out!" Whether it's because of what happened to Reagan or something else, to this day I still do not like being stuck in tight places. To illustrate that point, more recently at a UFC event in Minnesota in August of 2008, I was stuck for hours in an elevator with Reagan and a man named Burt Watson. I remained as calm as I could, we all did, but heard later on that Watson was as worried about the situation as I was. I have never really liked elevators in the first place because of that feeling that someone else is controlling you. There we were, somehow we were trapped in an elevator that only had to travel two floors. There were guys like Cheick Kongo who were trying to pull the doors open, but even he could not budge them. I found myself thinking about Reagan getting trapped in the suitcase and my furious struggle to get him out, yet Reagan was next to me, calmer than everyone. Maybe it's because he had faith that someone would free us, and as it turned out he was right—only this time, instead of me it was the local fire department.

I guess it's ironic that I would become someone who makes his living trying to trap people in positions they cannot escape from.

ONE OF THE THINGS ABOUT ME which has not changed since I was little is my ability to keep secrets, at least those that really matter. I can keep a secret of importance or those in which someone would be harmed if I told others, but little things, I do not keep those well. It is probably a good idea not to tell me what you bought your girlfriend for Valentine's Day, that you think a certain girl is really cute, or that you think someone is a jerk and you want to kick his ass. One of the things most everyone who knows me well is aware of is I am not very good at keeping my mouth shut, especially if I think it will make me laugh, or if I am already worked up.

Ever since I was a little kid, I have had this problem, if you want to call it a problem. I don't know if it's because I like to be the first to say something, or because I am just not scared to speak my mind, but I usually just shoot straight from the hip. I have always been in favor of having everything on the table. Whether this is something that developed because I had a big mouth as a little kid, or because as I got older I began to hate not hearing the truth, I don't know. I guess I like creating tension. Whatever the reason, it just is.

One of the stories people in my family like to tell about me is about Pop's birthday, when I was just four years old. My family had bought him a pair of gloves as a gift, and even though I was so young, I had found out. We were still in the old house, and everyone was waiting for my dad to come home from wherever he had been. I am sure he was working on something. My uncle and other people from the family were all there waiting for him. As soon as he walked through the door, the first thing I did was jump right up to tell him what we got him. My uncle was fast enough to cover my mouth to stop me.

Later on that day, after being told not to say anything by everyone in my family, I waited to make sure no one was around. When my father was alone I whispered in his ear, "We got you gloves," and spoiled it for everyone.

To this day even my best friends say that I'm incapable of keeping secrets, so I guess I've always tended to say things out loud. I do not do it to be mean, but I just cannot keep some things inside me. Friends have told me they think secrets just eat at me. Most of my friends have just taken to not telling me things they don't want others knowing. In a lot of ways it is a joke among my friends and family, but I would still like to think they all know I am someone they can trust.

But it's not only the secrets of others I cannot hold inside, it's my own as well. If I have something on my mind I have to let it out. I am always looking for answers, reasons, reactions, something, anything, to explain why I do things, why others do things. I like seeing how others respond when they find something out they did not know. It's my own experiment I am conducting on everyone around me.

LIKE A LOT OF OTHER KIDS my age around the world, I played a lot of soccer when I was younger. Soccer, soccer, soccer. From the age when I was first able to focus on sports of any kind, I wanted to be the best soccer player possible. I had dreams of being a professional. The most important soccer team in Hilo was the high school team, and from the time when I first started playing, I knew I would be on that team.

When I was five years old I already had a ball at my feet, and according to my parents, I knew what to do with it. I understood the rules, how to control the ball, and how to use my little body to keep it away from other people. We used to play soccer in the neighborhood, but mostly we practiced down in the town of Hilo, across the street from the ocean near Highway 1. In the middle of town there were a bunch of fields where all the teams would practice and play. Early on in my life that was probably my favorite place to be, on the soccer field. By the time I was eight years old I was considered to be pretty good among the kids I played with, and in 1987, my team became the first from Hilo to win the state championship.

I continued playing soccer through my younger years, dreaming of the day when I would be a part of the Hilo High School team. I made all the select teams and the all star teams in the area: soccer was my life. I was not a wrestler, I was not into karate, or judo, or anything physical like that at all, but at that time those sports were big and getting bigger in Hawaii because of the state's high population of Asians, particularly Japanese. Though my dad had been practicing for quite some time, it had not even crossed my mind that martial arts was a possibility. Soccer was what mattered to me, and I would keep on playing it forever. But oddly enough, it was soccer that led me into the first fight that had any real effect on my life in my years before high school.

My soccer coach was a good guy, and he used to have the whole team over to his house for different reasons. Sometimes it was to show us practice stuff, and other times it was so all of us could eat together, but whatever the reason, it was a place where we all gathered from time to time. I was fourteen. On one occasion when he was off the island, he let one of his soccer assistants who was eighteen, a responsible teenager that he and other people on the team knew, have access to his house. She decided to make us all dinner, and a lot of my friends went over there. Her meal was amazing. It was shrimp fettuccine Alfredo, a dish that single-handedly taught me just how good food could be. However, even more vivid than dinner was what took place after.

We finished our food and we were feeling totally free from parental control, just hanging around outside the coach's house. There was a guy who lived close by to the coach who was a bit of a loudmouth, probably around twenty years old, and on that evening, I had words with him in the street. He had a big mouth, and I had a knack for getting into it with anyone who had a big mouth, and regardless of the fact that he was older and bigger, I did not back down. We ended up fighting right in front of my coach's house, where I sort of got my butt kicked. During the fight I ripped the skin off of my heel completely, to the point where all you could see was flesh and blood. When I got home that night Uncle Manny was at my house, and he helped me nurse my foot back to good health. As it turned out, my foot was the least of my problems.

Back in the States an incident like this would probably just be chalked up as a fight in the neighborhood between young teenagers, but to Hawaiians, and more specifically, to my coach, I had done something very bad. I had made his home an embarrassment.

The fact that I got into a fight and made trouble at his house when he was not there meant that he could not trust me. The people in the neighborhood found out what happened and who did it, and this led to me having a falling-out with him. Even if the kid was a loudmouth who deserved it, I had disrespected another person's home. For me, I was just a kid, getting into a fight, shutting someone up. Well, this little fight ended up being the beginning of the end of my soccer career.

Complicating matters was the fact that my coach was also my history teacher, a man I had to see every day in high school, a man who knew me as a student. Growing up, I did not love school, but I had liked history more than most other subjects, and now I had a problem with my teacher. When I was a successful soccer player, whose biggest problem for my coach was messing with the refs, he could handle that. By fighting with someone outside his house, I had crossed a line. It made for an awkward relationship, and in a lot of ways, it was the end of soccer for me. I didn't play much after that fight.

Truth is, though, while I did love to play soccer, the rift with my coach was only one of many things that had been leading me away from the game. As a kid, the sport had always come quite naturally to me, but when I got older, the things you had to do in order to be on the team changed. Less and less we practiced the game, and more often we ended up just running endlessly through Hilo to the top of the river where this radio tower stood. It really soured me on the sport.

Ultimately, whether it was the running, the fight, or both, the result was that my soccer career was officially over.

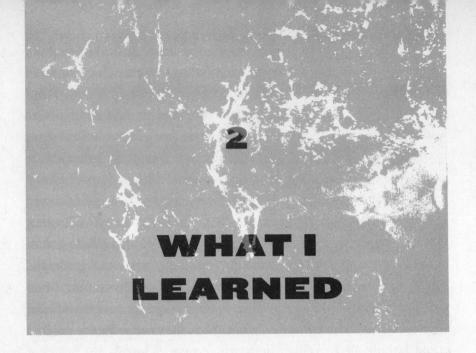

2

WHAT I LEARNED

DID NOT PLAN TO BE A FIGHTER; one thing just happened after another. Before I knew it I was standing behind a curtain waiting to walk out to fight Joey Gilbert. Maybe I made some questionable decisions before I arrived at that point, but I also made a lot of good ones.

With soccer, as well as the desire to be on the high school team, in the rearview mirror, I started living a different life. Since I was not going to be spending my days at the downtown soccer fields, I needed a new way to pass the time. Like most kids, I was a bit out of control, always looking for a good time and something adventurous. While I am not sure how they came into my possession, I ended up with some boxing gloves, and started using them all the time.

Fighting is something Hawaiians take to very easily, and at the time a lot of people were into the martial arts of one kind or another. While it is hard to say where the strongest people in the world live, it is often said the Hawaiian people, mainly Polynesians, are the strongest because they have so much muscle mass. If you walk around Hawaii and take a look at the people who are native, you will often see a number of very large people, with tree trunks for legs. Given the strength and size of many Hawaiians and the fact that we like to fight, or at least watch fights, you have as good a chance of becoming a fighter here as you would anywhere else in the States.

Right down the street from my parents' was the Hilo Armory, literally a quarter mile from my house. Today it is used for basketball, volleyball, and other events, but when I was a kid there were always fights going on in there. You could walk by on a Friday night in the 1980s and 1990s and see amateur boxing, kickboxing, and other types of events going on. I was not the kind of kid who grew up in the gym watching these guys all of the time, but I definitely knew it was happening, and that it got the locals excited.

I had a good number of scraps growing up, probably more than most people, so I knew fighting did not bother me. But I was not fearless when it came to fighting. When I first got hold of those boxing gloves, I would lace them up with some friends, and we would go at it. At first I was really timid about being hit, which is pretty natural since no one really likes to be hit, even professional fighters (not surprisingly we do a lot of training to avoid it). Like everyone else I worried about whether or not I was going to be hurt. I had no idea what my threshold for pain was like, or whether it would develop. I just knew being hit was not nearly as much fun as hitting someone.

Since I had brothers, especially an older, much bigger brother like Jay Dee, this boxing with friends was not the first time I'd been hit. It's pretty natural for most brothers to mess around, and we did just like everyone else. But boxing was different. Getting these gloves was not just fighting with your brother or wrestling with a friend, but a new sport altogether. I was taken by the fun of it pretty quickly without even realizing it was a sport. For me it was a fun activity.

One day I just walked into town with some friends and for whatever reason I decided to get myself some new boxing gloves. We brought them back to my house, and that's kind of when the real fighting began. Once I started sparring with friends in the neighborhood, I got over being timid quickly. I realized right away it was easy to take the punches, especially with the sixteen-ounce gloves we were wearing. After I'd gotten over my fear of getting hit, all I thought to myself was, *If someone hits you all you have to do is hit them back harder. Eventually they will fold, right?* That was basically my motto when it came to boxing, one that still holds up today: Cause more pain for the other person, and you'll win.

When we first got hold of boxing gloves, my friends and I just messed around with them around the house—nothing too serious since we didn't want to hurt each other. Then the whole idea of boxing as a daily activity started to take over, and we began to have all these kids from the neighborhood coming over to fight at our house. The house had a large wraparound porch and a veranda, where my parents' dining room table sits today. The wraparound made for a good corner, so we removed the patio furniture and closed off the two open sides, which created an area for us to fight in. It was like having our own little boxing ring. All the other kids who came over to box would be part of the ring, so you could make sure no one fell off the porch or over the edge of the railing. Though the drop is only like eight feet, that would have been a problem because it was eight feet onto cement.

On my parents' front porch, we taught each other how to box. None of us had any real formal training. Some of the kids wrestled and others had practiced some martial arts, but this was just a straight-up scrap. If someone did something interesting, you could pick up on it by watching, but there was no real teaching going on. There were big guys, small guys, fat, strong, skinny, short, tall—

every type of kid who was willing to fight was more than welcome to come over to the house, and they did. Fifteen to twenty guys would come on some days, maybe eight on another, but there were always people willing to scrap. In fact, one of my best friends from then (and still today), Saul, likes to tell people the only reason I went to school was to find more kids to bring over and fight. Right there on the porch, rain or shine, we had a covered area where we could just unload on each other. From when I was about fourteen until I was sixteen, we did this every day that we could. More and more kids from the neighborhood and surrounding Hilo would find themselves at my house boxing all the time.

After a while I didn't feel like I could be hurt with the gloves on, which made me more than willing to take a punch if it meant I had the chance to deliver one. There were times I'd get caught, but it didn't happen often. On the whole, I had a good ability to avoid punches compared to the guys I was fighting with. Still, boxing really toughened me up, and my friends Saul and Ipo, both pretty big, tough guys, played a large part in making me what I am now. If those guys hadn't beaten on me, who knows if I ever would have enjoyed striking or gotten comfortable taking a punch. Overcoming that timidity and the fear of getting hit when you are younger plays a big part in whether you will want to do it when you are older.

I never really had a hard time finding partners either. One of the reasons my friends took such pleasure in sparring with me has a lot to do with the games I used to play with them. I am definitely an instigator when it comes to messing around and having fun at the expense of others. My brothers are the same way, and I think my dad might be a bit of an instigator too, except he is a lot more direct about things, whereas my brothers and I like to play tricks on people. Saul and Ipo made for perfect targets.

When they came over the house to fight, I had a few kinds of gloves we would use. There were three sets, two sixteen-ounce gloves and one twelve-ounce set. When you train, or practice, usually people will use fourteen- to sixteen-ounce gloves. Professional boxers will use gloves between ten and twelve ounces. A standard MMA glove, like the ones the UFC, Pride, and others use is about five ounces. In other words, while the difference between sixteen-ounce and twelve-ounce gloves seems minimal, when you are punching someone, or getting punched, those four ounces makes all the difference in the world, and I made sure of it.

Saul was pretty easy to set off. If he was over watching TV or playing video games, I could usually get him going by throwing the larger gloves at his big head. Usually he would try to ignore me, and could brush me off for a few seconds, but after me hitting him in the head and face with the glove for a while, he would give in. If that did not work, I could call him "Saul Worst-and-Last" or "Last-and-Worthless," playing off his last name, Furstenwerth. Whatever I did, my plan was always to bother my friends long enough, leaving them with the larger sixteen-ouce gloves. Eventually they would chase after me, and I would grab the twelve-ounce gloves, which I had hidden somewhere else. Once they caught up to me, we would square off, and I started firing back. By this time it was too late. They would hit me with the big gloves, and I would just unload on them with the twelves. It is what you might call a dick move, but as I said, these guys were tough, so they got their shots in too. I was not exactly huge, but those smaller gloves could really make up the difference, especially if you landed one good punch, which I often did.

Of course, they got their revenge on me in other ways. My parents did not care too much about fighting, especially my dad. What he cared about was my grades. One day the guys were over the house, and report cards had just been issued. I tried to pull that move where you tell your parents bad news while your friends are over so that they will be less likely to yell at you or give you a hard time. Not my dad. Once he found out about my grades, he actually told Saul and Ipo to beat the crap out of me, so the two of them did just that. Since Saul and Ipo were bigger, they could use their size to hold me down and control me. Both of them started whaling on me with the gloves, taking turns, hitting me as hard as they could, back and forth, with my dad's blessing. Here I was using them as protection, and then my dad turned it around by using them as enforcers.

All in all, it was just a bunch of kids being kids. Occasionally someone got knocked out, maybe a black eye, or a busted-up nose, but there was no real damage to speak of. No one ever sustained life-threatening injuries or anything even close. We did not need an ambulance nearby, or make many trips to the hospital. Boxing was just a way to sharpen your hand skill and toughen yourself up because in Hawaii, especially Hilo, you are probably going to need to do this.

If you did not learn to fight in Hilo, you were going to have some real problems on your way up. Maybe you were the one guy who everyone liked that no one wanted to fight, but at some point even you would have a problem to deal with. Hilo's just too small a place to avoid physical confrontation. Even if you are just driving your car, and someone cuts you off, you know you are always going to see that person again. In fact, chances are you will see that guy tomorrow going down the same road. In Hilo, if you cross someone's path at the wrong place, and wrong time, you will cross paths again, so you better be prepared. Working out, boxing on the front porch—it all definitely helped me deal with being in Hilo even if I didn't realize it at the time.

Despite the problems that can arise from living in such a small place, Hawaii is not really about problems: it's about enjoying its natural beauty. While boxing was fun and it kept us occupied, in reality it was just one of many things we did outside. Whether it was surfing or riding bikes, everyone I knew took advantage of Hawaii's landscape in one way or another. In a lot of ways, everything outdoors was our playground. From the top of the Big Island's snow-covered mountain of Mauna Kea, the tallest mountain in the world from the ocean floor, down through the flowing rivers that reach all the way to the ocean in Hilo Bay, we covered all of it. Playing on the rocks, swimming in the rivers, hanging from trees, jumping off eighty-foot waterfalls—bridges, you name it, we did it. You connect with nature when you live here. It is almost impossible not to.

I spent my childhood with friends at all of these places, running down streams, jumping from wet rock to wet rock, knowing that if you fall down you could break your arms, ribs, back, legs, neck, everything. And we did this throughout our lives, climbing up wet trees, which were next to waterfalls. If you slipped when you were twenty to thirty feet up a tree, you could easily land on jagged rocks and kill yourself. If you jumped into a pool and you couldn't see the currents, you could be swept down waterfalls straight into rocks. In fact, Jay Dee nearly lost his life at Boiling Pots waterfalls once when the current swept him up and he went flying down the falls. Luckily he was fast enough, and strong enough, to grab onto the rocks and pull himself back up. I can tell you right now, had it been me, it might've been over. Jay Dee was a strong teenager, and no regular guy would have kept himself from plummeting down. But that's how close it was anytime we went playing there, and we played there daily.

These areas were where I grew up, where my friends and I barbecued, hung out with chicks, tried to hook up, went swimming, smoked pot, drank beer, all on wet, slippery, dangerous rocks—not exactly a great combination, but we'd been doing it so long it was second nature. Jumping off the fifty-, sixty-, seventy-foot waterfalls seemed like the least of our worries. I mean, all you had to do was jump out far enough and chances were you would make it. People have been known to break their legs, tear ACLs (anterior cruciate ligaments), and sustain other injuries from just hitting the water, but we'd been doing it for so long we simply knew how.

Another fun thing we used to do is jump off a sixty-foot bridge called Puueo Bridge, that crossed over from downtown Hilo into my neighborhood in Wainaku. This bridge was really only about thirty feet high, but it goes over the river just as it opens up to the ocean. Today it's mostly a place where people fish, but back when I was growing up, it was another place for us to jump. Once in the water, we would climb back up to the street through the forest along the banks.

It wasn't so much the distance of the jump that made Puueo Bridge scary; it was more that, unlike the waterfalls and cliffs I usually jumped off, the water beneath Puueo was salt. Hilo Bay is known to have more hammerheads than almost any area in the world, and they would often swim right up to the mouth of the river. Many times when we went to the bridge to jump, we'd see fishermen reeling out a hammerhead. This meant that instead of us encountering some harmless freshwater fish at the bottom, we were jumping into an area filled with hammerhead sharks, so once you jumped off the bridge and landed in the water, you would literally swim for your life to the shoreline. Even as I was in the middle of my fall and plunging through the air, I'd be thinking about those sharks.

This is how we passed the time living in Hilo, jumping off bridges, running around dangerous places, and basically just living on the edge all the time. There were people who did all the same things I did but were not as fortunate. People have died or been injured on the rocks by those waterfalls, others have drowned in nearby areas, but I never really got hurt.

It may seem like this was all just a lot of kids being kids, messing around and being reckless. But I truly believe growing up in this environment, spending all that time in very dangerous places, and needing to be constantly aware of my surroundings helped train me to be the athlete I am now. I really developed a sense of balance doing all of these crazy things. When you jump onto a wet rock running almost full speed down the middle of a river, and you slip, you have to be able to control yourself on one foot. Throughout my career of fighting I have been able to maintain near-perfect balance on one leg, and while part of that ability may be genetic, I am pretty sure a lot of it comes from growing up in the natural playground that is Hawaii.

WHILE THERE IS NO DISPUTING HAWAII is a beautiful place, one of the problems of being from there is once you tell people, they make a lot of assumptions about you. A lot of people think they know what Hawaii is, and so they jump to conclusions about your story. Maybe they've been there on vacation, or had a friend who got married there. They figure you grew up on a beach, all you did was surf, and everything was just one big chill time.

In my case, they figure I'm the exception to the rule in Hawaii, a fighter from an island of pacifists. A person who doesn't really know me—someone like Dana White—will say something like, "Yeah, BJ, he grew up in Hawaii, surfing and hangin' out on the beaches all day with his friends," but you don't know how inaccurate that statement really is. What many people don't realize is both the good and the bad parts of Hawaii were the central forces that made me a fighter. The boxing was a big part of what started me on that path, but so was living in Hilo.

When I was growing up in Hilo, there were a lot of shady people roaming around the streets. Literally, right down the street from where I lived, in either direction you could easily find problems for yourself. Like every city in the United States, Hilo had a "wrong side of the tracks," only in Hilo those tracks seemed to run in every direction. There would be a beautiful house up in the hills overlooking sugarcane fields and the ocean, and just a few feet away there were a bunch of vagrants living in a run-down house doing who knows what. The neighborhood itself was not very big, and it was laid out like a small grid, with two streets cutting into three streets. It was so small it didn't take long to go from a good area to a bad one, and avoiding trouble was not always easy. Some kids were always pushing their limits when it came to the bad areas of Hilo and they paid a price for it, but I was not one of them.

One of the worst areas in town was a place called Riverside Apartments, which was at the end of my street across from a park. There were only seven or eight homes immediately around the park, and quite a few of them had questionable people living in them. As if that wasn't enough, there were also the people who lived in the park itself, and seemingly came right out of the trees. Back then Riverside was totally overgrown, with one really big tree in the middle. It had this really old stone pavilion, and this old garage area, all covered with green moss. The entire park was green, with long grass, and trees that hung down everywhere like a set from *Jurassic Park*. As kids we used to call the garage part "The Cave," and the people who hung out inside and around it were "The Cavemen."

The street in front of Riverside was where people sold crack rocks all day and night. Because the weather was always good, nothing ever forced them to go inside. There would be a guy standing on the street, with no shirt on, maybe an old pair of ripped jean shorts, really tanned, with long hair, just relaxing by the park. In case there were any problems, maybe someone didn't want to pay, he would use the lead pipe he carried, or possibly a thick stick, to convince them otherwise. Next thing you know a car would pull up and head over to the guy, or maybe someone on a bike would stop, all looking for the same thing: crack. Meanwhile there would be a group of kids riding by on their bikes and the crack dealer would shoot them a wave and a smile.

Some of the kids got sucked into the Cavemen's world—mostly kids from poorer families who were looking to make some money. They'd start dealing or doing drugs with them, getting mixed up in a situation with no good way out. You had to have the willpower to do the right thing in Hilo. Not everyone makes the right decisions all the time, and not everyone has the support to overcome adversity. Personally I made decisions based on what was right and wrong, and what my parents and family taught me to do. But I can see how other people got caught up in that stuff; after all, these dealers were all over the place. These were guys you did not want to mess with, no matter who you were—real badasses—and the police at the time did nothing about it. There was this one really tough guy who used to sell rocks all day long in the street. He always had nunchucks in his hands, and he knew what to do with them. The second someone screwed him over, he would mess them up with the chucks.

He was one of the Hawaiian people you didn't see in postcards.

The fact that people have been shot at, or that bums suffering from drug addiction were sleeping just a few steps from where I grew up, makes me shake my head when those who do not know a thing about my town, or my life, have something to say about where it is I come from. Sure, some in Hawaii have it better than others, just like anyplace else, and I did not have it too bad, but where I was from was not what people talk about when they discuss Hawaii. It's strange for me because I never hear similar comments about other MMA fighters, how they grew up, unless it was in a country other than the United States. I wonder, were people shot and killed outside in neighborhoods throughout Canada? Were people selling crack rocks on the outskirts of farms throughout the Midwest, protecting themselves with nunchucks? I have no idea, and I'm not suggesting certain fighters had it any better, or worse than the next guy. We all have our own unique experiences in life. All I am saying is life in Hilo was not always pineapples and luaus.

Eventually people in the neighborhood got fed up with the Cavemen and all the bad elements in the area. People from all over Wainaku, including my parents, parents of friends, neighbors, and grandparents, formed little gangs and Neighborhood Watch groups. They started to walk around together to push all of these people away from our streets and out of Riverside. You would literally see grandparents walking around with flashlights, looking for anyone they considered part of the bad element. When they found someone they would threaten to call the police. After a little while the police started doing more to keep the area safe, allowing the parents to clean up the park as well. They cut the grass, knocked down the old pavilion and garage, then put up a fence around the entire thing. It became a different place entirely.

Today there's little about the park I recognize from when I was younger, but in my mind, it still represents all the dangers and bad choices which were once out there. It was a place where I saw people take missteps and pay the price for their decisions. It was a place where I learned everything people did came with a price.

For most of my childhood I attended Haili Christian School in downtown Hilo, just down the street from my house, like most everything else in a small town like mine. My father sent me there because he believed the school would teach me good morals and provide me with a good education. Although it was a religious school, my family was not very religious; it was more for the discipline the school offered, and because it was better academically than the public school. But this school and I never worked out that well together. I left the school for a couple of years, but then returned at the end of the eighth grade to finish up before I went off to Hilo High School. For me, like for so many kids, school was just not a place I liked being at a young age. Whether I was just impatient, or just did not really care that much, it was not on the top of my list of places I wanted to spend time. From an early age I had actually excelled in school, so much so I skipped second grade at Haili Christian; learning was never the problem. I was not a disruptive or difficult child for educators, I just had no real interest.

Since Hilo was not a huge place and I'd played sports with most of the kids, I knew most everyone in the town. High school would be different, though, since with more kids and less scrutiny than a private school, I had more freedom. However, not enjoying school and looking for other things to do became a bit of an ongoing problem. The first was my fighting, which no longer just took place after school. In just a short time at Hilo High School I was kicked out for fighting, and unlike earlier in life, these mistakes mattered and could follow me. Soon afterward, I found myself at St. Joseph's High School, where I had a few more problems as well.

Oddly enough, my dislike of school was definitely different from both of my brothers. Jay Dee was clearly more motivated than I was, and as I was entering high school as a freshman, he was thinking about college as a senior. (Eventually he went off to University of Nevada, Las Vegas, better known as UNLV.) Then there was Reagan, who just got straight A's in almost every subject, and always seemed to do really well even if he was not interested in his classes.

Meanwhile, I was not really sure what I wanted to get out of school. It is not that I couldn't do well, I just did not care to since I did not see the immediate benefits of it. Because I had already given up soccer, there was no real motivation by coaches, or even myself, to maintain good grades in order to be able to play some sport or be involved in an activity. There were my parents, who wanted me to do well, but you could always find the right words to keep your parents off your back when it came to school. I ended up doing just enough to get by, and while my grades were not all that bad, I definitely could have done a lot better.

Instead of school work and soccer, I found other things to do when classes ended. Besides fighting at my house, I spent time with friends looking for fun, and often "fun" meant finding marijuana plants in the sugarcane fields and along the rivers. This was definitely not as productive as playing soccer with the team, but at the time it was a whole lot more enjoyable. People planted marijuana through-out the cane fields, and as soon as the school bell rang at the end of the day, a group of about ten to fifteen of us would head toward my neighborhood and begin looking for it until we had to go home.

Since there was so much of it growing nearly everywhere, my friends and I hardly needed money to buy it, which is a lot different from the experience mainland kids deal with. In most parts of the United States, teenagers who smoke pot probably have to spend a lot of money on it, but the fact that we didn't have to pay for it, the relaxed environment, and the ease with which we obtained it made it so almost everyone I knew smoked. Pot smoking is a lot more accepted now than it was then, but even then we felt what we were doing was not a big deal. We were not doing hard drugs, or selling drugs, but to some people this did not matter. It was no different from anything else deemed illegal.

A couple of those people who did not like marijuana were my parents. It is completely understandable since they do not partake of these types of things at all (only on rare occasions do they drink alcohol). Putting aside the possibly bad health aspects, my parents could not see any benefits from smoking. From their perspective, if I was smoking pot I was probably hanging out with the wrong people. One bad thing could only lead to more bad things, which is the typical mentality of most concerned parents. I could see how that all added up to them, but I myself did not really see it that way.

So what's a high school kid to do with so much free time and an abundance of free marijuana? I can tell you what a high school kid is not supposed to do: smoke pot at school, which is precisely what I did. This was one of those bad choices which likely concerned my mom and dad.

It was probably the stupidest thing I had done in my life until that point, and most likely after as well. In high school, other kids used to smoke cigarettes in the bathroom, but smoking pot in the bathroom was a lot worse. However it happened, some friends and I were in one of the boys' bathrooms getting high. Someone tipped off some of the teachers and they came storming in as we were in the middle of passing a joint around. Kids were in the bathroom all the time, and most of the time got away with doing stupid stuff like this, so it was clear someone had ratted us out. As soon as the first teacher came in, I threw the joint onto the floor, but it was too late. The smell and smoke was in the air, and surely the guilty looks on our faces gave it away. My heart had already stopped beating and dropped into my stomach.

Next thing I knew I was in the principal's office, waiting for my dad to come pick me up. The school had notified him about what happened. In addition to Pop, the police were also notified, so they showed up as well. Not only had I been caught, but everyone in the school and town was going to find out. This was the type of public embarrassment I had always been taught to avoid because I knew I had a name to uphold.

Getting caught was a bad thing, but looking back on it, it was just so incredibly stupid to be doing something so obviously immature, and dangerous, in a school. My friends and I were not thinking about the future, or what this could mean, only about the moment and how much fun it was to be doing something reckless.

After Pop took me home that day, my school life changed drastically. The next time I would go back to St. Joe's was only to visit. From now on I was going to be homeschooled. To Pop, school was a place where I was just wasting my time and learning nothing that would help me in the future. At this point in time the only thing I was doing which didn't bother him was the boxing on the front porch. Pop figured at least that was productive! That was more than he could say about everything else in my life.

So I was sixteen and no longer at St. Joe's. Pop started forcing me to work out every single day; it was all he wanted me to do. In his eyes, the first order of business for me was to rediscover discipline. I had been destroying my body by smoking pot and drinking beer. Working out was his temporary solution to help me regain structure. This lasted for a while, as Pop worked me pretty hard—pushing me to walk and run on a treadmill for hours.

The ironic thing was I never wanted to go to school until I couldn't. Aside from the classes, I really missed just talking to my friends on a daily basis. I was fifteen years old when I left, and that's a pretty important year socially, so that certainly bothered me. Any way I looked at it, I was going to have to complete the part of school I did not like, that being the work itself, so only the fun part was removed.

My new life consisted of being alone and physical training. While the workouts seemed like a strange way to punish a kid, for Pop it was not really about punishment. He was truly concerned about my physical well-being, and whether or not I had harmed my body. All he wanted was for me to be healthy, and moving my life in a positive direction. In his experience, the best way to achieve this was for me to establish a new routine. It was unorthodox, but it was logical. The only problem with all this working out was I fell even further behind in school, causing the whole thing to snowball. Since I had already been having problems with my schoolwork, it seemed as if I would never catch up to my classmates. In fact, for a while I believed I would never graduate. At this time of my life when things went bad I did not dig in, work, and overcome. I tended to blow them off, which was creating the perfect storm.

Despite the difficult start, the homeschooling actually turned out to be a very good idea. As some of the intensity of the exercising tapered off and I began to study again, I found I was getting more work done than I had before. When I was one kid in a classroom of many, the setup had enabled me to do as little as I possibly could. Now that I was on my own, under the watchful eye of my parents, my mind was no longer free to wander off. With so much to make up, and the possible humiliation of never graduating, I started doing as much work as I could. Eventually I would catch up in the summer of my senior year, complete all of the requirements, and graduate at the same time my class did at the age of sixteen.

As a kid, I had always thought school never mattered, but at this time there was nothing more important to me than making sure I finished. It was no longer about what my parents, or anyone else wanted; it was about me realizing the value in all of it, and the shame I would feel if I did not graduate.

And of course, I still saw my friends and had a good time. In Hilo, and throughout most of Hawaii, other than Waikiki and Honolulu, there is really not a lot going on, so you have to make your own fun. As we were all getting older, we started doing the things that the older kids were doing, like driving our cars up to desolate areas where the cops were not likely to show up so we could hang out, play music really loud, and drink. And of course, there were fights all the time. Without a doubt, no matter where we were, there was going to be a fight, and a lot of times my friends and I were right in the middle of the action. I don't just mean two guys punching each other, rolling around on the ground, even though that also happened from time to time. I mean full-scale brawls between different groups of people.

These things were not happening because there was a lot of hate, or because there were rivalries. Occasionally two guys would get into a scrap over something stupid, like a girl, or someone said one thing about someone else. But on the whole, fighting was just something we did whenever we could. It was just the way we were.

At times these were brutal fights, with guys getting teamed up on or mauled by huge dudes. People would get blindsided, or maybe a weapon would be involved. You just never knew what you were signing up for when you showed up anywhere in Hilo—or Hawaii, for that matter. At the very least you better be prepared, and it was not something you could learn about in books.

3

UNEXPECTED CHANGES

SOMETIMES IN LIFE YOU DO the wrong thing, and maybe that wrong thing helps lead you toward the right thing. Like if someone goes to prison for a crime, and while there, they embrace religion or get an education, and end up coming out a better person for it. That has been known to happen to a lot of people. For me, I made a lot of questionable decisions in high school, namely the pot smoking, but I'm not sure I'd have found my calling if I hadn't made some of them.

In the summer of 1996, I was a sixteen-year-old kid who had no idea what was in store for him. I had struggled to finish high school because of mistakes I had made, and while I was definitely smart enough to go to college, I couldn't see myself following that path. Jay Dee was off at college, Reagan was in high school, Jay was working, and my other siblings were much older, living their lives elsewhere. In some ways it was just me, looking for a way to come into my own.

As summer began, I was definitely looking to take it easy but my dad had other ideas in store for me. He was still bothered by what went down with the pot smoking and the problems at school. He wanted to find some way to keep me productive during the summer, but wasn't really sure how to go about it. Luckily for both of us, the answer was dropped on the doorstep of my house.

That summer, Jay Dee was home from UNLV, and was very much into working out and lifting weights. One day while down at one of the local gyms getting in shape for the summer, he noticed a flyer posted near the exit of the gym. The flyer was noticeable because Hilo was not the kind of place where new things were happening without you knowing about them. Apparently there was a new guy living in town named Tom Callos, who was looking for people to practice judo, wrestling, and most importantly, BJJ— Brazilian jujitsu. On the flyer, he left his name, phone number, and what he was looking for, which was basically anyone who was willing to learn. Jay Dee took the flyer off the board and brought it home to show Pop.

In retrospect, it is surprising that Jay Dee took down the flyer. It was not as though martial arts weren't available in Hilo. Pop had practiced judo and kickboxing, and other forms were well established and commonly practiced. There was no BJJ going on in Hilo at the time, but there was no reason that the announcement should have gotten Jay Dee's attention since he was not into martial arts at the time. His only real involvement with sports other than weights was the ten years or so that he played soccer, no different than me. But Jay Dee always liked trying new things out, and doing things a bit differently.

Once my dad had the flyer in his hand, he immediately called this fellow Callos up and asked him what he was looking to do. At that point Tom had been in town for barely a day. He'd just moved in with his girlfriend, who was attending college in Hilo.

She had found an apartment for them before Tom even arrived, and he was moving in sight unseen. Moving to a totally new place didn't change the fact that Tom had upcoming martial arts trials in California that he needed to train for. As someone preparing to move forward with his training, he needed bodies to practice against, and the first thing he did after arriving was to post flyers all over town. He had gone over to the Relson Gracie Academy on Oahu a few times, which was the only established BJJ school in Hawaii, but realized flying to Oahu just for practice was not practical. When Tom arrived in Hilo the highest-ranking BJJ practitioner was a blue belt, which is only one up from white, the belt a beginner starts with.

While Tom was setting up his new house he plugged in his phone, and the moment he turned around to walk away, it rang. He did not know a single person in the town and did not remember giving out his number. He answered the phone somewhat surprised, thinking maybe it was the phone company, and was even more surprised to hear my father's voice. As it turned out, Tom's newly moved into apartment was one of my dad's rental properties and was located down the street from our house. Tom came over to explain face-to-face what he was looking for in training partners, and told my dad of his own abilities. Tom was working toward completing certain martial arts trials with famed martial artist Ernie Reyes in California. Having trained considerably in karate and kickboxing, he was becoming well rounded in as many arts as possible with the goal of being a complete martial artist. He had not had much experience with BJJ, but knew enough to teach decently. His goal was to learn and excel as quickly as possible, and having bodies helped him toward that end.

This conversation between Tom and my dad, and especially with Tom living right down the street, made it somewhat difficult to avoid him. Looking back on it, this was a really good thing. Most people who respond to a flyer like we did show up to work out once or twice, then never show up again. Our proximity to

Tom meant that wasn't an option, but still it took some prodding to convince me it was worth showing up the first time.

When I heard about my dad's discussion with Tom, I did not have any real interest. Pop told Tom he would send us down to wherever he was going to set up the training, but at first I did not show. Tom came over to the house a couple of times after, not only because he's persistent, but also because he's just a nice, outgoing guy, and liked knowing his neighbors. Even if he had not inquired about whether we had interest, he still would have come by just for conversation. However it happened, Tom managed to convince my dad how good this training would be for me, and that I should at least try it once. Pop was never one to force any of us into activities we had no interest in, unless it was for punishment or self-improvement, but this time he made me go.

"Just go down there once and check this guy out," Pop told me. "If you don't like it, you never have to go back. But go down there so maybe I can get this guy off my back."

I wasn't sure whether my dad had ulterior motives just to get me going in a positive direction. In the end, I went not because I was doing anyone a favor, but because I knew the subject would be brought up again and again until I showed up.

With Jay Dee back at school, eventually I showed up at the Waiakea Recreational Center, located on the west side of town, about a mile and a half from my house. The center was equipped with mats specifically designed for martial arts, since others had practiced there as well. I brought some friends along to see what this guy Tom was all about. On the very first day I began grappling with Tom, and he was already teaching me lessons, literally and figuratively.

Going in, I figured that because I'd been wrestling with my brothers and fighting on the porch and around Hilo for years, I knew how to scrap with the best of them. Next thing I knew, Tom was putting me into all different types of compromising positions, tapping me out, choking me out, and doing pretty much whatever else he wanted to do. When you looked at Tom you would not think this guy was going to be much of a problem. He wasn't necessarily big, or tall, not much taller than five nine and beginning to lose his hair. He seemed like your average haole from the mainland.

In the middle of all the grappling, after recognizing I could not beat this guy, a thought popped into my head: this is some unbelievable stuff. I am not saying it in a casual way. I felt it in the pit of my stomach that this was something wholly different than anything I had known. It's as if a small light went on in my head, a revelation telling me this is how a man can defend himself in a dominant way. There was this realization that I had just been introduced to something big, even if I was not exactly sure what it was.

I started going down to work out with Tom a few days a week, and train for a couple of hours at a time. Lots of people started to show up from all over the town, guys I used to see around town, but didn't actually know. Former high school athletes, older guys, younger guys, both tough and weak guys, people who were wrestlers in high school, or just those looking to blow off some steam. The center just started to fill up, and I was grappling with locals of all different shapes and sizes.

The basics of BJJ came to me pretty quickly, and I remember grappling with all these guys, huge guys, men, and I would just go at it with them. If there's one thing that sticks out in my mind, it's just how big some of these guys were. One guy was a former wrestler from Hilo High, and was just huge—maybe about six three, 250 or 260 pounds—and I squared off with him a number of times. Another big guy would just throw me to the ground like a rag doll, and I would end up tapping him out. At the time I was not very big at all, maybe five seven, 135 pounds, but the technique was what mattered. After a while a lot of the students just stopped showing up, finding that it was not for them. The good thing, though, was fighting against all these different-size guys with different skills helped me get over any fear I had of taking on men who were bigger than me.

Getting into BJJ was really easy because it was the opposite of how I thought about school. When I find something I like, I get really into it, sometimes to the point where it can consume my every thought. BJJ became that something, but it's not like I was an expert right away. It was something I looked forward to, but it was not like real martial arts training. My friends and I were still going to the rivers, hanging out at the beaches, drinking beers, and getting stoned. When not doing that, we were learning BJJ, and it was probably the most fun I have ever had working out and practicing anything in my life. I cannot put into words just how much fun it was. Even though it was considered training, it was fun in the way soccer had once been.

As time went on, Tom showed us all he knew, but it was a challenge for him since his knowledge was somewhat limited in BJJ. When it came to tae kwon do and kickboxing, he had a process and a formula for teaching. For BJJ, though, Tom was still trying to make sense of it himself, so it was not something that he could easily teach others. The fact that Tom was learning at the same time as we were meant he never acted like he knew more than he did, or that he had all the answers. He would even say things like, "Hey, go find some BJJ books and magazines, watch the videos, and whatever you learn we can practice together!"

I went out and did just that. It would be fair to say you cannot learn BJJ from watching a video; you have to feel it. Having experience with Tom enabled me to put the things I was learning from the videos and books to work. I remember we had a video from Renzo Gracie, one of the most well known practitioners and teachers in the world, and I watched it a lot. It was not the type of thing you could just watch and pick up if you had never practiced at all. If you had a little experience, you could try to incorporate some of the moves, or at least understand what it was you were trying to learn. It was the first time I started to think about BJJ outside of class, when I had to watch, listen, and learn from someone other than a hands-on instructor. I didn't realize that these little steps—

watching some videos, boxing, working with Tom—were putting me on the path toward being a fighter.

The free exchange of knowledge was incredibly important. With Tom, my brothers, and my friends, there was a give-and-take that was unique, especially considering most fighters and teachers these days try to act as if they have all the answers and solutions to make you "the best." Tom was never that way, which was a sign of real trust. He brought us to the water, but we all drank together.

Although my friends and I were all regularly practicing BJJ, it had not replaced our fighting at my parents' house. Outside of the guys who were practicing the BJJ, we still had a lot of people coming over to spar, and now we had taken it to the basement as well since occasionally the wet weather would force us inside. Over time we had collected more items to spar with, like headgear, a few mats, and gloves, so we were fully prepared to kick the crap out of each other, like we had been doing even before we had any of these supposedly necessary items. Afterward we would sometimes head down to the recreation center to fight some more.

While we still enjoyed the fighting at my house, we started listening to Tom, and seeing him as our responsible teacher. Without recognizing it, I was seemingly more into BJJ than anyone else I knew. When I first started working with Tom, I really did want to be a tough guy, someone who could take on anyone, but it didn't take long for me to get that out of my system. The more I trained in BJJ, the less concerned I was about fighting bigger guys. I did feel a surge of power and confidence from fighting them and tapping them out, but my interest in BJJ began to deepen and move beyond the personal satisfaction I could get from beating people who by the looks of things would get the best of me.

Looking back on it now, it shouldn't have come as such a surprise that I began to pursue fighting with such passion. I had been fascinated with it in one way or another since I was a little kid. Even before my friends and I started fighting on the porch, I had tendencies toward combat. In elementary school, I had been into professional wrestling pretty seriously. I had all of the magazines—*The Wrestler, Pro Wrestling Illustrated*—not to mention all the WWF stuff. While my brothers and friends were into other things, all I cared about was Hulk Hogan and steel cage matches. I'm told by the age of four I used to walk around with a fake championship belt and cowboy boots to mimic the wrestlers. As if that wasn't enough, *Rocky* was my favorite movie for ages, and I watched it over and over again as a kid. It was hard to say why I had a tendency toward combat, at least watching it, but it just seemed to make sense that I would gravitate toward fighting.

Coincidentally, it wasn't the film *Rocky* which made me believe I could be a fighter, but another movie I stumbled upon later on by chance. It all happened one night when I was about twelve years old, as I was lying in my bedroom unable to fall asleep. Reagan was out cold in the bed next to me, but I just could not rest. Rather than stare at the ceiling for hours, I got out of bed and went down the hallway to Jay Dee's room, where he had this massive big-screen television. It was one of those old screen projectors you had to actually open up to make work. It had those large round circular blue, red, and yellow lights which reflected off a mirror and then projected back onto the screen. The thing was huge. At my age the television was like a toy you could open, close, climb inside, almost like a spaceship. When we played the video game Super Mario Brothers on it, Mario was the size of a soda can.

With Jay Dee trying to sleep, and not very happy about me coming into the room around midnight, I turned on the television only to stumble upon a movie called *American Kickboxer*. I didn't really know what it was, but I figured since it was a fighting movie, it had to be better than anything else on TV, especially since midnight Hawaii time is 2 or 3 A.M. West Coast time. Not the best hour to watch television unless you liked infomercials. The movie was not very good. Its main character had just lost a fight at the very beginning of the film. They showed this guy, all upset, unhappy about the result, and then with his head down he walked back to his locker room alone. All of a sudden I hear someone say his name, and it was BJ Quinn. *BJ Quinn?!? That sounds like me!* I thought.

Even though I was just a little kid, but not too little, I remember telling myself, *That could be me. What if I just became a professional fighter? I could do that, right?* I was not really serious, or at least not in any real way, but the memory of seeing BJ Quinn and thinking about being a professional fighter never left me. Was it a coincidence? Was it meant to be? I have no idea. School was not a whole lot of fun, and BJ Quinn looked like a pretty tough guy who was having a good time. All I know is on some level a seed was planted that night.

EVENTUALLY WE STOPPED WORKING OUT at the recreation center in Hilo, and instead Tom moved into his own space so he could really teach classes. It was a more official place to practice both BJJ and other things. Whether he liked it or not, Tom had become the local teacher.

Going to the gym became something I enjoyed, something I looked forward to—a place where I had nothing to do but learn and grow. Starting at noon almost every day, this was my job: while other people were in school or working, I was left to do my own thing, which was BJJ. Unless I had a good reason I never missed a practice. My father sensed how much I had taken to it and pushed me to keep moving forward.

This went on for well over a year, with my only real responsibility being BJJ. BJJ became my job, but it was the best job a kid my age could have. At the time I had no real expenses since, like most of my friends I was still living at home. All I had to do was wake up, do whatever household things were needed of me (there was always something), drive over to the gym, practice, and then chill out. It was a stress-free life.

One day Tom decided he wanted to practice boxing with me

in the gym. Since he had a background in stand-up martial arts, was close to getting a fifth-degree black belt in tae kwon do, and was older and stronger, he definitely figured he would have an edge in hand-to-hand combat. The plan was to do some slap boxing, nothing too serious, so we squared off after class. He approached me, and before he knew it, I had hit him in the head four or five times then bounced away out of his range. Slightly surprised and frustrated, he chased me down, and again, "bop bop bop bop," I caught him with a few shots to the face, and then I was out of striking distance. This lasted for a few minutes, but throughout it, he was never really able to hit me.

Afterward according to Tom, he walked home with his head down, and that evening he started to think maybe he was getting old, wondering how this little kid could get the best of him on his feet. The night we boxed was the first time both Tom and I began to feel the training dynamic between us shifting. It was becoming clear to Tom he had reached a limit with what he could teach me in BJJ. He no longer was able to "pass my guard," which is the act of escaping from between the grip of your opponent's two legs while he has position on top of you. I too could sense how much I was improving because most of the guys I trained with had the same problem Tom did escaping my guard. Tom also could tell I was progressing at a pretty rapid pace, at least faster than most of the other people we trained with. In addition to my always showing up on time, rarely missing a class, and just being really involved and enthusiastic, Tom saw something more in me, but neither he nor I really knew what it was. As it turned out, "it" was a desire I didn't even know I had inside me.

IN A LOT OF TOWNS, BEING on the football or basketball team could make you a local star, but Hilo was not really like that. Don't get me wrong, sports were a big deal and were looked upon positively, but they were not as big a deal as they are on the mainland.

For my friends and me, our "sport" was fighting, everywhere, and anywhere. That is what we did for fun. On the weekends people would bring their cars up to the desolate cane fields, or drive them onto the beach, set up fires, drink, smoke, try to hook up with girls, and all of the things you do in your teenage years. But amid all of this, there were always fights, no matter where we went, no matter where other people went.

The fact that I was practicing BJJ did little to curb my instinct to fight without rules. On occasion a fight would start because one person would say something about someone else, or some guy would hit on another guy's girlfriend; the typical stuff. But for the most part, fights started because we had nothing better to do. We were bored. We had no excuse other than the fact that it was fun to have an adrenaline rush, to find out what you were made of, or just to kick someone's ass for looking at you wrong while you were drunk. It could have been any number of things, but if we needed a reason, we found one. Sometimes this meant a fight with just two guys in a circle of people going at it, and other times it meant full-scale brawls. Massive brawls. Just groups of people going at each other in the street, in a park, in the center of town, at a house party, at the beach, in some desolate area where there were no cops to stop anything and no adults to be found.

I was as much an instigator as anyone. Often, if I wasn't fighting on my porch, I was looking to start with them somewhere else. A lot of times I was joined by Jay Dee, who along with me did crazy shit to get people fighting, shit that even today I'm not that proud of. We weren't bad kids, and a lot of times we fought the guys who we believed *were* the bad kids; we just needed something to do. Sometimes we started fights, other times we just took part. There were fights which were justified, and others much less so, but I tried to pick my spots. However, more often than not I was the guy who always had to fight the guy who was a jerk to everyone else. I always had to take on the tough guy, the mean guy, the one who caused problems for others, and the one with the loudest mouth.

Those were the people I did not like, so I could always justify a reason to fight them.

On the whole, though, I usually fared better than a lot of my buddies, even if they were at least as tough as I was. I remember after one huge brawl, we all ended up gathered together, recouping. Mostly everyone in the group, especially Saul, had bruises, cuts, torn pants, bloody knees, broken noses, all types of injuries. Not me. I had definitely been hit a few times, but I guess not cleanly enough to cause any real damage. I guess I was just blessed with the natural ability to avoid punishment and move out of the way of incoming strikes. Maybe my friends were masochistic and liked being hit? Whatever it was, in the end, I did a little bit of a better job coming out relatively unscathed.

In the end, bumps, bruises, and injuries were the price you had to pay for passing the time and having some fun. Luckily for me, none of these were things I had to hide from my parents. Academics, working around the house, helping your family out, being respectful and productive, these were the things that mattered to them. Not fighting. To them, kids would be kids, and getting banged up was something kids did. My brothers, my friends, and I would come home from fights all bruised, and when my father saw us, he'd simply say something like, "So, how was your night?" or "Looks like you fell off the bed in your sleep," and nothing more. As long as the police were not involved and no one was seriously hurt, it was what he expected his boys to do. Coming as he did from a rough background, I guess maybe he saw a bit of himself in us.

Looking back on all of those fights, I'd say it was just plain fun. There were guys who I pounded on who you would never have thought I could by looking at the two of us. They probably still know who they are, and are still somewhere in Hawaii, probably Hilo. Then there were other guys who got the best of me, and I am even more positive they too know who they are. It happened, and I guess it was all a part of toughening me up and preparing for the harder fights I would encounter later on. In a lot of ways I thank all of those guys who spent part of their life tangled up with me. They helped make me what I am today. If they had not been willing to scrap with me, I have no idea if I would have ended up where I am today. All these people are part of a bigger family to me, people I still see to this day who are my friends—part of a group that pushed me and taught me. "My braddhas."

IN THE WINTER OF 1996, TOM approached my dad about an opportunity: he wanted to take me with him to California to meet some well-known people in the martial arts field. He was heading back there to celebrate the fiftieth birthday party of his teacher, the great Ernie Reyes Sr., and he felt he could introduce me to people who might provide me with the training I needed to take my BJJ further.

By that time, Tom had established a solid relationship with my parents. He was in his mid-thirties, well traveled, and responsible, which was why my parents were satisfied about my training with him in the first place. During the time he was working with me, he never stopped training for his own tae kwon do trials. Because of this he did a decent amount of traveling both in Hawaii and California, working hard to move forward.

When I first heard of this plan to bring me with him to California, it did not excite me. I had become very comfortable with my routine of practicing BJJ in Hilo and then hanging out with all my friends. Plus I had a high school girlfriend. Leaving would definitely change the comfort zone I had established. Still it was hard to argue with Tom; in terms of BJJ, there was not much for me in Hilo. My dad liked what Tom had to say and agreed that I had abilities that could be taken further and should be. Regardless of what I wanted, this was going to happen.

With no real excuse to stay in Hilo, I went with Tom to the San Jose area shortly after my eighteenth birthday in February of 1997.

We flew out to California with Malani, my girlfriend at the time, whose family was also close with mine. Having my girlfriend with me would make the trip more fun, and help put me at ease. It was not only a big trip, but it was the first time I had ever left Hawaii, or taken a long-distance flight as an adult. I had been to Disneyland as a child, and across the mainland to the East Coast once with my family, but all of that happened when I was a small child. Understandably I was nervous about the whole thing.

We ended up getting two rooms in a hotel in Mountain View, California, but I had no idea where I was in relation to the world. I could have been anywhere. I had grown up seeing the ocean, rivers, and trees from my house, and now I was in some big city area in between mountain ranges, next to suburban houses, buildings, and traffic everywhere. I was officially out of my element.

That week we went with Tom to the Ernie Reyes Sr. fiftieth birthday party. Malani and I said hello to people, shook hands, and were very respectful, but had no idea what to even do, or how to act. I did not know it, but the fact that Tom had brought us to this event was a pretty big deal. He had worked very hard to reach a level in his career where he would even be invited to a gathering such as this, so to bring me and Malani with him meant something. He had a lot of faith in me, and he had been able to convince the party's host I was someone worth meeting, even if I had yet to accomplish anything.

After showing me around for a day or two, Tom started introducing me to people who would have a very large effect on my life. One of those people was Ralph Gracie (pronounced "Halph"). Since we first planned this trip, I had known that meeting Ralph was the real reason for me to come to California. Ralph's school was just a few blocks away from where Tom had been training under Reyes, and the martial arts community was small enough that Tom and Ralph knew each other. So that's what we did, we visited Ralph's school, and I was introduced to a number of people. The name Gracie was then, and is today, the biggest name in the world of BJJ. Having the opportunity to visit one of the Gracie academies was a big deal, and I knew it.

While I was quiet because of the unfamiliar surroundings at Ralph's school, I had a bit of a chip on my shoulder. Before arriving in California, I remember thinking I would show up, tap Ralph out, and that would be the end of it. Looking back, the fact I even thought that was ridiculous. Here I was, a white belt who had only been grappling with people in Hilo, and I thought I could dominate anyone I encountered, including a black belt like Ralph Gracie. I was naïve to say the least; naturally, things did not go as I had imagined.

During my week there, I had the chance to train at Ralph's school. He set me up with two of his better blue belt students—Kevin Graham and Dave Camarillo—to see what I was made of. It was a funny thing for these two guys—who were both a few years older than me—to suddenly have to roll with this random kid from Hawaii. Ralph told them I was considering moving to Mountain View, where the school was located, to train, but they probably figured I would stay for a few days, be gone, and they would never see me again.

The first person I grappled with outside of Hawaii was Graham, and he was definitely as good as, if not better than, anyone I had worked out with up until then. Graham was a lean guy with a shaven head, not much taller than me, but definitely strong for someone with his build. I remember he and Camarillo, who I call Dave, really wanted to do well against me because it was not considered a good thing for anyone to walk into someone else's school and excel, especially someone of a lower belt level. Initially I thought there was no way this guy could beat me, but learning a bit of humility turned out to be a good thing. Graham did things to me I was not prepared for, but I learned from my mistakes—even if it was a bit painful. (At one point he got me into an arm bar so successfully that I thought he'd ripped my arm out of my socket.)

As we continued grappling, there was a point where I had him in my guard, and he couldn't pass me no matter how hard he tried. Graham was really trying to take it to me, but I was not letting him have his way. Dave was standing next to us watching, getting a little bit ticked off by it all. It bothered Dave at the time because he didn't want to see some white belt kid from Hawaii make his school look bad. Dave liked to say he was a "Ralph Nazi," and would do anything to defend the school. The best way to describe it would be to compare it to how the Cobra Kai kids acted in the movie *Karate Kid* that no outsider would come in and make them look bad. Even though it got Dave worked up, I kept Graham in my guard for most of our grappling sessions.

In order to truly protect the image of the school, Ralph, having noticed what was going on from afar, decided to roll with me. As one would expect, he had no problems doing whatever he wanted to me. I could tell how good he was immediately. Within a very short time I had rolled with the two best guys I had ever worked with, Ralph being far superior to anyone I had encountered previously, on video or in reality.

Before I left the school, Tom and Ralph had a conversation about me. Ralph mentioned to Tom that I was very good for the little time I had trained and had the ability to get even better. He wanted me to come back out to Mountain View to learn more. Tom really didn't know whether I would return for the long term, knowing how comfortable I was in Hawaii among my family and friends. I told Ralph I definitely enjoyed the visit, but in the back of my mind the only reason I made the trip in the first place was to meet a Gracie, and maybe have a chance to grapple with one of them; and I'd done that. The truth was, I didn't know if I was ever going to go back to California because Hawaii was the world to me. Outside of it, not much else mattered, even though the trip had made it very clear I had a lot to learn, and the place to be was California. On the flight back to San Jose, I was sitting next to an older woman, and we started to talk about different things relating to my life. I was still pretty young, and I remember discussing what my plans for the future were. I told her, "Maybe this is it for me. Maybe BJJ is what I am going to do for the rest of my life." She expressed how I would be lucky to find a career I loved. In that moment I started to wonder what could be if I really stuck with this.

BACK IN HAWAII I WAS ABLE to take some of what I had learned at Ralph's school and practice on other people. But I hadn't been in California long enough to absorb anything substantial. Still it was reassuring to know that Ralph had expressed some interest in me. At least I had the option of returning if that was what I *chose* to do.

When my dad asked me about the trip, I told him I liked it, but I was not looking to head back quickly. Despite my lack of interest, Tom told my dad what Ralph had said and pointed out that it would not be very hard for me to find a place in California I could easily adapt to. There were a lot of other kids my age training over there. Tom mentioned Ralph was a good person, someone who could be trusted to train and watch over me, and that a lot of kids my age were already off to college and on their own anyway.

Through Tom, my father was aware I had reached the end of what I could learn in BJJ in Hilo, and there wasn't anyone else qualified enough around. So it was not surprising Pop seemed to like the idea of me trying out California. He was always supportive of me doing things I wanted to do and against the idea of me wasting time. To him all the signs pointed to this being an opportunity I needed to pursue, an opportunity to grow as a man and as a martial artist.

My dad approached me with the idea of moving to California for a little while, at least to check it out in the same way he had originally wanted me to go down to Tom's "to check it out." Only this time I was not just walking down the street to the recreation center; I was leaving all that I knew behind. I told my parents I was not into it, hoping maybe to get sympathy from one of them, but

Pop was not going to let it go that easily. He offered me a deal I literally could not refuse: "You can either get a job, or you can go to school. But before the summer begins, if you are not working, you're going to California."

He gave me a couple months to figure it all out, which seemed like a good amount of time to not deal with it. I figured I could do a lot in the next couple of months. At the very least I would not have to leave my girlfriend, or my friends, the beach parties, the barbecuing by the rivers, the gym, and all the other things I looked forward to doing. All I had to do was get some kind of part-time job, and I could stay in Hilo, practice, and continue to do what I enjoyed. The time passed quickly, and after about two months, Pop brought it right back up, as if he'd been crossing off days on a calendar.

"Okay, time's up!" he announced with a smile on his face.

"Huh? What? Already?" was about all I could get out. I had no job. I was not enrolled in school, nor did I plan to be.

But that was it for me, I was going to San Jose, California, to live and train at Ralph's school. I was pretty upset by the whole thing because I knew the fun of growing up in Hawaii had finally come to an abrupt end. Even though I wasn't leaving forever, in some sense I really was. I knew this would bring my relationship with Malani to an end on some level, and part of me knew when I came back nothing would be the same. People would grow up, maybe leave, get married and have kids, or all of the above. But all the things I was leaving behind—the porch boxing, beach drinking, the rivers, my friends—all these things, I knew would never be the same. But I didn't have a choice.

4

RALPH AND DAVE

FLEW BACK TO CALIFORNIA WITH MY dad at the start of the summer of 1997. He came with me so that he could meet Ralph and help me find a place to live near the gym. I imagine it's like what parents do when their kids go to college, only I was going to learn about fighting.

Dave Camarillo was also around to help me get settled, since he too lived close to the gym, and it quickly became obvious Dave was someone I was going to see quite a bit of. He was under Ralph's wing already, and since I would be too on some level, we were in this together. Seeing me return, Dave realized I was serious, not just someone who was going to walk away. Because of this, he was willing to help me out. He was not an old guy, only about twenty-one, but since I was so young and going to be there alone, I think he felt a sense of obligation, or maybe Ralph had requested his help. I think he respected that I was not just some kid who showed up a couple months ago talking about how I was going to move there, but someone who actually did it, which surprised everyone at Ralph's school.

After I found an apartment and got the basic things I needed to live, my dad left to catch his flight. Standing there by myself watching his car pull away from my new place, I wanted to run after it. Was I ready to be doing this? Was I ready to be alone? What was I even doing? I had never been alone in my life. By no means was I a child anymore, but being shipped off to California after leaving all the comforts of Hawaii—it was a lot to swallow.

Other than Dave, Ralph, Kevin, and these three other guys I had met at the school named Alex Oxendine, Greg Rivera, and Bobby Southworth, I did not really know anyone. (And how well did I really know even them? I ask myself now.) I had no one to call, no one to hang out with, nothing to really do—I had no experience to compare my life in California to. Since I would be alone most of the time, it was going to be a hundred percent up to me, and no one else, to make this opportunity work. I really didn't know how I was going to handle it, but then again, I didn't have many other options. I'd been thrown into the water and told to swim.

My new life was going to be BJJ, full-time. Since I was going to be at training and only training, not working a job like a lot of other people, I was expected to be involved right from the start; there was to be no sightseeing or settling-in period. I was not sent there to screw around and waste time. Ralph would be my head teacher, while Dave would be left to spend most of his time with me at his side, almost like his apprentice. I had no excuses not to be at the school, and really I had nothing else to do.

LIKE EVERYONE ELSE IN THE SCHOOL, I started out as a white belt, despite the fact that I had a little more experience than a standard white. That was how it went for a while. I attended class every day and worked on all of the positions, transitions, and moves someone of my level should—the same as everyone else. Maybe I had been considered something a bit more special back in Hilo, but here in California I was just another student. It was a daily process in which I repeated everything I was learning over and over until each move was perfect. In BJJ, technique is everything; not power, strength, or brute force, but technique is dominant, and you learn this early on.

Not too long after I arrived, it seemed I was entering BJJ competitions around California. When Dave and Ralph signed me up for my first one, in Bakersfield during the summer of 1997, I finally realized how different this was than what I'd been used to. When I started doing BJJ in Hilo, it was all about having fun and using the judo to dominate fights. In California, it was competition, not fights, something that I didn't understand at all.

I remember one day I went with Greg over to Dave's house, and we started watching a video of a BJJ tournament in Brazil. It featured these two guys, Shaolin and Leozinho. I kept asking Dave and Greg what was going on because I hadn't realized until then that BJJ was something you competed in; I thought it was only for fighting. I was slowly coming to realize that with martial arts came respect, understanding, learning, and many other things to help give you discipline. This is not to say Tom didn't tell me this when I was in Hilo, but being in Hilo just made everything looser. We were respectful of Tom and the school, but life did not revolve around our studies. In Hawaii, we wore board shorts and maybe a T-shirt, but under Ralph, I wore the standard gi, essentially as a uniform.

Dave drove me down for this first competition with some other guys from the school. It was the first time I had competed in something official since I had played soccer as a kid, so I was definitely anxious. I was only a white belt, but I had been entered in my weight division and the open division as well. It was how the tournaments worked: you fought for two different divisions—your own and with everyone in the tournament within your belt class. For a little while I just watched some of the other guys rolling and doing their thing. I had no idea about point scoring or the way you could win a match based on control. I had been training, but I was not thinking that way at all. My focus was just on getting better, not really winning tournaments; fighting was still in my head. I just figured I would try to dominate, not think about points, scoring, or any of the other stuff. After all, *If I dominate my opponent I can't lose, right?* So that was the plan.

When the announcer called out my name, I was as nervous as I'd ever been and I almost started crying. Here I was in some gymnasium in front of an audience waiting to see me perform. Unlike soccer, where you went onto the field in front of all these people you knew, as part of a team, I was now entering this thing alone. It felt like the eyes of the world were focused on me. I walked out to the mat, and I didn't know what to do, so I just did what felt right to me.

Luckily everything came to me quickly and naturally. I won my own weight class rather easily, and even won the open division, despite fighting a guy who was about 220 pounds to my 135. I flying triangled him for the submission, which is when you take your body from a standing position, grab your opponent's arm, and jump up, throw your legs up across his neck and head, all while holding his arm. It puts your opponent's arm in a position where he can either have it broken or he can submit. Either way he is going to be pulled to the ground because your opponent not only has to worry about the arm, but is also carrying the weight of your body. Naturally, you can bring someone right down to the ground with this move. It is a pretty high-level move, but it is something you can use to stop a much bigger man, so that's what I did to stop this guy and win.

Ralph and Dave were excited that I'd been able to win, which made me happy. Dave had won his division as well, which in turn made me happy. When the competition was over it felt as good as anything I had ever done in my life. I had moved forward on instinct and that carried me to the top.

EVERYTHING SEEMED TO BE HAPPENING really fast. I'd barely had time to adjust to California and already I'd won a competition. As if that wasn't enough, Ralph and Dave started to introduce me to the larger fighting scene in the area. California seemed to be where a lot of the best fighters were living and training (at least in the States), so naturally a lot of these guys came through Ralph's school. In addition to BJJ, guys were training for mixed martial arts (MMA). Ralph had already fought four or five MMA matches himself before I had come along, so he was connected to what was a growing sport.

Ralph is Brazilian, and in many ways the Brazilians are responsible for the growth of MMA. They practiced a style of fighting called *vale tudo*, which basically means "no holds barred" or "anything goes." This style of fighting goes back years and years into Brazilian culture, and Ralph was someone who carried that tradition from Brazil to the States.

One afternoon I was hanging around the school when this guy walked through the front door. I didn't notice who he was, but he saw me standing there. He looked like a real confident man and there was something familiar about his face that I couldn't quite place.

"Hey, is Ralph here?" he asked me.

"No, he isn't," I replied.

"Well, tell him I came by, and I'll be back later," he said.

"Okay," I told him. The guy was heading out the front door when I realized I didn't even know who he was, even though he carried himself in a way that implied I should. I called out, "Hey, who should I say was looking for him?"

He looked at me like I had to be joking and said, "I'm Frank Shamrock," nodding a bit as if to say, *Of course I am.*

"Okay, I'll tell him." The door closed behind him as he left. I just stood there thinking to myself how I had just met Frank Shamrock, one of the best-known MMA fighters in the world. The first name people say when they talk about MMA is Gracie, and the second is Shamrock. I had seen him fight many times on TV and in videos. He had already been competing in different organizations like Vale Tudo in Brazil, Pancrase in Japan, and of course the Ultimate Fighting Championship (UFC) here in the States. This guy was already a legend, and probably no more than twenty-five years old. To him, I was just a white belt kid who did not know who he, Frank, was.

Later on that evening Frank returned to the gym to work out with Ralph, and to my surprise Ralph told him he should roll with me. Talk about a great opportunity. The other guys at the school probably had rolled with Frank before, so maybe to them it was no big deal, but I was beyond excited. I'd been in California only a few weeks and I was already working out with Frank Shamrock. No one in Hilo would believe this.

Even though I was just a lower-level student and Frank was an established, strong fighter, I was confident I could handle myself. I had grappled with much bigger guys than him before. Ralph and some other guys told me what he liked to do, and I had seen him fight a few times. Plus, it was only practice, so no one was going to get hurt here. At the very least I knew I had my guard, which was proving difficult for most people to escape from. Frank was the type of guy who wanted to grab hold of your leg to pull off a submission with a heel hook, knee bar, ankle lock, or something in the leg area. I was told he loved leg submissions; they were his bread and butter. Fortunately for me, I had always been really good at avoiding getting my legs trapped in those types of submissions. If there was one area of BJJ where I always excelled, this was it.

For nearly forty minutes we rolled, back and forth, trying to work submissions on each other. Like I was expecting, Frank kept going for my legs, but it was not going to happen. Other areas of my game he may have had luck with, but not there. Basically the two of us rolled to a stalemate, which in BJJ is quite common. For those not well versed in the art, it can sometimes seem boring because there's a good chance no one will dominate, or gain any real advantage. It can look like two guys just holding on to each other.

After rolling with me, Frank then grappled with Ralph for a while, and those two really went at it. They were both about the same size and had a similar look, at five nine, somewhere between 170 to 180 pounds, and both with dark hair, although Shamrock looked Latin while Ralph had the sharper features of a Brazilian. Watching the two of them was an experience. The entire school was gathered in a circle around the mat, and to be honest I felt really good having been able to hold my own as well as I had with Frank. Made me feel like I was part of something important, which, thanks to Ralph, I was.

Later on I would get to know Frank really well and would spend a lot of time working out with him, but there was nothing quite like the first time. From the moment I met Frank, I knew I liked him. All at once I came to see these were the types of people I could meet living in a place with more fighters, a place where martial arts was becoming a world of its own.

At the school I was still no different from anyone else as far as moving up the ladder and striving to achieve a higher belt level. Some days I was up, other days down, taking my bumps and bruises as they came. I was battling in the gym with other guys on my level, which I had not done a lot of in Hilo. What also made things tough was working with the same people over and over because they get to know your game, making it hard to do things they're not expecting. Because of this, I always had to be thinking of new ways to get better, create new moves, transitions, whatever I could do to get past whomever I had to face. I started to have BJJ on my mind all the time—not just at the gym.

Dave worked with me constantly, and he picked up on things I did well that I'd never realized were different from what other people could do. Ever since the week I'd first visited, he'd noticed I had a difficult guard to escape as well as good flexibility. It is not common for someone my age to have extreme leg strength and BJJ flexibility, and according to Dave, I had both, which probably helped me be successful early on. I have always been flexible without really working at it, which may be one of the reasons I like BJJ so much: it came to me naturally.

One day when I was on my back stretching, Dave and Graham noticed I could take my right leg and bring my foot up next to my ear. I could literally scratch my ear with my foot. Dave and Graham started calling me an "alien," meaning I was from another planet because of my flexibility and leg strength. They started to refer to my game as "Alien BJJ," which never really stuck, but it was the first time someone had given me a nickname relating to my BJJ ability.

HAVING WON MY FIRST TOURNAMENT, I was eagerly anticipating my second—the Joe Moreira Tournament, also down in Southern California. According to the guys at the school, this tournament was definitely much bigger than my first BJJ event in Bakersfield. The Moreira, as it is called, was considered a national competition, which meant at the very least there would be guys coming from all over California, maybe even farther away. It was going to be my third martial arts competition and I had barely been in California for two months.

For this one I would be fighting in the blue belt division even though I had yet to earn my blue. The guys in the school felt I was ready for it, especially Dave, who was a blue himself. This was something Ralph had been known to do to students: put them in a tougher division to see how they performed. It would either humble them or give them a chance to excel. Since I was able to at least hold my own with Dave, and he was very good, I did not think I would end up embarrassed.

My goal here was to have a good showing. I had prepared for the possibility I would lose rather quickly, and I never really handled losing well, so I was going to work as hard as I could to succeed on some level. I wanted to win outright, but who knew how I would do having never competed on this level? The competition was definitely tougher than in Bakersfield. The blue belts knew what they were doing, and there was a higher level of intensity. Once you reach the blue level, you can consider yourself skilled at BJJ, so this was truly competitive BJJ.

There was definitely tension in the room, and it seemed certain teams, depending on where they came from, carried different chips on their shoulders. Not everyone got along well, something I learned firsthand in my final match of the day.

I was able to move through a competitive field, and make it to the finals by submitting three opponents. However, the first fight sticks out most because it was against a very aggressive guy who fought for Gokor Chivichyan's school in Los Angeles, a school that would eventually produce fighters like Karo Parisyan and Manuel Gamburyan, both very successful in high-level MMA. Chivichyan's school was known to have very tough guys, and they wore it on their sleeves. Maybe not the most technically sound BJJ guys around, but at the very least you were going to have to earn everything. If you were going to beat them, you were also going to pay for it.

The referee for the match was Rickson Gracie, a very well-known and accomplished BJJ practitioner, considered by many to be the best of all the Gracies. I wanted to represent my team and myself the best way possible, so winning it all was extremely important to me. Of all the matches I would fight that day, the first was the most memorable. The match was rough from the get-go, as my opponent was trying to push me around and use his superior size over me. I was still only around 135 pounds, and my opponent probably had me by at least 10 to 15 pounds. While size does not necessarily matter, if two fighters are identical in every way, but one is heavier, it could make a difference. In this match, no matter what my opponent tried, I would not let it go his way. Every time he saw an opening to rough me up, even if it included trying to hit me in the head, or slam me, he took it. Rickson tried to keep things in control, but they still got a bit out of hand. One time I had him in my guard and he picked me up and slammed me on my back into the mat. He was warned to stop doing this, but because he was frustrated from being down on points at the time, he went on to do it again. My technique was better, and his brute strength was not enough to overcome it.

Finally, I caught him in a triangle choke, which is when you trap an opponent's head and arm between your legs, while on your back, which will cut off his circulation and ability to breathe. Again he tried to pick me up while I lay on my back with my legs wrapped around him, attempting to slam me a third time. He got me up in the air, and the moment he slammed me, Rickson came in to separate us. As the guy was getting up, I mule-kicked him in the chest with both feet to push him off. At heart, I was still a fighter first, and I was ready to trade fists at this point. He was going beyond disrespecting the sport and was attempting to disrespect me simply because I was winning and had just defeated him. Both teams ran to the middle, and a brawl nearly broke out. Rickson and Ralph were able to keep everyone calm, but I am usually not easy to mellow out after near altercation. Ultimately, despite the fact I had just beaten this guy, I had to maintain my composure because there were more matches to come. This kept me from really exploding and going after the guy. It was a good thing too, because I would eventually go on to win the blue belt tournament as a white belt, by defeating one of Rickson's students in the finals.

When we returned to the San Jose area, Dave received his purple belt from Ralph, and I got my blue. I had not been there a long time, but I had been successful pretty quickly, and obviously I proved I could compete on the blue level. Right after the competition, Ralph started to tell people about me, how I could really be successful in this sport. This was when I put the thought of fighting for its own sake behind me and focused more on competitive BJJ. Hearing his words made me realize all at once how serious this could all be for me if I remained committed.

EVEN THOUGH TRAINING WAS GOOD, and I knew where I needed to be, I still missed home. I would always call my friends in Hilo to find out what was happening without me, but it was costly. This was before everyone had a cell phone, so calling Hawaii was pretty pricey. When my friends told me about things they were up to, everything sounded like such fun. Even things I had done so many times before which I knew I was tired of seemed exciting. Guys in Hilo were still training BJJ, including Reagan, who had started working with Tom and this new guy named Charuto, who Jay Dee had trained with in Las Vegas while at UNLV. Hearing stories from Reagan reminded me of how much fun I'd had, and how far away I felt in California.

Had I not been completely committed to BJJ, there is no way I would have been able to ride it out. Other guys at the school had other things going on in their lives, like longtime friends, wives, girlfriends, families, cars, school, jobs, and just a general familiarity with the area. I was in California for the sole purpose of BJJ. Though I was working toward a goal, I was living a somewhat lonely existence. Every day, over and over, wake up, eat, ride my bike to the gym, ride it back home, watch television, call people, play video games, eat, sleep, maybe hang out with Oxendine, Southworth, and a few others. That was it.

Since I was left to myself so much and was training constantly, I had a lot of time to think, and the one thing I kept thinking about was BJJ. It was not enough that I really had nothing else to focus on, and that I was always at the school. Even in my spare time, it was on my mind. Whenever I was riding my bike, or sitting on the couch, the beach, anywhere, it was rolling around in my head.

How could I transition from this move, to a different move, back to another move? I would start to conjure up my own moves altogether. I could start to see patterns forming on how and when to do things, even things I had never been taught, things I wanted to try. There was always a way to transition to something new, like an endless flow from one thing to the next.

My saving grace during this time was the connections I made and the people I met at the school. Southworth and Dave were like saviors to me from the get-go. Had I not met them, two guys I really liked being with, who knows if I would have stayed. I owe a lot to those two in particular when it comes to making me comfortable. I had grown up with friends and brothers around me at all times, on an island where hardly anyone left. Now it was kind of like I was on my own new island, so I had to make do. I did not have the means to go anywhere far, having only a bicycle, so San Jose was also like an island.

I stayed really focused, always thinking about the whole idea of competitive BJJ. The atmosphere at the gym and the competitions were changing. Having these victories under my belt gave me confidence, not just that I could win, but that I was here for the right reasons. For much of my life, I'd had conflicting feelings about whether I was actually good at the things I was doing. I didn't know whether I was good enough to take on certain challenges even when I had success to fall back on. The only way I'd actually recognize I was good at something was by someone challenging me, or telling me I was good; I never innately knew it myself. I lacked the confidence to recognize my abilities, or at the very least I was embarrassed to be complimentary to myself.

IN THE FALL OF 1997, SOMETIME around October, at the urging of friends and family, I decided to travel with Dave and a guy named Greg Rivera, who had also trained with us, to Rio de Janeiro, Brazil, for a tournament called the Brasileiro. Brasileiro falls under the International Brazilian Jiu-Jitsu Federation. The federation oversees all the major BJJ events of significance. While there are smaller events around Brazil at different schools, just as there are in California or anywhere else, this governing body presides over all things important to the larger BJJ community throughout the world.

I knew just being in Brazil was going to be an overwhelming experience, regardless of the competition. When we landed in Rio, I looked out over the city and saw this huge mass of buildings and large ships in port. Like California this was another huge place with millions of people I knew nothing about. Being in California had been strange enough, but Brazil? The sight of the Rio skyline awed me, and I found myself thinking about how much there is to do in the world. It might sound simplistic, but for a kid who was not even 19 years old to suddenly be competing in Brazil was incredibly eye opening.

We stayed at a small place not far from the competition, and the three of us were together most of the time. We were representing Ralph Gracie's school, but we fell under the larger organization of Gracie Barra (Baha), which is one of the largest team associations in the world and represents many of the Gracie schools. Before the competition began, Dave and I had the chance to go over to the famous Gracie Barra Academy, which in many ways is the place where BJJ began. Just a year or so earlier I had not known very much about BJJ, but now everything I knew started and ended with the Gracies, and for them it began at Gracie Barra.

When we entered the school, we felt like we were looking at superstars. The average person on the street wouldn't have known who they were, but we did. These were the guys we hoped to be, and we were about to work out in the same room as them. It was akin to playing basketball on the other side of the court from Michael Jordan. Dave and I worked out alone. For whatever reason, no one took much interest in us. It didn't seem like a very welcoming environment—more like a club we didn't belong to, but were allowed to use their facilities. Regardless, Dave and I practiced the way we always had with each other, as if it was war. It ended up being great preparation for the Brasileiro.

On the day of the competition, there were all these guys walking around—black belts, brown belts, groups of people, different schools—and I just thought to myself about how far I had to go to walk among these fighters. Back in the States you could enter an event and have maybe four or five guys competing in a certain division at a certain weight, and that would be the entire field. You saw white and blue belts, with maybe a brown or black sprinkled in to the group. In Brazil, it seemed the numbers were endless. It certainly made me aware of how much I could gain just from being around all these people. To win here meant you'd really accomplished something special.

When the event finally did take place, I remember the competition being a lot more difficult than I was used to. Not to say I had expected to win the Brasileiro outright because that would have been a bit too much too fast, but having been successful back in California, part of me expected to at least do well. By the tournament's end, I felt satisfied. This time I managed to finish in fourth place, after five matches at the blue level, one shy of receiving a medal. I lost by a point to the guy who went on to win the whole thing, so I felt very good about my performance. Finishing in fourth place was not my goal, but it was something I could be proud of. Besides, I knew I would be back there; it was just a question of when.

BACK IN CALIFORNIA, I CONTINUED to enter more and more local tournaments, and I won almost all of them. The competition was pretty good in the area, but nothing like I had seen in Brazil. Winning local tournaments was good for my confidence, but it didn't necessarily mean I was getting better against the people I would want to beat in the future. In the back of my mind, I knew the next big thing I needed to accomplish would probably be in Brazil, so I stayed focused on preparing myself for that.

Dave and Ralph worked closely with me, as Dave and I were pretty much on similar tracks: two young guys trying to get to the top of the BJJ world, working together. Dave was also trying to figure himself out at the same time I was. Even though we were always together and great friends, it does not necessarily mean we were the same type of person. He loved grappling, and like me was lucky to find himself working toward something he enjoyed. The biggest difference was that I had been a kid who grew up fighting all the time, and he had more of the martial arts mind, trying to become at peace with himself. In a lot of ways our differences helped us help each other. Because we came from two different backgrounds but were looking to go in the same direction, we could take our differences and use them to understand ourselves as individuals.

At the same time, though, Dave was really Ralph's guy. He really looked up to Ralph in a different way than I did. Of course, I respected Ralph as a mentor, teacher, and great martial artist, but to me it seemed Dave saw Ralph as an example of how he would lead his own life. Ralph saw it the same way, as it was obvious that Dave was his most trusted student.

The many ways in which Dave and I were the same and different played out at the school, and this was most evident the first time we decided to put on some gloves for sparring. We didn't do much sparring at the school, and that first time was the most memorable. Since Ralph was an MMA fighter in addition to being a BJJ coach, he liked to work on stand-up fighting. Dave really had no experience doing it, but Ralph always pushed people to try things whether they wanted to or not so they could challenge themselves. Ralph's desire to test people was a very good thing for a martial artist in training because it built confidence and tested limits. Dave knew I liked to fight, and I knew he didn't, so the advantage was mine before we ever threw a punch. He had seen the tapes I had of my friends, brothers, and myself fighting in my basement and on the porch. He knew I was into aggressive sports like wrestle-boxing, and anything else physical. He also knew about many of the fights I had gotten into around Hilo. I was not one to brag a lot, but when you're a teenager, a lot of times getting into fights is the biggest accomplishment of your life, so surely I told him a couple of stories because they were the only stories I had. While I had no formal training in boxing, Dave had none at all.

THIS FIRST TIME RALPH HAD US box I pretty much beat Dave up as Ralph coached from the sides. Ralph yelled at Dave to "stay in there . . . be aggressive," and Dave did his best to comply, but I really was pounding on him. At one point I hit him in the nose a little harder than I should have, and he started to bleed. As he moved to end the fight because the blood was getting all over his shirt, the floor, his face, and my gloves, Ralph yelled at us to "Keep going! Keep fighting!"

"Don't stop!" I heard Ralph say as Dave's face became covered in blood.

"Ralph, I'm bleeding!" Dave looked at Ralph; he was trying to cover up. Ralph refused to let him stop, but at some point the session ended. Whether you agreed with how Ralph did things or not, it was his way and his school. You had to keep going until you couldn't go any more. His nickname was "The Pit Bull" for a reason.

After Dave's and my session, Ralph decided he also wanted to box. After all, if you beat someone's student up at a school, it's usually the teacher's responsibility to put you in your place. It's almost like a pit bull taking a piss on a tree; that's just how it is.

I was a little scared at first—not of getting hit by Ralph, but because you're not supposed to hit the coach at his own school. I didn't want to disrespect him or his school. When I first started training BJJ in Hilo, we had gone over to another school and tapped out some other judo practitioners. Tom was not happy about this and said, "You always respect the sensei." Those words never left me.

Ralph didn't seem to care too much for the rules, or at least he didn't on the day we went at it. At first I pretty much let him have his way with me, not really hitting back much, but it was not natural for me to let anyone hit me without punching back. Still I did what I had been taught to do: respect him. He could see what I was doing, but just as you would expect from a guy like Ralph, he wasn't happy about it. He expected to be hit.

"If you don't hit me back, motherfucker, I'll beat you worse!" he said to me as I continued to hold back my punches and block his. That was his mentality: you either bring it, or I am going to beat on you. There was no shame in defending yourself. His words were all it took for me to flip the switch. Not only had he asked me to hit him back, but he had threatened to beat on me. I have always responded well to those types of threats.

From then on, I more than held my own against him standing up. We were in a fight, or as much of one as you could be in with your coach. This is how Ralph was with some of us. He taught you and toughened you up in the process. This was not the only time it happened either. On another occasion he had just beat up Dave pretty thoroughly, and he asked the class if anyone else wanted to fight. So naturally I raised my hand. Within seconds he had me mounted in a triangle and arm bar, he but kept on hitting me, so much so that I wanted to cry. While it might seem too aggressive, it really was nothing more than teaching. It toughened me up a lot and put on display just how good someone could get. No one was ever severely hurt, and amid all of these fights, Ralph could sense my potential for fighting MMA, even though it wasn't on my mind at all.

While I was happy to have reached a level where I could hold my own on my feet with Ralph, a man who had fought professionally, I had no plans to work on my stand-up. No matter what, I was there for BJJ, and Dave was teaching me all he could, all the time. It was not the right time to even consider a change of course. As fate would have it, though, the road to MMA was a lot shorter than I expected.

Apparently Ralph knew of upcoming fights in the San Jose area, and he thought maybe he could interest me. He approached me about it, and in his own way suggested maybe I wanted to do it, which was more like him telling me I wanted to do it. He was not the type to force you into something, but he could persuade you with his aggressive style. It had never crossed my mind to actually get into a real ring in front of other people at a sanctioned event. I'd had thoughts of boxing in Hilo, but those were the daydreams of a kid. At the same time, though, I loved to fight, and even more loved to challenge myself, so why not? I figured it couldn't hurt to try, when it actually really could!

Ralph laid out the situation for me, where it would be, when, what I could and could not do, and how much I would be paid if I won. *Paid if I won?* That was something I had never heard before. When it came to fighting someone, I had heard things like "You might get arrested" and "That guy is huge . . . do you think you can take him?" But "paid"? Brand-new concept to me. The purse was $400, and to a kid my age, at that time, well, it was a lot of money. There were certainly a lot of things I could buy with $400.

It was weird too because the whole idea of mixed martial arts— while it was growing in California, it was definitely not a legal sport yet. It was still underground. California legalized MMA in December 2005, and here I was sometime around 1997, fighting in some gymnasium while wearing a pair of tight little black Speedo-style shorts, up against a kickboxer in a pair of long black karate pants who had to be at least twenty pounds heavier than me and quite a few inches taller. But whatever, a fight's a fight. Now I just had to pay attention to the actual rules.

Before the fight, I was back in the locker-room area, if you could call it that. It was more like a room with a few mats in it, with cinderblock walls and not a lot of heat. I sat there looking around at the other guys getting prepared for their fights. It seemed like a weird setting, like no one knew what we were doing there. Ralph connected with some of the guys from Cesar Gracie's school, which was a bit farther north in California. We stayed as a group, waiting together for our fights to start. One of the guys was David Terrell, who would eventually fight in the UFC's middleweight division. He was one of the better students from Cesar's school, but he looked slightly anxious, almost shaken up.

We talked for a minute and then I told him, "I'm really nervous about this. I had a hard time sleeping last night."

Terrell, who was looking down at the floor, picked up his head and in all seriousness said, "Hard time sleeping? I haven't slept in three weeks!" I believed him. I would rather have been fighting two or three guys in a Hilo street fight than doing this. I had never really been on a raised stage of any kind like this boxing ring was. Even though at home in Hawaii I was outgoing, joking all the time, and at times loud, I was not that way in California. I was still learning my place, watching others, getting used to being in these new situations. This was a brand-new stage for me, more intimidating than the others, and Terrell's reaction did not exactly put me at ease. But this was going to happen whether I liked it or not. Once you agree to a fight, you can either hit or be hit.

The time passed quickly in the back room, and soon I was walking out to my first fight in front of about a hundred or so people. These people had to be the most hard-core MMA fans in the world if they were here at this event. Ralph and Dave were my cornermen for the fight, and I was told by Ralph what I should do, to take this guy down, because no matter how big a kickboxer is, he will not be able to handle himself on the ground.

I entered the ring, and within seconds the referee checked our readiness. As soon as he motioned for us to begin, I went right at the guy. The only way I knew how to fight was to go full speed and jump on my opponent before he could jump on me. The guy tried to throw a knee, or a kick, but I was already in his corner and had my arms wrapped around his torso. I was able to get him to the ground immediately, as Ralph had instructed me. We rolled over near the ropes, and I had him in side control, with my body on top of his, lying across him and controlling him from the side.

While on his back, he was still able to get his hands around my neck, which kept me in a headlock. I pulled my head out, got my legs over the top, and mounted him. In full control, I started throwing as many punches as possible into his face, one after another. He was helpless in this position, and naturally tried to avoid the punches, which forced him to roll over. Once he gave me the opportunity, and now that I was on his back, I sank my arm under his chin and went for a rear naked choke. He started flailing his left arm, trying to punch me without being able to see his target, but there was no way I was letting go. I held on to his neck like I was hanging from a rope off a cliff, just waiting for him to give up. He did, and it was over. The whole thing seemed to last about ten seconds, even though it was closer to a couple of minutes.

There it was, my first MMA victory against some random kickboxer, for $400, in Stockton, California. The details of the event may be a little vague, but the fight itself I will never forget. Afterward I felt as good as I ever had. It had been a while since I'd gotten to take someone on like that, and doing it in front of an audience was just a huge adrenaline rush.

There was one thing about that night that I regret. When Ralph asked me for a cut of the purse for having been my cornerman, I completely laughed it off, thinking he was kidding. I didn't realize that someone got paid for coaching. I always wish I had given him some of it, because now I know it would have been the right thing to do.

• • •

THE YEAR 1998 ARRIVED AND IT was bound to be a year in which I would learn a lot about myself. I still had a little less than twelve months to go before I was no longer a teenager, but the last year had been the most unique I'd ever had. Like everyone else who makes New Year's resolutions, I already knew what I wanted to achieve in 1998. I was going to get better every day, and at some point, hopefully, I would find myself once again competing in Brazil.

I continued to compete in local tournaments all around California, winning my weight class every time. It may sound a bit unrealistic to hear that I was winning so many of them, but the competition was not always the best. At the white belt level, there were a lot of people competing, but as you moved up higher and higher, facing blues or purples, the ranks thinned out. Many times you would see the same people again and again, or groups of guys from different schools you had faced before. Winning was definitely a good thing because you have to learn how to win, even if you are good. We competed mostly to stay sharp and roll with new guys. Seeing new guys, no matter what level they were at, was an opportunity to see and learn new things, as well as to test what I had learned.

As for what I was learning, it was not just what was taking place at the school, or what Dave, Ralph, or anyone else was showing me. I continued to think about BJJ all the time—every day, every hour, whenever I was awake. There came a point where I was not even able to shower without thinking about it. The only time I was not thinking about BJJ was when I was actually putting it to work either during practice or in competition. Alone, though, when I was just hanging out, I could not get it out of my head.

On some level the whole thing was making me a little crazy, but I had to focus and work around it. It may seem weird to be training for something and viewing the idea of it being on your mind all the time as a problem, but it was. I was not dating anyone, I did not work in some office, I just had this thing in front of me I was trying to figure out. I couldn't understand why it was consuming me like this.

With this commitment, and this constant practicing and thinking about BJJ, the only thing left for me was to focus on getting back to Brazil. Dave and I had discussed going back to compete in the Mundials, which is the Brazilian World Championship of BJJ, or more accurately, the most important BJJ tournament in the world. Dave would say to me, "Why stay around here and just dominate the competition when we can really test our skills against the best guys?" Ralph was not very into the idea. One time we were talking about heading there to train and compete, and Ralph just said, "Why do you motherfuckers want to go to Brazil? Stay here and train here!"

Well, we were doing that already, every day, and while we were definitely improving, the allure of getting back to Brazil in order to take on the best was something we both could not ignore. We had been watching these grainy VHS tapes of earlier Mundials, black-and-white copies on a crappy TV, seeing these guys, one after another, pulling off all these phenomenal moves. Why not us? If you were not going to test yourself against the best, what is the point of showing up at school every day in the first place? It is why I was there; it was why I was competing.

My desire to go to Brazil had nothing to do with what I was learning from Ralph. He had invested a lot of time in me and was always pulling me aside to show me different things he was not showing the others. He was there for me in a lot of ways, trying to mold me into the best BJJ competitor he could. It is something I will never forget, but still I was a kid who wanted to see and do more things. Brazil was one of those things. In fact, it was the only place that mattered. Brazil gave me one of the answers for why I had always loved to fight. It was a chance to compete against the best, and in the summer of 1998 I was going to go to the Mundials in Rio no matter what, to compete against the best people on my level.

• • •

As I was preparing through the first months of 1998, Reagan decided he wanted to come to California. He was still living at my parents' house at the time. Since he had done well in school, as always, he had lots of opportunities. He had been practicing BJJ a lot in Hilo and wanted to come to California to check it out. I was definitely into the idea of having him with me, so he moved out to San Jose.

With Reagan now in Mountain View and working out at the school, I had a new partner to practice with. In the year since I'd left home, Reagan had become really good and had no problems keeping up with the guys at the school. Reagan was taller than both Dave and me, and slightly bigger too, so he was a different type of partner.

As the 1998 Mundials approached, I was working harder than ever to prepare. Even though I was approaching the level of a purple belt, which was Dave's level, I remained blue heading into the summer. Reagan was also going to compete as a blue belt, but he was not as intense about the whole thing as I was. His plan was just to accompany me since Dave was not going this time. Not surprisingly, Dave had listened to Ralph and decided staying in California was the better move, but Reagan and I were going to go no matter what.

This would be my second trip to Brazil in less than a year, and rather than be the younger kid following someone else's lead, it was my turn to lead Reagan. Reagan was always a confident kid, so I didn't have to worry much about him, but he was definitely excited to be there. We both were. After all, this was the biggest tournament in the world.

This trip would be a real eye-opening experience for me because unlike my first trip, with Dave, I was traveling with Reagan, Jay Dee, and my friend Hoyt. In addition, Jay Dee's friends from Las Vegas, Charuto and another named Steve DaSilva, were also going to be there, providing us with places to stay in Brazil. Unlike the last time, when Dave and I were in a more uncomfortable situation, we now had guides.

Unlike tournaments in the United States or anywhere else in the world, this was Brazil's world championships. If you were from France, Japan, or anywhere else in the world, you could show up and say, "I'm the best guy from Paris. I'd like to compete." Anyone from elsewhere was allowed to try their luck, but he was probably going to get smashed. The Brazilians, however, could not just enter at will. They had to compete within all of the different schools, and there were many of them. There was the well-known Gracie Barra, another called Nova Unãio, others like Alliance, as well as a number of other Gracie academies. Countless numbers of guys, just little packs, all working together, pushing each other. There were fighters who would later become more well known, like Travis Lutter, Ricardo Arona, and Paulo Filho. From the Ralph Gracie school in California, it was just us. We met some other people who we hung around with, but we were there alone.

Reagan had really just come to watch and help. At that point he had only been at the Ralph Gracie School a couple of weeks and had not really competed on the levels I had, but since he was already there, he figured he would also compete in the blue division, one weight class heavier than me. The competition was going to be very difficult for both of us, especially for Reagan, who was new to a lot of this.

Team competition in Brazil was very different in that if you were the best in your school and had defeated your teammates, you did not have to fight the same number of matches as guys who were not as successful. Once you'd defeated someone from your school, if you faced him again in competition, you leapfrogged over him, which saved the best fighters from exerting themselves early on. Reagan and I would have to fight at least five or six times to achieve a medal of any kind since we had no team to speak of, but we were both able to do so.

I reached the finals in my first Mundial and faced a very talented guy from team Nova União named João Vitorino. In what was a very competitive match, Vitorino was able to defeat me on points, which meant he executed more moves than I had. I made it to the top of the blue belt division in my weight class, and I had lost, but just barely. I wasn't satisfied with the result because I really wanted to win, especially having come this far. Thousands of people were there to watch me on the biggest stage there is for BJJ, and I let it slip away.

For Reagan, things definitely went better. While I had almost become a world champion in BJJ, the first Penn to do it was my little brother, who had a lot less experience. In a very tough division, as a white belt, he defeated Daniel Dias and Alberto Crain to win the gold. It was really impressive, and in many ways, the best thing that could have happened. It was one thing to win something for yourself, but to see a member of your family succeed, especially my little brother and best friend, was amazing. He came out of nowhere to do this. He had been at Ralph's for a really short time, and working out with guys in Hilo who were not nearly the level of the guys I had been with, or the ones he would face, and yet he was still able to come out on top. He always manages to amaze, but never surprise.

ON OUR RETURN TO CALIFORNIA, MANY people at the school congratulated us for winning the gold and silver medals. For Reagan, this whole thing was still new to him, but he handled it pretty well. For me it was an accomplishment, and I had just moved one step closer to achieving my goal of becoming a black belt. Almost immediately after returning, Ralph awarded me with my purple belt. I had been a blue belt for about a year, and since I'd done very well locally and now in Brazil as well, he thought it fit that I move up to the next level.

It was now the summer of 1998, I had come to the San Jose area about a year earlier and achieved my purple belt. I had worked extremely hard to move up and was now on the same level, to some extent, as my mentor, Dave. Things were starting to take shape for me, but I really still wanted more.

The summer moved along the same way as the weeks leading up to the Mundials had, with a lot of training. Jay Dee made plans to transfer from UNLV to San Jose State and live with me and Reagan. This was definitely going to be a good thing for all of us because it would be the first time we were living together for quite a while and for the first time without our parents. In addition to school, though, Jay Dee had also been practicing BJJ in Las Vegas, so he would be another partner to work with. We never knew what Jay Dee was going to bring to the table as far as training went. Coming from another school, he probably had new things to offer. At the very least I knew he would be bringing good vibes with him, as he always did.

I needed a bit of a change of pace too. Having traveled as far as I had to compete and having done all the training I had, it would seem natural to want to take a little break or a vacation from it all. For whatever reason, though, I did not have vacation on my mind. I would still hang with my friends and hit places like Santa Cruz with Southworth from time to time, but I could still not shake BJJ from my head.

I would be sitting on a beach with friends, and I'd start asking questions: "How do you do this?" "Then what do you do if he has your arm caught?" "Can you do that? Can you show me how to do that?"

"BJ, is this something you need to know right now?" my friends would ask.

"YES!" was the only answer I could give them.

I was not only driving myself crazy, but anyone else who spent time around me. All I could do was go back to the school and work as hard as possible. Maybe, if I perfected something or figured out the answers to all BJJ's questions, maybe then it would stop, or at least I hoped. That seemed to be the only solution, so I had nothing left to do but keep at it.

5

NEW
BEGINNINGS

N THE FALL OF 1998, JAY DEE finally arrived in San Jose
with a plan to attend school and train on the side. Having my
older brother around was good for a lot of reasons, and not
just because he was so close to me in age: he was always bringing
something new to the table, which I really needed. With the BJJ
in my head all the time, Jay Dee would be a necessary distraction,
someone who could help me relax so that I didn't get too crazy
about my training. He was the type of guy who would pull your
leg and try to make you laugh, whereas Reagan was quieter and
more reserved, like me. Jay Dee could defuse a situation or help you
figure it out, which is what older brothers do.

At that time I needed someone who could help me figure some
things out—mainly whether I should stay in California or go back
to Hawaii. Part of me still itched to go back home even though I

knew it wasn't the best idea as far as moving forward with BJJ. I was almost twenty years old, and I still wanted to do more than what I was doing. Seeing Brazil, visiting Jay Dee in Las Vegas, and just traveling around California showed me that I didn't want to stay in Mountain View all the time, that there was more out there. Adding to this restlessness, I had reached a point of understanding with competitive BJJ, had taken on the best in my class and done well, and had the work ethic to succeed wherever I went. After my trips to Brazil, it was becoming clear that just as I had to travel to California to go beyond the small BJJ culture in Hilo, I'd have to go beyond California if I hoped to continue to grow. This was not to say that I wanted out of my situation at Ralph's, but I did need something new.

This was where Jay Dee was able to help. When he was in Las Vegas, he trained at the Nova União school under a guy named John Lewis, at his Academy J-Sect, which is also known as Lewis-Pederneiras Brazilian BJJ. The head coach was a guy named Andre Pederneiras, who lived in Brazil but was extremely well known to anyone practicing BJJ seriously, and frequently visited Las Vegas. Nova União stood for "New Union" and was created by Pederneiras and his partner, Wendell Alexander, by bringing their teams together to create a single team able to compete at the highest levels.

When it came to teaching, Pederneiras was known as "The Ultimate Master." Everyone I trained with seriously seemed to feel this way. It was just understood that learning from Pederneiras and alongside his students could only be a good thing. Pederneiras was the first guy to put together the Brazilian BJJ Championships back in 1993, before the Gracies started hosting their own a few years later. He himself had received his black belt from Carlson Gracie Jr., one of the best in the world, but had decided to blaze his own trail. Pederneiras helped BJJ spread, and now he had developed his own high-level guys who continued to study under him.

At one point earlier in the year, I had gone back to Hilo to see my family, and one of Pederneiras's students, a guy named Renato Verissimo, also known as "Charuto," who had accompanied us to Brazil for the Mundials, was living there and helping to teach at Tom's school. During this trip, I had the opportunity to work out with Charuto, and from the moment we started grappling, I knew immediately this guy was good. Not good in a "I could learn a few things from this guy" kind of way, but good in the "Holy shit, this guy is real good" kind of way. It was my first time rolling with one of Pederneiras's guys, and I was impressed. He was definitely going to be good for BJJ in Hawaii, if he decided to stay. I had known Charuto was already helping guys like Reagan, but having first-hand experience with him really convinced me of his abilities.

I'd met John Lewis one time when I visited Jay Dee in Las Vegas, and from my experience with Charuto, I knew he was training good guys down there. Because of Jay Dee's connection to Lewis, this became another option I could explore. At the very least it would not hurt to go to Las Vegas just for the fun of it, even if the training was not what I had hoped. I was young and wanted to do some things people my age were doing. I needed to have more fun than I was having, since I never took a break.

As the fall of 1998 wore on, I started making more and more trips to Las Vegas to hang out and train with some of these new guys. There were so many guys in the Vegas area who were into martial arts, and the entire vibe was just different there. J-Sect had future MMA fighters like Marvin Eastman and Tony DeSouza, as well as a future world BJJ champion, Robert Drysdale, who was just starting out as a young teenager. Future BJJ and MMA coaches Mark Laimon and Todd Lally, who have gone on to create their own schools and camps, were also there training. Just a lot of new people, new faces, and new techniques to learn with countless fighters. I was there to soak up anything I could, and bring it back with me to California, Hawaii, and of course, to Brazil.

I had no plans to stay in Las Vegas for an extended period of time, but it was so much fun. Las Vegas is obviously like no place else in the world, so it was a great escape for me, and connecting with more and more fighters could only be a good thing. It just made sense for me to keep exploring and looking for new people and challenges.

As for the grappling in Las Vegas, some of the techniques were very different, but the way my partners dealt with me was the same. Lewis was a black belt, and his students were very talented, but guys had a hard time passing my guard or getting me in leg locks, no different from how things were in Hawaii and Mountain View. I had learned a lot over the last two years and had competed on a pretty high level, and the things I was able to do when I began I now did even better. Passing my guard would always be difficult for most fighters, no matter how big or small, and even the guys at Nova União could sense this was a strong suit of mine.

Meanwhile, back in California, Jay Dee, Reagan, Dave, and other guys I had worked out with were still grappling at Ralph's as much as possible. Ralph also brought in students from his cousin Cesar Gracie's school, like Dave Terrell and Gil Castillo, also very talented fighters. There were just so many guys showing up from all different places it was unbelievable. Everywhere you looked, it seemed there was a new guy to work with. I could sense BJJ was growing rapidly and we were all in the center of it.

Having so many new guys, in addition to the frequent trips to Las Vegas I was making, helped me shed the feeling that I was not growing as a fighter. At the same time, though, my travels did not help my relationship with Ralph and his school. I had stopped showing up there for quite some time and began seeking new places to study.

Complicating matters was the fact that I also had new opportunities from my old friend Bobby Southworth. When I first arrived at Ralph's, he had been one of the main students at the school, helping Ralph run the place. Unfortunately, their personalities clashed, so Southworth moved on. He found a new home with a guy named Javier Mendez over at a place called the American

Kickboxing Academy (AKA) in San Jose. Mendez had opened up AKA officially in 1993 and had been training people since the mid-1980s. AKA was one of the first schools to really focus on mixed martial arts. At the time not many places were doing this. Schools were teaching different martial arts, but in terms of viewing MMA as a sport in and of itself, encompassing all types of fighting, there were very few: the Lion's Den in San Jose, run by Frank Shamrock, his brother Ken Shamrock, and Guy Mezger, and a school in the Midwest run by Pat Miletich. Miletich was not only a great fighter; he was training future MMA stars like Jens Pulver and Matt Hughes.

For a while I'd watched MMA take shape around me. The guys were all mix-and-match. Learning in one place, taking it to another, improving every aspect any way and everywhere possible. Though I knew a lot of them from various gyms, MMA wasn't yet my thing. Still, Southworth provided me with a place to train and introduced me to other helpful people. In particular, I met this guy named Garth Taylor, who had been practicing BJJ for about eight years. Taylor was a big guy, who looked like an NFL offensive lineman, and in addition to BJJ, he had a solid wrestling background, having competed for the West Valley Junior College team.

Between Southworth, Taylor, my brothers, and our friend Alex Oxendine, there was a little circle forming of guys who got along and liked to train. Almost like our own team was forming without us even realizing it. I was still tight with Dave, so he was not really far outside the circle, but he was always training at Ralph's or working for him. Since I was not showing up at Ralph's as often as he would have liked, our relationship fell off slightly. Taylor and Southworth were right there to pick me up, though, always providing me with places and people to train with. We had our own crew, all helping each other in our quest to achieve our individual goals.

Things were changing very quickly for me in late 1998, and it was hard to make sense of it all. For a number of months, I was all over the place, whether it was Hilo, Las Vegas, or parts of California. It seemed I was never in one place for more than a week or two at a time. As soon as Jay Dee had arrived, it seemed I was always on the road, going in circles, but at the same time competing in all of the local tournaments and taking everything in. All the while I was winning the tournaments I was entering into, I was pushing myself to keep going, justifying all the training and traveling. Throughout the period before the 1999 Mundials, I won just about every event I entered.

The break I took from Ralph's was necessary to keep me from burning out. Just like a student of U.S. history can't just study the Civil War but has to study the Revolutionary War, World War I, and Vietnam, so I had to learn other ways besides Ralph's. I had no designs on leaving Ralph's; I was just spreading my wings, doing what came naturally, moving forward, trying new things. Leaping from rock to rock, jumping off bridges.

As 1999 BEGAN, I WAS TWENTY years old and was setting my sights on Brazil again, this time in the purple belt division. With that, I expected the competitions to be tougher, but I was training harder than ever and I knew that come summer, I'd be ready.

The biggest change in how I prepared myself for fights came about because of Garth Taylor. Before I started to work out with Taylor, I'd never done much working out, the way most people recognize it. I had not been lifting weights, jogging, doing springs, swimming, cardiovascular exercises, none of it. My entire training consisted of the martial arts activities I was doing. I knew that other people (especially those in MMA) were supplementing their martial arts workouts with cross-training, but until I met Taylor, I never felt my strength was lacking in any way. In fact, it was just the opposite, since I often had people commenting how I was surprisingly very strong for someone my size. And again, BJJ was a lot more about technique than it was about power and strength.

Taylor was able to convince me of the benefits of a cross-training workout. He had been involved with a new training program called CrossFit, which at the time was somewhat revolutionary. CrossFit was started by a guy named Greg Glassman, and he was helping Taylor take his physical skills to another level. This company was on the cutting edge of athletic training, and Taylor was one of their first pupils, if not the first. It has since been used to train military personnel, police, and countless others who want to be in top performance shape.

Even though I did not work with CrossFit on a daily basis, it definitely opened my eyes about training methods, and helped me see how much more I could do physically and the impact this would have on my career. I knew the days of relying on my natural abilities were numbered. While I had no desire to enter the MMA world at the time, even with BJJ, more people were getting involved and the competitions were growing. This meant that the stakes were getting higher, and I'd have to work harder to stay at the top.

IN THE WINTER OF 1999, I was fighting in the biggest BJJ competitions in the United States. One of them was the Copa Pacifica in Los Angeles, known as "The Copa," and in winter of 1999 it was my goal to compete in the purple belt division and win it. The previous year I'd done quite well, winning the blue belt gold by finishing Javier Vasquez, who was probably my toughest opponent stateside at the time. I knew that the competition in the purple belt division would be much stiffer—even though I'd have to fight fewer guys. As it turned out, I only had to fight two to win the gold, but the first ended up being tougher than the second. My first opponent pushed me to the max with neither of us really able to gain an advantage throughout the fight. Eventually I was able to sweep him and win on points, but I left that match feeling fairly anxious about what the competition would hold from this point forward.

Fortunately for me, the second match was much easier. I fought a guy named Sabatini, someone who I had not seen before but who I was told was pretty good. I was able to control him from the beginning of the match until the end, and I may have even finished him with a submission from his back before the end of the match.

One belt higher, and one year later, I had won the Copa again. While I might not have been a household name anywhere in Brazil, I was definitely establishing myself as one of the better guys state-side. Little did I know that this victory would come with a price—my friendship with Ralph.

I'd entered the Copa tournament fighting for Team Nova União. It was the first time I'd done that in a major competition, but it felt like the right thing to do because I'd been training so much with that group of guys. It didn't seem like a huge deal; it was just a name, and I was just a kid who was competing.

Not everyone saw it that way, though. Ralph Gracie was not happy about it. In his eyes it was bad enough I'd started to spend most of my time training with the guys from Nova União, but for me to fight under their name made him pretty upset. In his mind he'd probably viewed me as someone from his school, someone he invested in, and for me to be anywhere else was a slap in the face.

That wasn't how I saw it. To me, I was just competing, meeting people, traveling, and having fun. I was proud that I'd earned my purple belt from Ralph and not someone else. There was nothing malicious on my part; I had just been training with the Nova guys and went with them to the Copa. In any case, Ralph was very unhappy about the situation and would let it be known. When he found out I'd competed for Nova União at the Copa, he told both Jay Dee and Reagan not to come back to his school.

My leaving Ralph's wasn't something I had planned on doing; I did it because I needed to keep growing as a fighter. It wasn't personal, but Ralph took it that way. I guess to him things were either black or white; there could be no gray. It was as if he had an unspoken rule that if you trained at his school, you were obliged to stay there forever, or at least keep him informed of all the things you were doing. I never signed up for that. I did not sign up to compete for Ralph or Gracie Barra for life. I was twenty years old, still figuring out my path. But he took offense at my decision to fight for Nova União, and as a result we were through. I have always respected Ralph for the help he gave me, so I have tried not to do him wrong, but it just seems we will never see eye to eye on how things transpired.

THE TRANSITION FROM RALPH to Nova União happened pretty naturally. Ralph did not want me around if I was not exclusively with him, while Nova was pretty excited to have me on board regardless of where I trained. Whatever it was that took me from one place to another, it all seemed to make sense. In a lot of ways I was having a growth spurt, both physically and mentally. This period of training in different places with different people was really paying off and was reflected in my expanding abilities.

After the Copa, I heard Pederneiras would be in Las Vegas with some of his guys, so I took another trip down there. From time to time these guys from Brazil would come in to give seminars around the States, especially Vegas. Even though the city was not even hosting large fighting events outside of boxing, it became home to a lot of martial artists.

The day I arrived in Vegas I was rolling with Steve DaSilva for most of the class, as Pederneiras was pointing out some new things to us. DaSilva was a student under John Lewis and quite a bit older than me but was a fantastic guy to be around because of his huge personality. I had spent time with him in 1998 when I first went to the Mundials, and had instantly become a friend. He was a long and rangy guy, with a big Afro and an even bigger smile. In fact, when I first came to Las Vegas, after watching me train for a bit, he moved past the name "Alien BJJ" and coined the nickname "The Prodigy." It stuck, and it was fitting someone creative like Steve was responsible for it.

After the class, I was resting up with Steve when Pederneiras and Lewis came over to me. Pederneiras told me to stand up, and then he approached me with a brown belt. Even though I had not been a purple belt for very long, they believed I had accomplished enough to move up to the next level. My purple belt was removed from my gi and the brown belt was tied around my waist by Pederneiras. In a few short months I had made a major jump, since I would now be competing not just with brown belts but with black belts as well.

A lot of people may think the jump happened very quickly, but I was being judged by the best in the world. I had been able to finish off guys who were black belts, and even though this is not what qualifies you to move up, they believed I had reached the next level. No one understood the situation, or what it meant, more than Pederneiras. I was not there to judge his decision, but I was extremely happy with it. If there was ever a lingering question about which team I would end up with, it had officially been answered.

AS THE 1999 MUNDIALS APPROACHED, a group of us connected to Nova União—Jay Dee, Charuto, my older brother Jay, Marc Laimon, and me—flew to Rio de Janeiro. This time I was traveling as part of a team, which meant not only that I had the support from coaches, teammates, and friends, but that I was representing something bigger than myself.

The guys on Nova União in Brazil were not just a bunch of guys who had come together because they liked BJJ. To be a part of this team, you did not just show up at a school; you had to earn your way into it. Nova União was the team we wanted to be a part of, the guys we had been trying to emulate for years. A lot of people had come to know the Gracie name, but to our crew these were really the guys we were looking up to. We had all watched the videotapes, read the magazines, and found out everything we could about them. Now we had the opportunity to train with them, learn from them, and compete alongside them.

We arrived in Rio about a week before the tournament so we could get acclimated to our surroundings, and wasted no time getting ourselves started. First thing we did was grab our luggage and take a car over to the gym where we would be training. We left our bags there because we had to go meet up with the Nova União guys who were training at the University Gama Filho. Gama Filho was located in Rio, and not the nice part.

Gama Filho is a really big school, and had a large sports complex with swimming pools, gymnasiums, and anything else you would need to train. As we walked over to the gymnasium, you could hear voices, sounds, and bodies just going at it. We finally came through the door, and it was just this huge place, about the size of two basketball courts, with mats all over the floor. There must have been about thirty black belts in the room, working with each other and doing their thing. We were all a little bit in awe of what we were seeing. In the States, if there was a black belt in the room, there was a really good chance he was either teaching the class or owned the school. Now we were in a room filled with them—guys we wanted to be just like.

I put down my things, and just went right to it while my brothers and some of the other guys watched. The way I figured it, this was the reason I'd come all this way, so why waste time? From the moment I put my things down, I started matching up with anyone willing, and held my own.

There were black belts and brown belts grappling with me, sweeping me off my feet only to have me sweep them back. These guys were all so good because they pushed one another, and this is what I wanted and needed. This was the type of preparation you must have to compete on the highest levels. You had to have guys on your own team who could beat you. You had to have teammates who could win it all. You want to be part of the best, pushing to be the best. Whether I could ever win the gold at the Mundials at the highest level, the black belt level, would be decided before the competition ever began. If I could not defeat my Nova União team-mates, or at least do to them all that they could do to me, there would be no point in going forward.

I could sense most of the Nova União guys had each other's back. When I was at Ralph's, I felt I had the support of the guys at the school, but with Nova União it was just a different atmosphere altogether. These guys were tough, and they stood by each other. I wanted to be a part of that, and I got the sense if I could prove my-self to them and show them that I could make them better, I would have all the support I needed to do well.

The fighters of Nova União did not act privileged and did not grow up doing BJJ because their moms or dads took them over to the school to learn. These were young men who started off on the street, fighting, looking for a way out, and maybe BJJ could offer it to them. A lot of the Nova União guys had grown up in the "favelas," which are those tiny homes you see everywhere in South America. They're built one right on top of the next with metal roofs and clothing lines that stretch from one wall to the next. These are places where no one has ever used a washing ma-chine, and people are lucky to let alone have electricity. If you think there are places to buy liquor and cash checks in American ghettos, take a walk through Brazil's favelas. It seems like there are five bars on every street, but if anyone has a check to cash, it would be a surprise.

The streets of the favelas are packed with kids kicking balls down alleys, and maybe one in a million will be able to make it as a "futebol" player. For the rest, fighting is also an option, and just like in Hilo, it's not an option that leaves you with a lot of choices. You either fight to get out of the favela or fight to stay in it. Either way you are going to have a fight. A lot of these guys were fortu-nate to find BJJ, and none of them ever forget the fights they'd had, which toughened them up and helped them become a part of this team.

I did not grow up without a roof over my head or something to eat, like some of these boys, but I certainly grew up fighting. I knew what it meant to hold my ground if you wanted to get something, and as a result I felt very comfortable with the team. But even though I had Pederneiras as a supporter and Charuto by my side, I wasn't sure if these Brazilians would accept me. While I was a teammate, I was not part of the family yet.

On that first day in the gymnasium, I felt I did enough to show them I belonged. As I trained that day and for the rest of the week, there was none of the unease that had marked my two previous trips to Brazil. This setting, these new people, and my friends from home combined to make this a much easier experience. Being accepted by Pederneiras and having Charuto as a guide made Brazil a place I wanted to be rather than a place I had to be.

WHEN THE DAY OF THE COMPETITION finally arrived, I was as ready as I'd ever been, but still a little nervous. By the time we got to the facility, most of Nova União was already there. After spending the last week earning my place on the team against guys like Vitor "Shaolin" Ribeiro, considered to be one of the best, I was confident I would do well. For someone my size, Shaolin was as good as they came, and he would go on to win the gold medal in the black belt division. If I was capable of holding my own with him, I could at least challenge anyone.

The competition was very good. There was not much that separated a lot of these brown belts from the black belts. As a purple belt, I was able to do very well against some black belts, so this level was that much better. This was the second year in a row I would not be fighting in my normal weight class of 135. There were many more senior fighters in my natural weight class (which at the time was around 140 pounds), and I had shown up late for the "selections," so competed at 147 pounds. The selections were a process of fighting the guys in your own school to see who moves on to compete in different divisions. There were two Nova União fighters in the brown belt division around my weight who had done well in the selections. One of them, Rodrigo Antonio, was competing in the weight below me—*pena* (featherweight)—while the other, Marcos Mello, was in *pluma* (superfeatherweight). Because they had done well in the selections, they had as good a chance to win in my natural weight division as I did, which was featherweight. Because of the selections and matters of seniority, I was relegated to the *leve* (lightweight) division, which was two divisions up from my weight at the time. This happened a fair amount in BJJ, so I didn't see it as a huge problem, but still in a place where the competition was this tough, every advantage mattered.

The roster of guys who competed for the brown included some notable names like Gabriel Gonzaga, Matt Serra, and Ricardo Arona, who would all go on to become big-time MMA fighters. And those were just the browns. You still had Murilo Bustamante, Paulo Filho, Royler Gracie, and guys of that level fighting to win the black belt competitions. At the time all of these guys were just pictures in magazines, images on videotapes—none of them connected to me in any way except in our desire to win a gold medal. Now we were all in the same room competing to be the best.

The tournament was tough. I had been matched up with a good opponent right from the start. Other tournaments in other countries, maybe you get an easy fight out of the gate, but not here. While my first opponent was difficult, I was able to finish him by submission. The next fight was even harder—possibly the hardest fight I'd ever had either in the gym or in the street. I did not know the opponent, and my teammates had no advice. It was an all-out war from the moment we began to the moment it ended. We had both swept each other and both had moments when we were in control of the fight, trying to survive. As if that wasn't tough enough, the guy was flat-out bigger than I was, and he was able to use his size to wear me down.

I won by advantage, meaning that although the match was

within one point, I won because I'd attempted more in what had been a dead-even match. Debatably, a subjective decision.

I was able to rest up for a bit, get some energy back, and focus on the next match. It was at moments like these where training with Garth Taylor could make the difference. I had reached the semifinals of the tournament, and had to face a very well-respected fighter named Fernando Augusto, or "Tererê," as he goes by in Brazil. Tererê was a great fighter, as skilled as they came in BJJ. He was at least two weight divisions up from me, taller, and more experienced. He was also very flexible, strong, and lanky. I figured whoever won this match between us would go on to win the gold medal.

Tererê fought for a team called Alliance, one of the most respected in the world. As good as Nova União was, Alliance had still won the Brazilian Team Championships earlier in the year, so they were just as solid as we were, if not more so. Just being part of Alliance, Tererê had all the help he could have needed against me, and vice versa. Lucky for him, though, he received a little extra help along the way.

Though it had been a few months since Ralph had asked my brothers to leave his school, from everything I'd heard, my former teacher was still bothered about what had happened with me. Whenever he had a chance, he would tell anyone willing to listen that I was a "traitor." Some say he does this even to this day. As it turned out, apparently his family couldn't let it go either.

There were multiple Gracie teams in the Mundial tournament that year, as there are every year. Teams like Gracie Barra, Renzo Gracie, and Gracie Humaita covered the lineup, and it seemed that almost every team had some connection to the Gracies. The famed Gracie Barra team basically runs the Mundials, and Carlson Gracie Jr., the head of this team, is a first cousin of Ralph and his brothers. Ordinarily the Gracie teams and Alliance were opponents, but during my match with Tererê, I was surprised to see Ralph's younger brother, Ryan Gracie, actively rooting against me.

The match with Tererê was an all-out battle. He was an explosive fighter, and for much of the fight things were very even, with both of us struggling to gain control. He was trying to avoid my guard at all costs, and he knew to do this because Ryan had been instructing him to avoid it. Tererê decided to pull guard first, which was a great way to avoid mine, but he was unable to score any points there. It was only when later on in the match, after a lot of back and forth, he was able to push me out of bands while he was attempting to sweep me. The referee awarded him advantage based on that, even though there was no way he had gained an advantage. But again, there was Ryan Gracie, shouting at the official to credit Tererê.

Throughout the rest of the match neither of us was able to gain any real advantage. At one point I had Tererê down in his guard, fighting for control, but was unable to do much. Toward the end, with the two of us tied up on the ground, Tererê went for my foot in an attempt to get a heel hook, or a foot lock on me. I was able to lunge forward and stop him, or "stuff" him, as they say, and the match ended. They awarded Tererê the victory by advantage. I had come up short, but just barely, left to wonder how much influence Ryan's yelling had over the match, although I did not have to think very hard to know.

No one otuside of the Gracie Barra group viewed the fight as fair, and anyone who has viewed the match since, or who was present for it, agrees that it was complete bullshit. It was not even for the gold medal, but at the very least, had I won the match, I would have taken the silver. That was not the point, though. It was just the fact that one member of the famed Gracie family would act that way in a tournament where their family name meant so much. And for what? Because Ralph Gracie was upset that I left his school? It really was a shame. I was still just a kid trying to accomplish something great in my life. I have no problems with the Gracie family at all, for they have done as much, or more, for BJJ than any other single family has done for any sport. It was just so disappointing to see Ryan act in such a manner toward me at such an important time in my life.

In the end I placed third and received the bronze medal, two weight divisions above, as a brown belt. I truly did feel robbed, but at the same time I felt Team Nova União really did have my back. Everyone knew what had happened was ridiculous, and something that as a team we would fight against happening again. Ultimately Nova União did very well in the tournament, and I had been part of it.

I was starting to like Brazil a lot more, but it seemed there was a lot of unfinished business.

6

UNFINISHED BUSINESS

WITH THE MUNDIALS BEHIND ME, I returned to Northern California to continue my training. There was no vacation yet for either the body or the mind. So much had happened in Brazil, and it was difficult to process it all. While I had the opportunity to meet all of these new guys and move forward with Nova União, the circus surrounding the end of tournament pissed me off to no end. There was only one thing I could do: continue to get better and return next year to prove I was one of the best.

Meanwhile, back in San Jose, I started spending more and more time at AKA and the other gyms in the area, as did Jay Dee and Reagan. Getting stronger and cross-training were things I needed to start taking seriously. Even though I had seen a lot of guys working out and getting big, it never added up for me when it came to

BJJ. For MMA, I could understand doing it because of the toll all of those disciplines take on your body, but I just wanted to practice BJJ and was a bit too lazy to dedicate too much time to the other stuff.

One thing I had noticed in Brazil, though, was how Shaolin worked out like he was a MMA fighter. A lot of the others were naturally big, or in shape just from the training, but he took it to the next level, which was one of the main reasons why he was as successful as he was. Between being at AKA and working with Garth Taylor, I was determined to take myself to a higher place. Slowly but surely I started working out more and more, usually with new people all the time, which meant I was meeting even more people.

Meanwhile, over at AKA, Frank Shamrock and a partner of his, Bob Cook, started something they called the Universal Submission Academy. Javier Mendez, Cook, Shamrock, and Southworth all recognized the importance of MMA, which was growing in popularity throughout the region, with more and more fighters looking to train in all aspects of martial arts. Because of this, Mendez was comfortable giving these guys the room to push the BJJ and other submission fighting arts inside his gym.

While MMA was getting bigger and these guys were trying to make it a reality, I still had no interest in it. I just was not sure there was a real future or a career in it for me. With BJJ, I knew I could become a highly skilled champion, head back to Hawaii, and then teach for the rest of my life. MMA did not offer such a clear path. You could make more money teaching people and living a nice life than you could putting your life on the line inside of some cage in Lake Charles, Louisiana, which is where Shamrock was scheduled to fight Tito Ortiz.

These guys were impressive, and I was interested in watching all of the UFCs and other events, but the payoff did not make sense for me. Such a huge risk and so little reward. Guys like Dan Henderson, a former Olympic wrestler, were fighting twice in one night, and outside of a small circle of devoted followers, no one really seemed to care. Credit to Henderson and the others who were laying it on the line solely out of the desire to compete, but I had not yet reached the heights they had.

Even though I was not into the MMA, I did from time to time like to hit the bag, or practice hitting mits with people at AKA. I guess after a certain period of time I yearn to hit something, so it might as well be the bag. From time to time, I would work out with Mendez, who in addition to being the owner of AKA, was a celebrated kickboxing champion. He had a lot to offer, and like Ralph, Pederneiras, and Tom Callos, he was older than me and had been around. He knew how to coach striking as well as anyone I had known.

During one of our first workouts, Mendez held up the hand pads for me and had me work on my jabs and straight right hands. I had done this before, but not with a guy who was as talented as he was. He liked what I was able to do from the get-go. After a couple of sessions with the hand pads, he started to instruct me on how to move my feet and throw standard combinations with my hands. I was able to pick up all of the things he was pointing out to me pretty quickly. Even though I lacked formal training, punching is a natural thing to do, especially if you have practiced like I had over the years.

Mendez was impressed by how hard I hit for a guy my size, and how good my reflexes were. It had to be a product of all the wrestle-boxing I did growing up. Anyone can throw a punch, but to do it with accuracy and power while moving—that is different. The reason I was able to pick it up so quickly was because of the young age at which I started.

I could sense some of the guys at AKA wanted me to make the transition to MMA in the middle of all of this BJJ, but it was not going to happen, at least not then.

• • •

Right before the New Year I took another trip down to Las Vegas to get some work in over at J-Sect. If you're in Las Vegas as often as I was, all the days blend together. Obviously it's one of the craziest towns in the world, but for the most part I was there for business, with a little pleasure sprinkled in from time to time. Of all the days I had spent there, there was one day that has had a more lasting impact than any other, even more than the day I received my brown belt.

In addition to being a teacher at his own school, John Lewis was a mover and a shaker. He was the kind of guy who just made things happen, involved in many different things—acting, singing, fighting, promoting—and always just waiting for an opening. He had a natural ability that enabled him to connect himself with the right situation, which, like fighting, takes a lot more work than luck.

One day he told me about this superrich client he was teaching BJJ to, and asked me to work out with him for demonstration purposes. Lewis specifically said, "Don't show me up, let's just have some fun."

We went over to this rich client's gym, which was located underneath an office building not too far west of Las Vegas Boulevard. I remember thinking this would be a weird place to train, but once I got into the building, I saw there was a full gym, with a boxing ring and mats, all set up on the ground floor. At least this guy was serious about working out, so much so that he built his own gym. On the other side of the gym from the entrance there were two guys who looked to be in their early thirties working out together in gis, both wearing white belts. Two white guys, one about six feet tall, pretty slim, and losing his hair, and the other about my size, maybe a few pounds heavier, pretty unassuming-looking. Lewis introduced me to both of them; one was Lorenzo Fertitta and the other Dana White.

Fertitta was the guy Lewis had referred to as superrich, but to me, a twenty-year-old kid, I didn't even know what that really meant. The concepts of having money, needing a lot of money, or making money were not really ones I had thought about, so it didn't matter to me what the guy was worth. The two wanted to grapple, and that was why I was there.

Lewis started the instruction and showed them a couple of things to work on, using me as his demonstration partner. Once we were done, they both tried these things slowly on us, and practiced the moves a couple times over. Neither was very skilled, and I tapped them both out a few times, which is what you do to show them what not to do. Even though they were not skilled white belts, they did seem enthusiastic, which is always fun when you are teaching someone.

When we were finished training I noticed Dana was on the phone trying to get a match scheduled for a fighter he managed. He was haggling over a deal that would pay his guy $700 to fight, and $700 more if he won. That fighter's name was Chuck Liddell (my, how far we've all come). In addition to Liddell, Dana was the manager for a fighter named Tito Ortiz, also relatively well known. Lewis had been doing work with both these guys as well.

After Dana was done with his call, he turned to me and said, "So what do you think about all this MMA stuff? You thinking about getting involved?"

"Nah. Right now I'm pretty much just focused on jujitsu. I want to be the best and get ready for the Mundials in Brazil."

"BJ has some serious grappling skills," Lewis chimed in. Dana thought about that for a second and turned his attention back to me.

Finishing my thought, I told him, "After I accomplish that, I'll start to work on my hands."

Looking over at me, Dana said, "Just want you to know, hands are hard to get. It's going to be a while before you get those." He had presented himself as a boxing coach, but I just blew it off because MMA was not really a concern. I wasn't all that worried about my hands, and if I was going to worry, I had Mendez and others to teach me. I had no idea that this chance encounter would lead to something else, much further down the road.

I TRAVELED BACK TO HAWAII for Christmas and New Year's and continued to work with Charuto, who was now running Tom's old school all by himself. Tom had moved on to focus on his own trials and career goals. Things were going really well for Charuto, and I think he was enjoying having his own place, as any teacher would. Charuto had helped build the school up to another level, bringing a set of skills not yet seen on the Big Island. He was teaching more and more people and was as tough a partner as I could find anywhere. Charuto was over six feet tall, so he had me by a good four or five inches, and he had that wiry strength that comes from years of training. My plan was to train in Hawaii for a couple of weeks before heading back to the mainland for some big tournaments.

To be able to come back home to my family and friends, relax a little bit, train, and show my parents that they had not made a mistake in sending me to California was a good feeling. It was also nice to see Tom and show him what I had learned as well since he was so instrumental in pushing me onto this path in the first place.

Now that I had a place to train and partners to compete with, Hilo had fewer pitfalls than when I'd left home a year and a half earlier. Being here was no longer a vacation or a waste of time. Still I did not want to get too comfortable because I knew how easily I could fall back into my old ways of just lounging around and having too much fun. Coming home under these circumstances probably prepared me for the life I would one day lead, and the sacrifices I would have to start making.

On that particular trip home, my brother Jay and other guys at the gym helped me prepare for a major stateside event in February of 2000, the Pan Americans of BJJ, held in Orlando, Florida. The

Pan Am was a pretty big competition as far as the overall numbers of fighters was concerned, but it wasn't huge for the brown belt division. Since it was international, and competitors from Brazil made their way to it, I definitely thought it was necessary to compete. It was probably the closest stateside tournament for competitors living in Brazil. Fighters from all the biggest schools—Carlson's, Barra, and Nova União—would make the trip, in addition to all the best guys based in the States. If I wanted to truly be serious about this, I had to make all the trips to the big competitions, just like everyone else. Maybe there were not a lot of guys to fight among the brown belts, but the most committed and skilled fighters would probably show.

I had a bye in the first round of the Pam Am, but in the second, I faced off against a guy named Francisco Neto, who is currently a black belt at the Yamasaki Academy in Washington, D.C. The name may sound familiar because it is the school where UFC and MMA referee Mario Yamasaki trains. The match stayed close most of the time, as neither of us scored many points.

With only a few seconds left in the match, knowing time was about to run out, Neto jumped toward my leg in a last ditch effort to secure a heel hook, or some other leg lock, hoping to tie up the match. He was unsuccessful, but he held on to my foot, and was twisting it after the time had expired. I guess he did not hear the referee end the match because he kept going at me well after I stopped. My foot had come free, and he had moved onto my leg now, but only because I figured it was over. I wanted him off me, so at the same moment as he realized time was up, I was in the process of smacking him on the back of his head. I basically just wanted him off me. He popped to his feet and smacked me back. After that, I bounced up and lunged into him with a wrestling takedown, but neither of us was looking for a real fight. We were just two guys who had the adrenaline pumping after a match, one misunderstanding leading to another.

Both Neto's team and my own, as well as all the officials, came running out to the mat to make sure nothing serious happened. Neto was really heated, but probably more because he had just lost than because he got smacked. In the end, though, we both paid the price, as the referee, a BJJ fighter by the name of Edson Diniz, disqualified us. Clearly I lost more than Neto since I was the one who had won the fight.

While I wanted to win, the disqualification taught me a lesson—one better learned at the Pan Ams than on a bigger stage like the Mundials: Even if a guy is in the wrong, you cannot retaliate. BJJ is a nonstriking martial art that came from Japan, and one where you are always supposed to show self-restraint. Neto had acted first, but his action was just a mistake. I was in the wrong, but he then retaliated. This was the last time I was ever disqualified from any sanctioned fight.

Having come away from the Pan Ams empty-handed, I was pretty disappointed I'd let my emotions get the best of me. I was also concerned the guys from Nova União would think I had done something wrong. I had not represented the team at many events and did not want to be viewed as the kid who lets his emotions get in the way of success. Lucky for me no one saw it that way. It was a competition, a fight, and at times emotions can get the best of you, especially when your limbs are at risk. In fact, the Nova União guys were all such fierce competitors that some would be happy to learn that I hit a guy who cranked my ankle after the time was up. In the end, though, it was still something I viewed as a lesson.

Ultimately the incident, as unpleasant as it was, just reminded me that I was with the right guys, the kind of guys who would move toward a fight like moths to a flame.

WHILE I HAD NOT BEEN COMPLETELY successful in some of the bigger tournaments with Nova União, Pederneiras and Wendell Alexander still regarded me as a very good fighter and someone they wanted to see compete alongside them at the highest levels.

Pederneiras expressed a lot of confidence in me, which in turn boosted the faith I had in myself. In the summer of 2000, before the Mundials, he had me travel back down to Brazil to compete in the Campeonato Brasileiro de Equipes, known in English as the Brazilian Team Competition. This was where the best guys on all the different teams, at different belt levels, competed in a tournament to see which team was the best overall, top to bottom.

There were many unique things about this tournament, but none more than its location. It was held on the beach in Copacabana, Rio de Janeiro. We were right there outdoors, on mats, set up along the beachfront next to the ocean. As a kid who grew up on an island, even I had never done anything like this before, but it was not the first time I had fought near a beach.

To even be considered for this competition was an honor. Once I arrived, I had to compete at the school against different guys to see who would make the team. I was confident they would select me with a good showing since they had me travel so far in the first place. Within the school, I had already done well with the best guys, like Shaolin and Robson "Robinho" Moura (they beat me too), so I was pretty much assured I would make it. This event only had two weight divisions, *leve* and *pesado,* or lightweight and heavyweight. At Nova União, lightweight was clearly our best division, even though quite a few of us could fight at lower weights.

Pederneiras and Alexander had to choose their top seven guys, and put us in ranking order. Basically, your top guy would fight the top guy of another school, so you had to be somewhat strategic when selecting. I ended up being ranked third on the team, just after a black belt named Leo Santos and ahead of Robson Moura, another black belt, with Shaolin as our top guy. One additional component to this tournament was that the guys who were ranked in the top three had a really good chance of being on television. It wasn't going to make me famous, but who doesn't want to compete on television if given the chance?

This tournament was a mix of brown and black belts, which

meant I could be matched up against either. The way the matchups were set up, I would definitely end up facing at least one black belt, and sure enough, my first match was against one, the first black belt I'd ever faced in competition. I ended up finishing him by submission, as I did with my next opponent, who was a brown belt. The wins helped my team secure the overall championship. It was a tremendous day for Nova União, as our school finished either first or second in six of the ten divisions.

It was my first gold medal in a brown or black competition, and the first time I could really consider myself a world champion of any kind. Even though I had not won the Mundials, I had come in as a relatively new brown belt and finished off two guys who were probably favored to beat me. The victories made me feel as if I had accomplished almost everything I had ever wanted to. Almost.

IN THE SUMMER OF 2000 the only thing on my mind was the gold medal at the Mundials. With about two months between the Equipes and the Mundials, I could think of nothing else.

I had been spending time in California, Las Vegas, and Hawaii, but most of my time was spent in Hilo to clear my head before the Mundials. When they finally did arrive, I traveled to Brazil with a few friends from Hilo. We arrived in Brazil about three weeks before the competition and stayed about a block away from where Nova União trained at a place called the UPPER Academy.

Every day at noon, all the Nova União guys would meet at UPPER for practice. I remember heading over there the first day—it was on the second floor of this old building, probably built in the 1960s. We had to walk up this dark and steep staircase to get into the school. As I used my hands to feel my way up the steps, I could hear all of these people inside, and I knew I was about to walk into a lair of fighters. Sure enough, when we got inside it was filled with tons of guys—black belts everywhere, groups of people working out, rolling, little bands of fighters from the same neighborhoods, just ready to go to war with you.

When the competition was about a week out, I had to go through the selection process with Nova União once again. I had to compete against the other brown belts to see where I stood in the hierarchy of the school. This mattered because according to the rules of the academy, if a fighter had to face one of his own teammates, and they had already competed in selections, he could just pass him over. If I had run into one of my own guys in the finals, and I had already beaten him during selections, the tournament would already be over. This preserved the best fighters' energies for competition, which in turn helped the team overall.

Since I had been so close to winning the year before, I had expected to have few problems in selection. I was more than holding my own with everyone in the school, and the more you know guys, the harder it becomes for both competitors.

Shortly before we started selection, Pederneiras pulled me aside and told me what was expected of me. I remember him saying, "BJ, I know you can do this, you can compete on this level, but you have to prove it to the school." In order to compete in a very crowded *pena,* or lightweight, division, I would have to take on the top two guys within Nova União.

Both guys knew me well, and I knew them very well too. One was Leandro Nyza and the other Rodrigo Antonio. Of the two, Nyza was one of the guys who I had become good friends with. At that time, though, nothing but winning mattered. This is where teammates became fierce rivals. They wanted this as much as I did, maybe even more, since maybe they had expectations that selection would be easier. With me involved, it was not going to be.

Right there on the spot I had to go at it with Nyza, and it was a battle. I remember both of us were unable to do very much, which would also be the case with Antonio. We had spent too much time together and knew each other's strengths and weaknesses. That was not an excuse, though; I had to win and I did. Both matches were incredibly close, and I defeated both of these guys by advantage. It could have gone either way, but this time, it went my way.

Once it was over Pederneiras brought me before the entire class, and in what was somewhat of a controversial move, he removed my brown belt and tied a black belt around my waist. It was an indescribable feeling that almost made me want to cry in front of the whole class. I gave him a hug, and then turned back to my teammates and sat down. I was now the top guy in the black belt lightweight division for Team Nova União going into the Mundials.

THE DAY OF THE COMPETITION I packed up my things and headed over to the Tijuca Tênis Clube, in Rio, where the championships were held. I had learned to control my nerves a lot better than I had in the past, and I was feeling calm, relative to past events. It seemed the number of fighters had grown from years past. Team Nova União had definitely grown and become more of a force to reckon with. After winning the Equipes, we were all expecting to really make a mark this time around.

Since I had already defeated my two teammates in selections, I would only have to win four matches to capture gold. It was a good position to be in. I felt Nyza and Antonio had been good enough to win the whole thing, so my confidence was high.

Right from the start, I was in control of my first match. I immediately pulled my opponent into my guard, and from there was able to finish him via submission without too much difficulty. My next opponent was more of the same, as I went up against a Gracie Barra student named Alexandre Soca. He was one of the better-known and established guys in the tournament. It seemed the Gracie Barra guys had this attitude like they were supposed to be there, supposed to win this, so fighting one of them was always an opportunity to show them how strong Nova União had become.

The match with Soca was a good one for me. He was tough but unable to do much when I had him in my guard. We went back and forth attempting moves, but throughout I was able to outpoint him. He was never really able to get control of me, and I was ahead from the start. I swept him once in the beginning and from there I had his back. I tried to go for the finish as I always did, but I had to be cautious as I knew Soca was the kind of guy who would try to get the submission at the expense of points.

Remaining patient until the end, I stayed in control of Soca and the match. Like Soca, I wanted the submission, but was content riding this out and keeping the lead until the end. I was in complete control of the fight, even though I was unable to score a lot of points. Control had to be enough to reach the finals and sure enough it was. Time expired in the match, and I'd done enough to win, just barely, on points.

My next match was the semifinals, and before I had to fight, there was some time to rest up. When I was by myself, I started thinking about the match from last year, and how I had been so close against Tererê. This was the second year in a row I had reached this level, and there was no way I was going home without the medal. But even as big as the Tererê fight had been, this was for the black belt, which was a whole new level, literally and figuratively.

My opponent in the semis was a fighter from Team Gracia Humaita named Fredson Alves. He trained under Royler Gracie, the man who'd won this division a year earlier. I had desperately wanted to fight Royler for many reasons, most of all because he had won the championship four years running. Before the fight I was aware of Alves's skills, that he had a great half guard, which is when you have one leg tangled between your opponent's, and one free. It was a good place to attempt arm submissions from, so it was something I definitely wanted to avoid.

Having reached this stage in the black belt competition in 1998, Alves had lost to my teammate Robinho in the weight class just below this one. I am sure he wanted this match every bit as much as I did, and I expected a battle, which is exactly what I got.

Neither of us was able to do much from the moment the match began. We came at each other cautiously, and eventually I pulled guard and worked from my back. It could have gone either way. I used my athleticism to avoid his strong positions, keeping him out of half guard from the top. I was in control of the match but unable to score any points. The good thing was he couldn't do much either, and because I was a lot more active than he was, I was awarded the victory in a somewhat uneventful match.

Now I had to start preparing for the final match against someone I knew but had not faced—the 1999 brown belt champion of this weight class, Team InFight's Edson Diniz. The name was familiar because Diniz was the referee who had disqualified me earlier in the year during my Pan Am match against Neto. Often referees were fighters from higher levels, or different weight classes, which is why Diniz had presided over my Pan Am match. Diniz himself had taken second place in the black belt division during those very Pan Ams. Now I had the opportunity to face him head-to-head. I mean, how many times in your life do you really get to square off against the referee who may have had a hand in taking something from you?

The nerves I had been able to suppress until then came roaring back before the finals, but I just kept telling myself, *I will not be denied. No matter what happens, I cannot quit, I cannot lose. If my arms or legs are broken, or my neck is squeezed so tight I cannot breathe, I will not be denied. Who knows if I will ever have this chance again?*

The entire Nova União team was excited about the match, and never before had I felt so much like one of them. It was my chance to do this, and they were there rooting me on from the sidelines and bleachers. When it was finally my time to go, I walked onto the mat, looked back, and could just see the support of everyone. Guys were jumping up and down, flags were waving, and everyone was shouting and hollering. There was an anticipation that, one way or another, something big was going to happen.

With the arm of my gi, I wiped the sweat from my forehead and prepared to fight. As soon as I approached Diniz, he moved side to side to avoid my grasp, but I dropped down right to my back and tried to pull him down between my legs, into my guard. He was still trying to avoid me a little bit, but from a seated position I was able to grab hold of his right arm and pull him inside and downward. Still attempting to pull him into my guard, I had him close enough, so I slid slightly underneath him, brought my legs underneath his body, and swept him over me. Essentially, I had tossed him onto his back with my feet, and ended up rolling on top of him. Next thing he knew, I was in control, and he was on his back. I was awarded two points for the sweep almost immediately.

It is a bit of a risk to always bring people into my guard because escaping the guard is worth three points, whereas a takedown or a sweep is only worth two. But I had such confidence in the guard position, I rarely worried about the downside, no matter the opponent.

Once I had him down, Diniz tried to grab hold of my foot to control me, but I was keeping his legs apart and was applying a lot of weight on his front right leg. He was in a pretty bad position on his back as well. From there, I just tried to throw his legs aside, pass him, and get control of him from the side, which is known as side control. He was doing a good job of keeping his other leg between my body and himself, which made the pass tough.

After a lot of work, I eventually was able to pass, but only for a split second. He was soon able to get his leg back in between us to maintain something of a half guard on me, but for him it was more defensive and offered him no control of me. I kept working from this position until I was able to grab both his legs and throw them and his body to the side, which rolled him over a bit. Doing this opened up his back for me to jump right on it, which I did. Now seated, I was in full control of his body with my legs wrapped around his waist and my arms underneath his armpits, controlling his hands and arms. This was a really bad position for him to be in, being down on points already. There was no way I was going to give this position up unless he found a way to get himself out of it.

Once I had gotten his back, the two of us rolled really close to the end of the mat. The referee came over and tried to bring us farther in bounds, closer to the center. Inch by inch I tried to pull Diniz back toward the middle so I would not have to give up position. Even when you do give up position and a referee resets you, it may not always be exactly the same way. In this case, the referee eventually stood us up and brought us to the middle, but unlike the year before when I lost my position, the referee did the *right thing* by putting us back into the same position we were in.

After we were back in the middle, I looked over my shoulder at the time and saw the match was coming to a close. I continually looked over to Pederneiras to see if he had any advice to give me, but I was doing well on my own. All I had to do was control Diniz for the last five minutes of the match. At the same time as I was in control, I could feel the energy from my teammates and the people in the stands. Everyone was going absolutely wild, screaming and shouting, still waving the flags back and forth, jumping up and down. I could hear the pounding of all their feet together and could feel the vibrations in the floor. I could sense my time was coming.

Diniz did everything to try to get free. At one point he started to turn and I could see the opportunity was there for me to mount him by coming around the side of him and rolling one onto the top of his chest. I had my right leg over his side, and was turning him slowly. As I tried to pull myself over, he was finally able to turn over himself, pushing against me and falling into my full guard. This made things a little dicey, but I still had a solid lead, and was not in trouble. He tried to posture up, which means to back away and create space, but I used my legs to keep him tied up. I raised them all the way up under his arms as he pressed down on top of me.

While it looked like he was in a better position than before, from my back I started to maneuver myself to the right a little bit. He was seated with his legs underneath his body. At that point I unhitched my legs and started to roll forward, which swept him off me, straight into an arm bar on his right arm. Time was about to expire, but nothing was going to save him at this point. I was up 5–0 on points, and he was in the process of tapping out. Either way, the match was over.

I was the first American to win the gold medal in the Brazilian Mundials as a black belt. I really could not believe it was happening. I was a world champion. In just under four years, and at age twenty-one, I had worked tirelessly to become a black belt, and now I was considered one of the best in the world. It was also a great day for Nova União overall. Robson "Robinho" Moura and Vitor "Shaolin" Ribeiro both took the gold medal in their divisions. Just incredible the kind of team Pederneiras and Alexander had built, and to be a part of it was special.

Moments later I was standing there receiving my medal, looking around the room at all the other great fighters, thinking to myself, *I am one of these guys. I am now up there with the Santoses, the Shaolins, the Mouras.* A truly amazing feeling.

I WOULD NOT RETURN THE FOLLOWING year, or any year thereafter, to defend my title, or even compete in the Mundials again. When I was leaving Brazil, it had been my plan to return. At the time I probably figured I would go back many times over, as long as I could defend my title and fight for Nova União, but it didn't work out that way.

7

MOVING FORWARD

F OR THE FIRST TIME SINCE I'D left Hilo for California, my head was finally clear. I was no longer consumed with BJJ, and I felt a weight had been lifted off my shoulders. It was hard for me to even realize how much I'd been struggling with it until I no longer was.

I went back to Hawaii to visit my family and friends again, not so much to show them what I had accomplished, or celebrate it, but to truly relax. I had not known what that felt like for a long time. I was finally going to take some time for myself, and maybe see the world for a bit.

Everyone who had been following what I was doing showed incredible support, and in many ways I had won this not only for myself or Nova União, but for the people of Hilo. I may have been the first American to win the gold as a black belt, but it was a double victory for me in that I had also won it for the Hawaiians. Upon seeing me soon after returning, my friend Hoyt said, "I am looking at a different guy. A new man." It took me a moment to understand what he was saying, but he was right on the money. I was no longer a kid; I was a new man.

Now I had time on my hands, and my only concern was what came next. I thought a lot about opening a BJJ school, but while it seemed simple in theory, in practice it was a lot more difficult.

Charuto had become the established teacher of BJJ in Hilo, and this was becoming his home. There was no way I would ever open a school in Hilo. The most I would ever do is work alongside him, but even that was not a serious consideration. Instead of dwelling on the school proposal too much, I took a long-needed vacation with DaSilva over to France to teach some seminars, make some extra money, travel, just live day to day, and see some more of the world. Heading to Europe was the start of two firsts: the first time I was paid to teach somewhere overseas and the first time I had traveled on my own while not preparing for BJJ. One week was probably not long enough for me to figure out what I was going to do next, but thankfully no one was pressuring me to make any decisions. I had become used to having a goal, something to work toward. Having too much time on my hands would ultimately be a bad thing.

Complicating matters was the fact that the previous year I had enrolled at West Valley JC, so now there was the question of pursuing my education after the summer. Garth Taylor had gotten me involved there by saying that it was a good opportunity to learn wrestling, and I'd been redshirted my first year, which meant I could only practice until the fall of 2000. With a few options on my plate, I felt heading back to California to wrestle and take classes was the best one.

The wrestling program at small West Valley was very good because of head coach Jim Root. Root was well respected around Northern California and had even hosted the Jim Root Classic

Wrestling Tournament, which was held at the school in Saratoga, California, for a long time before I had arrived. Not only was I able to wrestle, but I was learning from a highly skilled and well-respected coach.

Right from the start I loved wrestling, and I was pretty good at it. I did not go on to win any major titles or anything even close, but I competed in a couple of events and did well. In addition to the wrestling, there were the classes, and although I wasn't a very serious student, I decided to learn more about fitness and took classes to become an athletic trainer, classes like first aid and nutrition, which worked with the lifestyle I was living. The idea of being a trainer was not a serious one, but this path helped me learn things useful for my life.

Ultimately, I got a lot out of the time I spent at West Valley, both physically and mentally. It was not like going to San Jose State, or a big university, but it was the right thing for me at the time. I have always had a bone to pick with myself about not going to a regular four-year college. I think my frustration is really about wondering what other people experienced more than anything else. BJJ was my college, my trade, my schooling, but it was something I did mostly alone. Having the "college experience" is something I will never get, and also something I envy a bit in others.

Even though I may seem like the type of person who would not be a huge proponent of education, I think it is the most important thing in the world. I try to make up for neglecting it when I was younger by learning as much as I can now whenever I have free time. You can lose your legs, your arms, not be able to walk, run, or compete, but in all likelihood you will not lose your intelligence. Not to be a preacher, but education is the most important gift you can give yourself, and something I wish I had approached as seriously as I approached the martial arts.

● ● ●

WHILE I WAS HEADING TO WEST VALLEY in the fall of 2000, my brothers and I got together with our friend Alex Oxendine to try something new. Oxendine was a big guy, around six three, with dark skin because of his Native American background, and another guy with a big personality. We'd all originally met at Ralph's, and in a lot of ways he'd grown up on the same steady diet of wrestle-boxing that we had. He'd started practicing muay thai when he was thirteen and had since become involved with the BJJ, which gave him the well-rounded skills fighters need in no-holds-barred fighting. Like us, he'd basically been doing MMA long before it was defined as a sport.

Oxendine fit in with us like he was another brother, and in the fall of 2000 we all decided to turn his two-car garage into a gym. We padded the cement floors and the walls as best we could and made a sign out of cardboard that read LEGENDS and the acronym BJJ underneath. We all signed our names to it, and just like that, we had our own gym.

Even though we called Legends our "gym," it was really just the four of us—myself, Oxendine, Reagan, and Jay Dee. Sometimes other guys came over to train, but it was really just us. In a lot of ways it helped us get back to having fun with it all, as if it was our basement in Hilo. It was completely serious, though, not just a place to mess around.

I was relatively content with all the working out I was doing—grappling at Legends, training with CrossFit and at AKA, as well as teaching. But there was still a void. I did not have much else going on, but I knew there were many other things I could focus on, like MMA. No one was clamoring for me to come fight in a show, but I still had an interest in it, so I just started practicing in addition to doing BJJ.

With Mendez running AKA, and Shamrock and Cook doing the submission grappling with the school, I had a lot of skilled guys to learn from and continue my martial arts training. One day I decided to focus a little more on other aspects, so I went to Mendez and asked him to work with me. After all, he was training Frank Shamrock, who was certainly a great fighter, maybe the best. I decided to tell Mendez exactly what I was looking for. "Jav, I have accomplished all I ever wanted with jujitsu, and now I think I want to train MMA. Can you help me?"

He did not even hesitate in accepting. From the first day I had hit pads with him, he'd been a bigger fan of my striking than I was. He wanted to bring me to the next level. The way it all worked out almost seemed too easy. I took to punching and kicking quickly. I already had the fighting background from my childhood, which Mendez thought was a big reason I was able to excel. I had kicked enough soccer balls in my life, so using my feet was not really difficult either. The biggest thing I had to work on was just understanding my footwork, developing my base, and being able to control and generate the power in my strikes. I liked striking, though, since it brought me back to my basic fighting instincts. Mendez felt I was a "natural" at fighting and that I had really good reflexes and a deceptive, instinctive ability to avoid being hit squarely.

Just as with BJJ, I was all about MMA from the start. I constantly worked on whatever Mendez taught me while picking up more from other guys around AKA. With no fight on the horizon, there were enough fights in the area if I felt the need to test myself.

Over time, AKA was slowly transforming into a place for MMA fighters, mostly because of Shamrock's presence. Mendez was still kickboxing first, but did not resist the trend. There was no reason not to bring everything under one roof with so much going on in the area. It took a while for the MMA concept to take hold, but once it did, AKA quickly became one of the best MMA schools you could find anywhere, and I loved being part of it.

ONE DAY, OUT OF NOWHERE I received a call from John Lewis, who was still training BJJ down in Las Vegas, and he had an offer for me. I remember the call like it was yesterday. I was about to leave my apartment for the gym when the phone rang.

"Hey, BJ, I've got your next fight. King of the Cage is looking for a lightweight to take on Caol Uno. I think you should do it."

This hit me out of nowhere. I had no idea how KOTC even knew who I was, and Uno was a talented fighter who already had about fifteen MMA matches under his belt. Lewis had been in contact with a lot of fighters in Las Vegas, notably Marvin "The Beastman" Eastman, who trained at J-Sect. Uno had fought Andre Pederneiras in Japan the year before to a draw, so maybe Lewis and Pederneiras thought I was capable of taking him on. I had no idea if I was ready to fight someone like Uno, but I didn't care. I had nothing else to do, so why not?

At the time, Indian reservations were the only places in California where an MMA event could take place. This fight was scheduled for late February 2001 at the Soboba Casino in San Jacinto. As far as preparations were concerned, I knew nothing about what I was supposed to do and had no idea what MMA fighters did.

These days there are all kinds of ways to prepare for a fight. If a guy you're fighting likes to "lay and pray," which is to hold a man down and hope to win on points, you prepare for that. Maybe the opponent is a great wrestler, so you train to sprawl, which is one method for avoiding takedowns. Nowadays fighters will fly to Brazil to train for BJJ, maybe Boston for muay thai, and finally Las Vegas for the last few weeks for sparring partners. Back then, no one had the money to do something like that. Simply put, you just trained for everything and hoped it was enough.

The only worry I had leading up to this first fight was over-training and burning out. With the CrossFit guys instructing me, I started swimming, carrying waterproof medicine balls underwater, and trying other physically challenging drills. In truth, though, I really didn't know what I was doing, but it felt good. I figured if it was difficult and made me tired, it was probably working.

Mentally I wasn't sure I was prepared for this type of thing. I had said yes without even thinking it through, which was typical of me at the time. Once I started watching Uno's fights, the whole thing took on this new reality for me, and I started to actually overthink it all.

The mental aspect of fighting is a big part of the training—perhaps even more crucial than the physical workouts. If I wasn't careful, the mental component could break me before I even went into the cage. Garth Taylor and I would discuss how the mind processes fighting—not just in preparation but also during the actual fight. During a fight, whether in the street or an arena, I always found myself having different thoughts, sometimes extremely quiet moments when I'd ask myself, *How in the world did I get here?* If I wasn't careful, these quiet moments could become distractions that could cost me the match. Inside of a cage, in front of a large crowd, against a talented fighter, I would have to stay focused to win.

Just a couple of weeks out from the fight, I felt as good as I had ever felt preparing for a fight. Then one day, out of the blue, I was sitting in my apartment when I got a call from Lewis.

"Hey man, bad news. The fight's off . . . Sorry." That was all he said. And just like that, all the talk and preparation, the mental adjustments—as quickly as they'd come, they all left.

I had never signed a contract detailing what I was going to make, or my obligations, whether I could pull out. This taught me a lesson: Make sure you get things in writing, signed on the dotted line. My first moment dealing with the business of being a professional athlete.

Meanwhile, Uno had not only gotten out of our fight, he had signed with the UFC to face off against Jens Pulver for their lightweight championship. Here this guy had been training for me, and now all of a sudden he was getting a shot at the belt in one of the top organizations in the world.

What I didn't realize then was that the UFC was being purchased by a company called Zuffa, and one of the people who owned Zuffa was Lorenzo Fertitta, the white belt Lewis had asked me to grapple with a while back. Oddly enough, the other white belt I met that day, Dana White, was the new president of the UFC. The first UFC event under their control was to take place on February 23, 2001, in Atlantic City. It was UFC 30: The Battle on the Boardwalk, the first of Zuffa's many great events with not-so-great titles.

In order to make a big splash, they needed another championship fight, and Uno was one-half. To their credit, both Uno and Pulver had a lot of experience, had been in battles, and deserved the opportunity. Uno was a big deal at the time, and I am sure KOTC would have been happy to have him, but KOTC did not have the money these new UFC owners did. I am guessing it wasn't hard for them to pry Uno away. From the moment Zuffa purchased the UFC, they were in the business of going after other organizations' best guys. It was a practice they would continue, and eventually take to new levels.

The wheels were in motion for the UFC and Zuffa. Thanks to the adoption of rules that protected the fighters, the sport was becoming acceptable in more places and growing rapidly. For years, the previous owner of the UFC, Semaphore Entertainment Group, had been lobbying hard to get the UFC sanctioned in Las Vegas, since the city was home to the biggest boxing matches. Coincidentally, Zuffa ended up purchasing the UFC shortly before the rules were codified and accepted in Las Vegas. Soon afterward MMA became legal in Nevada, the UFC also returned to pay-per-view after a long hiatus. All things just happened to work out for Zuffa.

A couple weeks later, I watched Pulver and Uno battle it out, wondering what it would be like had I been in there. Both looked really good, but I thought I had the ability to stand there and trade punches with either of them. On the ground, I believed I could hold my own, but what did I really know? I still had never been inside a cage—not even for training—but as it turned out, I didn't have to wait for the chance.

Oddly enough, when my friends and I discussed trying out

MMA, we usually talked about the Pride Fighting Championships instead of the UFC. Pride was based in Japan and at the time was bigger than the UFC. The UFC was more of an eastern and southern U.S. thing, and not as big on the West Coast. With Pride's Asian roots, fighters from the West Coast flew over to fight, and with Hawaii's Asian roots, it seemed to be more of a natural fit for someone like me. In the back of my mind, though, I found the UFC to be more interesting, more raw. It was something I really wanted to do at least once in my life, especially since I had a connection to Lorenzo Fertitta.

In March of 2001 I was sitting in Jay Dee's room in our apartment in San Jose, when I received a phone call from the UFC's Lisa Faircloth, who at the time was seemingly responsible for everything over there. John Lewis had once again worked his magic. Faircloth let me know the UFC wanted me to fight at UFC 31: Locked and Loaded, in Atlantic City against Joey Gilbert, and asked if I had any interest. They could have offered me Andre the Giant. There was no way I was saying no.

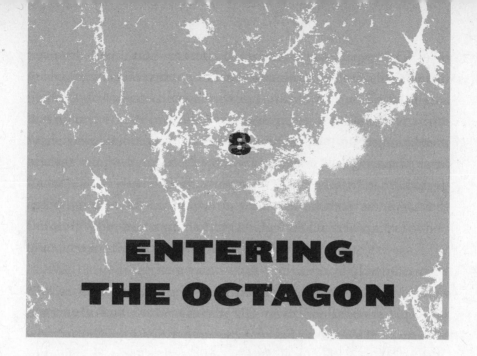

8

ENTERING
THE OCTAGON

MY FIRST CONTRACT with the UFC was almost un-
forgettable, except for the part about the money. I
can't remember exactly, but I think I was paid $1,500
to fight and $1,500 to win. At the time, though, I remember
thinking to myself, *Man, they're going to pay me fifteen and
fifteen!* That is how fighters refer to the money they're going to
make, "fifteen and fifteen" because you often get paid to fight,
and paid to win.

Everything seemed so simple with the UFC, from the moment
I heard from Faircloth up until the time I actually fought. This
would not be like King of the Cage, where my fight got pulled off
the table. This fight was definitely going to happen. Faircloth called
me a few times beforehand to make sure I knew where I would
be staying, when my flight was, who would be coming with me,

what time I would have to be in certain places, and whatever else I hadn't thought of. It was like a small business trying to get up and running, and she checked up on everything. Even though the UFC had already been established, in a lot of ways it was a brand-new business since brothers Frank and Lorenzo now owned it.

In a way I was starting over myself, as I had to prepare for a brand-new opponent in Gilbert, and more importantly, a new sport. I did not know too much about him other than he had a couple of MMA fights under his belt and he was eight years older than me. Not that the age should make much of a difference, but there was a chance the experience would. Either way, we were both making our UFC debuts with this fight.

One thing I did know was that Gilbert had a really strong wrestling background I had to be prepared for. Since I was training with the West Valley team, I was confident I could overcome this. He had also been submitted in Japan by a heel hook in the Shooto organization by Naoya Uematsu, who had beaten Caol Uno. There was this guy named Joe Silva, who at the time was pretty much a huge MMA fan, and he had in his possession countless videos and photos from nearly every event, whether it was UFC, Pride, or Shooto. He sent us some of Gilbert's footage to help me prepare for the fight. I don't even know who called him, or who knew to call him, but someone did. These days Silva is a vice president with the UFC.

I was now training for this fight full-time at AKA with Mendez, Cook, Southworth, my brothers, and toward the end Frank Shamrock. It was an interesting collection of characters, to say the least. A lot of headstrong personalities were helping me, and there was a lot of great knowledge when it came to preparation, so one of the most important things for me was being able to process it and keep some balance with the team. Luckily Jay Dee and Reagan were around because at the end of the day, they could keep some order around me.

While everyone was helpful and intelligent, they all brought their own intensities. Some guys were more comfortable in their own skin when it came to their roles regarding my training, and others naturally wanted to be more involved. It was a balancing act. Luckily for all of us, Mendez had transformed the gym for my training, so everything took place under one roof, and I avoided having to travel. At the same time, since it was his place, Mendez was also the head coach for the most part, and more than anyone else, he could keep a healthy balance among everyone. He was the consummate professional.

Though turning the gym into an MMA gym sounds simple, it was quite an undertaking. One must understand that at the time MMA was not even legal in California. MMA was (and is) dangerous, so Southworth and I had to push constantly for Mendez to let us do things—such as kickboxing with takedowns, and boxing while shooting on people into throws—that have become commonplace in MMA training today. In addition, there were all different types of exercises, including using a wall for balance to do drills to increase speed, plyometrics, and exercises that were not very common at the time. We didn't want to reinvent Mendez's gym, but this was the direction fight sports were going in, and true to his great character, Mendez was both patient and willing to work with us as we tried to figure out our rhythm.

Similar to the training methods at Nova União in Brazil, we started something called the "Noon Training," where we worked on everything we could. Just like we were doing at Legends, we would go five or six rounds with a new partner every round. Sometimes we even changed partners every minute to keep the intensity up. These are things that are practiced at nearly every good gym today, but at the time we were just trying to push ourselves, making things up as we went along. Given the limited knowledge we had of MMA training, we basically had to make up our own model based on trial and error.

There was no shortage of drive and talent at AKA, but one of the better things we had going for us was Shamrock. He brought his own brand of passion to the gym. No one knew more about MMA fighting than Frank, and in addition to having been a fighter in the UFC, he was their commentator. When Shamrock was around, the level of fighting in the gym went up another notch. Maybe because he came really hard, or because we all wanted to impress him. Whatever the reasons, he managed to raise the level of competition while also providing a calming presence. For a young guy like me, his presence alone those last few weeks helped tremendously in controlling my nerves.

I FLEW OUT TO ATLANTIC CITY with the guys from AKA. I had never been to New Jersey, and approaching Atlantic City by car, I thought it looked like Las Vegas but on the ocean. It was not Las Vegas, however. Not the worst place I had been, but it definitely could use a bit of a face-lift—and that included the Trump Taj Mahal, where we were staying. You hear that name, Trump, and you instantly think it has to be beautiful. It either once was, maybe had the potential to be, but at the time it was something short of luxurious.

I started to meet all of the people who worked for the company, including Faircloth, who I could now see really was doing *everything.* It was like wherever I went, or whenever I needed something, she was right there. It was nice to have someone like her around, helping me every step of the way, since it was all so new. Then there was Dana White, of course, and Lorenzo Fertitta. They were really happy to have me there, and I was excited to see them again. I mean these two guys were all of a sudden heading up this whole thing, it almost seemed strange to me. They were definitely not white belts in the business sense. While it was the Fertittas' money making all of this possible, it clearly seemed to be White's show to run. He was the guy doing all the hugging, handshaking, and of course, the talking.

John Lewis and Tony DeSouza, two of my main BJJ partners back in Las Vegas, were there as well. DeSouza had competed in

MMA before, but this was also his first really big show. If all went well, we would both be going home happy. What I learned during this first trip to Atlantic City still holds true today: All of the guys show up happy and excited, but only half of them leave feeling the same way. At least for the time being, I could enjoy being a part of this, staring at all the UFC stars just like a fan would. MMA may not have been very well known, but Randy Couture, Kevin Randleman, and Pat Miletich were the big names in the sport and all had had success elsewhere. The only name the general public probably knew of was Matt Lindland, who won the Olympic silver medal for the U.S. Greco-Roman wrestling team.

It was so completely different from the UFC you see today. Even something like the weigh-in, where we had our weights checked to make sure we could fight, was a world apart. It was held in some tiny room, just large enough for the fighters and their corners. No one was in there except a few other UFC employees and maybe someone from the New Jersey Athletic Commission. No one was recognized, and no one acted like a big star because nobody was a big star. Not Couture, not Chuck Liddell, no one was much of anything except in relation to each other.

I remember being in there looking at guys in sweatsuits attempting to "make weight," thinking how much it would suck to be doing that. While cutting weight has become a bit of a hassle in my later years, at the time I did not have to worry about it since I already weighed under the 155 pounds required for the fight. I was one of the first guys in the lightweight division, along with Pulver and Uno.

Though I had not done anything in the UFC, strangely there was a lot of hype surrounding me. Part of it was from Shamrock talking me up to the people in MMA who mattered, but it was also because I was the first non-Brazilian ever to win the Mundials, and that seemed to matter to those in the know. One of the founders of the UFC was Rorion Gracie, the oldest child of the great Helio Gracie, and in many ways the UFC was really just the Gracie challenge to see if jujitsu could take on other, more violent martial arts, since BJJ was considered to be a more defensive art than, say, karate. Everyone discussed how I would fit into this tradition, but what they didn't realize was while I loved jujitsu, I had been trying to knock people out with my hands, knees, and feet long before I ever put on a gi. Gilbert was prepared to take this fight "to the ground"; I was preparing to leave him there.

FIGHT NIGHT ARRIVED PRETTY QUICKLY, and I was definitely anxious. We had spent the last few days working out in small training rooms set aside for us and had little else to do to kill time. There's a tendency to want to have a good time and relax a bit, but it's impossible, especially since I needed my aggression to fight. All you can do is wait for it to come.

When the day arrived and I made my way down to what they called the locker room, it was a couple of hours before the fight. It was not a locker room in any real sense, just a room with some curtains in it dividing one side from the other. The "red" corner was on one side and the "blue" on the other. It was a real makeshift operation, and it was evident that not a lot of thought or money had gone into it. Or maybe they just had so few options in this venue that that's how it had to be. There was nothing stopping one fighter from looking around the curtain to check out his opponent, but by then, it didn't really matter.

On my side of the curtain was Liddell, who was previously managed by White. Liddell was also tight with Lewis, and trained with him, so he was with DeSouza and me. Randy Couture was also on our side of the room, and we were looking at him like he was the man, flat out. Liddell was an up-and-comer, but he had to fight this guy Kevin Randleman, who seemed like the guy to beat. Everyone talked about Randleman as the big deal, so you could only imagine the tension flowing around me from guys like Liddell.

I warmed up for my first fight simply by hitting some boxing mitts with the guys on the team, and grappled a little bit on the gym mats the UFC provided for all of us. The vibe started off good on our side after DeSouza won his match by unanimous decision. Before I even had a moment to congratulate Tony, someone called my name, and it was time for me to go. When I heard them say it, I had no idea what to do. *Is this how it works? They call your name, and you walk out there to fight in a cage?* It almost didn't make sense.

Now I was standing in front of this black curtain, and the UFC's own music started playing. I had Mendez, Cook, and Lewis behind me telling me how ready I was for this, and this was "my night . . . my time to prove myself!" Right before I walked out, my emotions were getting the best of me, and out of nowhere, I started to cry a little bit, but they were tears of joy. I could not believe this was really happening to me. This was who I was becoming, and it all seemed to be making sense, even though in a weird way none of it did. I took a few deep breaths, listened to my guys offering support, gathered myself, and walked out alone to the Octagon for the first time in my life.

The fans in attendance on this night were absolutely unbelievable. Really the truest of the true. Before anyone even cared about who I was, these guys were screaming my name, yelling for me to "kick his ass!" These were not just random people who came to town to watch a fight; these were people who really cared about MMA and the UFC. They knew more about all the fighters than I did and probably anyone else back in the locker room. Before all the glitz and the glamour, there were these fans.

I stepped up to the Octagon with Gilbert already inside and waited for the referee to call us out. As soon as he did, I was across the ring to take control of the Octagon. I wanted this guy to know I was there to knock his head off. I threw a punch straight down the middle, landed it, and then immediately tried to get my hands around the back of his neck to secure a "clinch." We separated and moments later I threw another big right hand but just missed.

Compared to a lot of fights today, which start off slowly because of the pressure, we went right at it, maintaining a very fast pace. We were both throwing knees and attempting to clinch each other. Gilbert pushed me against the cage, and tried to hold me there, but I spun around behind him and was able to take him down. From then on, there was no way I was going to let this guy beat me.

Before Gilbert was able to get into a good position, I was already moving to mount him. From his back Gilbert held on to me with a headlock, but I was punching him in the ribs so he would loosen up. When I finally got my head free, I was fully mounted and trying to hit him in the head and face. Wrapping his hands around my waist, he pulled himself against my body with me still straddled on top of him. He was trying to cut down the angles so I would be unable to land any punches, and since striking an opponent in the back of the head is illegal, I had little to hit. This was only a temporary solution for him to buy time. He tried to stand up with me on his back, but I started punching the side of his head and body with my left hand, while my legs were hooked around his body with him unable to stand. Not only was he not able to defend himself, but he was also carrying me on his back. It doesn't get much worse than this.

The guys in Gilbert's corner were yelling at him to roll over, which is a great idea if your opponent does not know it's coming. It's a lot easier to hear your corner when you're not getting beat up, and I was not, so it was easy for me to hear their directions. He tried to roll, but he just basically collapsed. I was holding on to him from behind, continuing to beat on him and go for submission chokes. Eventually he was able to get up, but soon we were back on the ground in the same position. There was just no way I was going to be denied.

Finally, I had him in a no-win situation, lying on his stomach with me mounted on top of his back. I threw punch after punch, over and over, into both sides of his head until the referee came in and stopped the fight with two seconds left in the first round. It was over. I had won my first UFC fight in convincing fashion.

Right after the fight, I received a lot of compliments and accolades from everyone in my camp, and even some of the other fighters. I had apparently lived up to some of the hype surrounding me. Shamrock had been singing my praises on the broadcast during the fight, which really helped me among the fans and fighters. On many levels, he played an essential role in shaping my early UFC career.

It was a good feeling to be acknowledged by your peers. Getting compliments from a guy like Liddell, who had as big a night as anyone after knocking out Randleman, meant a lot. Back then, though, when it came to being "hyped up" before a fight, it was not received like it is today. Nowadays, hype is not always a positive thing. You hear people bashing a guy before he even makes it anywhere. Let's say Dana White calls a guy the next great fighter, and the guy does not achieve greatness. People jump all over—not just White, but the fighter too! A guy gets hyped up and he fails, these days people call him a bum, overrated, a guy who fought nobodies. There are few nobodies in the UFC, regardless of what people think of a particular fighter's abilities.

When I first began my MMA career, hype was looked at as being a good thing. When a new fighter was coming onto the scene, people were excited at the prospect of seeing something different, something good. Maybe he could teach us something none of us had ever seen. This was true for both the fans and the fighters. We were all about seeing this sport grow, and when someone came along who could do something different, maybe better than the last guy, everyone took notice. If there was hype surrounding a fighter and he did not live up to it, we just hoped the next guy would.

On that night, though, I lived up to mine. I called my family back in Hawaii to tell them the news, but they already knew. Apparently I had made the pay-per-view broadcast, which had not been a guarantee going into the fight, since at the time, they only showed the main card fights. If you were lucky, you made it onto the montage they pieced together from video clips of the other fights. Having made it, knowing the people back in Hilo, my family, friends, and everyone else, saw me on television in the UFC, was the most exciting news I had ever heard in my life.

After the event, I hung out at the bar with some of the other fighters, all of whom were getting to know each other a little better. That I was now one of them was almost like a dream. I took a walk to think for a second and clear my head—to soak it all in. While standing by myself in the casino of the hotel, some old guy motored past me on one of those electric carts older people use to get around—more like a really slow scooter with a basket in front than a wheelchair. When the man got closer I said to myself, *That guy looks like Rodney Dangerfield . . . Wait, it is Rodney Dangerfield!* He had been with a woman who walked alongside the cart. Then I thought to myself, *It looks like he's gonna die . . .* The man did not look good. The whole situation was just surreal. *Where the hell am I, and how did I get here?*

EVEN THOUGH FEW PEOPLE in the media cared about what we were doing as MMA fighters, at least I had done my part in helping the UFC put on a good show. Unlike BJJ, where a fight can be slow and boring, we were expected to entertain. As soon as I was back in San Jose, I received another call from the UFC, offering me my next fight, which would be against Din Thomas at UFC 32. White had even called me himself this time to tell me how "amazing" my performance was, and that I had to fight in the very next event. I hardly had a second to reflect on what I had just accomplished, and next thing I knew they wanted me right back.

When this all began, I had told myself I wanted to fight in the UFC just once, and that was it. Since I had accomplished the goal, was it enough? I had also been telling myself on the flight home that the UFC was going to offer me Din Thomas, who was a chiseled black fighter with good boxing skills and a solid ground game. I had already been making plans inside my head to fight again. Even though Thomas was not in the UFC, he was the number one lightweight challenger for the belt. Knowing as I did that Thomas had already beaten Pulver by submission, it just made sense for them to match us up. So I figured this call was coming, and before it did, I already knew I would accept.

This fight was a much bigger deal than the first one. It was again being held in New Jersey, this time on June 29, 2001, at the then-titled Continental Airlines Arena, as part of UFC 32: Showdown in the Meadowlands. While not the most exciting-sounding event, it was the largest venue outside of New York City, where MMA was still not legal. White offered to make me the co–main event alongside fighters Tito Ortiz and Elvis Sinosic.

Dana also offered me more money, since it only made sense that the "co-main" fighters receive more. This also meant I had to renegotiate my contract. It only made sense, right? Right. They renegotiated the deal so I would get paid more, but I was not really too concerned about the numbers. The UFC's goal was really to get me signed to a longer deal, before the next fight. The one thing about Fertitta and White early on was that it always seemed like they wanted to pay us more money. White used to say things like "You guys deserve to get paid a lot more" and "Why do boxers make so much money, but you guys don't get paid shit? We're gonna change that." In the beginning you had the feeling these guys were on your side—at least until you started really negotiating with them and asking for things. I honestly believe they started off with the intention of taking care of fighters, but in the long run it turned out to just be business for these guys. To them, every fighter is expendable.

When they offered me more money for my second fight, I took them at their word as to the reasons why. Even though the money was not really occupying my mind, I just assumed they were doing right by me and other fighters. Deep down, a part of me felt like I did not deserve any more money since I had just started fighting. These guys were helping to make me famous, put me on television, and there was more to come, as I was always led to believe.

I was too young and naive to think about the business side of things, and I didn't really care. At some point before the fight I spoke to Dana White about the payout for Thomas, and he mentioned I would be paid "eight and eight" if I won. "Eight and eight!" At the time $16,000 seemed like an enormous sum of money, and the thought of being paid so much to fight someone was unheard of to me.

Truth is, all I really wanted to do was kick Thomas's ass, and a few months earlier it was the sole reason I fought anyone: for the love of it. Having money involved changed the dynamics of it all, but at twenty-two, I was still too carefree to consider what any of it really meant.

I STARTED TRAINING for Thomas immediately, working with the same guys at AKA but preparing a little differently. I got into the habit of watching tapes of an opponent, and with Thomas I could tell I would have my hands full since he had already defeated Pulver. Being submitted was not a very big concern; I had full confidence in my ability to stop BJJ style submissions. What bothered me was experience, which Thomas had, with thirteen professional fights under his belt and an impressive 12–1 record.

Back in the gym, things intensified both for me and the guys working with me. More and more people were getting involved with AKA, which only helped me prepare. Sometimes things got out of control, though. There was this one younger guy in the gym who was close with Cook and was helping me prepare for the fight. He seemed like a character out of *Beverly Hills 90210*, concerned with his looks and having a "punk" attitude, but unlike an actor, he liked to fight. For whatever reason, he always came at me hard, whether it was because he had something to prove or because it was his nature. On one particular day we were sparring, and he hit me pretty good in the face. I had a fight coming up, and had had enough with his antics. I started beating on him as hard as I could in front of everyone in the room, to the point where he started calling for Cook to help him out. Cook jumped up onto the ring as I was on top of the guy, and instead of helping him, he yelled out, "Thirty seconds, BJ! Finish him!" I just continued beating on him for thirty more. This is the way it was at AKA, sometimes serious, sometimes fun, but always unexpected and entertaining.

My same crew made its way out to New Jersey for UFC 32, including Reagan, Jay Dee, his then girlfriend Jodi (now his wife), and the guys from AKA. They put us up in some small hotel near the venue, nothing fancy with little surrounding us. This time, though, the UFC wanted me to take part in other things besides fighting.

While everyone always likes to point out the $2 million the Fertittas paid for the UFC, they don't always remember the money they poured into it to make it successful. It was more like buying land with oil underneath as opposed to buying pumping oil wells. It took money to build and fix this thing, and one of the first things they spent money on was billboards and advertisements, one which, in New York City's Times Square, had my face on it.

The UFC shuttled me into the city with Thomas, Ortiz, Sinosic, and some of the other guys to promote the fight at the ESPN Zone in Times Square. I hadn't been to New York City in a long time, and didn't remember the first trip. I was a bit overwhelmed, especially when I looked up and saw myself on a billboard. The whole thing was just weird. The UFC machine was in high gear. A few months ago, no one had known who I was; now my face was plastered on a sign for millions to see, alongside a few other guys hardly anyone knew.

Well-known model and actress Carmen Electra was hired to do

PR, and she told everyone how she loved martial arts and practiced Tae Bo. She and White had something in common, since he had previously done aerobic-style boxing instruction in Las Vegas. Before I knew it, I had to say some things about myself, so I mentioned how excited I was to be there and what a great fighter Thomas was. Thomas did a little more hyping than I did, saying we could "expect some early fireworks before the Fourth of July." Tito Ortiz, the great self-promoter, took it even further, commenting about the "explosions from his fists" we could expect, in addition to any fireworks.

Some of the press people there wondered how I ended up as the co–main event, and White responded by letting everyone know he'd received a lot of e-mail from fans expressing their desire to see me on the main card. How I would not be on any more undercards ever again if I kept fighting like I did against Joey Gilbert. I was getting a sense of what the Fertittas and White had in store for the company, and as strange as it all was, it was definitely exciting.

WHEN I ARRIVED AT THE VENUE, I started realizing how big this thing really was. The arena was huge, with about ten thousand people in attendance. Jens Pulver was there, scheduled to provide commentary for the fight. When I saw him I thought to myself, *That's him. That's the man, the guy everyone wants to beat*. Half of me was in awe, thinking, *Wow, the champ!*, and the other half, *He doesn't look special, but I guess he is*. Pulver would have a front-row seat at the fight UFC announcer Mike Goldberg claimed was "as big as a title fight."

My emotions were much more in check this time. The biggest difference was having to wait for six fights to finish before my turn, watching them on the closed circuit TV in the locker room. As the evening went on, the suspense grew as I witnessed the emotional highs and lows of the fighters who had already won and lost.

DeSouza was on the card again, and he won somewhat easily by submission, which boosted my confidence.

When I was called to fight, I walked straight from the locker room to the cage with the UFC's theme music hovering in the arena. Things happened fast, and I hardly noticed the size of the building as I walked through the crowd. I had come to beat this guy, which was all that mattered. Thomas and I stood across from each other inside the Octagon, and I was amped up to fight. Referee Big John McCarthy asked us if we were ready and gave me my first "Let's get it on!"

I did the only thing I knew how to do, go forward, so I went right across the cage toward my opponent. Thomas threw a big right hand, but I ducked out of the way. Even though Thomas had submitted most of his opponents, his real advantage was his seventy-six-inch reach, which is longer than most guys' in the lightweight class. Mine is only around sixty-nine, which means he could stand seven inches farther away from me and still land punches. All our other measurements were pretty much the same.

Once he missed with the first punch, I immediately grabbed hold of him, took him down, and pulled him into my guard by wrapping my left foot around his right leg and using my arm to drag him to the mat. We worked from that position until I was able to grab his right leg and arm, and pull off a omoplata on him, which is a position that applies a lot of pressure on an opponent's shoulder by keeping the entire body weight on his arm. He got free after a few seconds and unloaded a few punches on me while I was on my back, hitting me cleanly in the face at least once. The crowd started to get loud. I scrambled to my feet immediately and backed up.

Now we were both standing again in good position, no one really damaged at all. I could hear Mendez and Cook shouting instructions for me to throw punches. You could always hear those two, especially Cook, who was great at instructing ringside. He has an unmistakable, piercing voice when cageside.

I started to throw some jabs, but then Thomas came toward me, confident he could land some shots standing. He threw another big left hook that missed, and then a short right which I caught with my hand. In one motion, I clinched the back of his neck with my left hand and threw a right knee to his face. I was ready to attack at that point, but he fell back to the canvas, almost in slow motion. He was sprawled out in front of me, unconscious; the right knee from the clinch had knocked him out cold.

Naturally I went to jump on top of him to finish the fight because you just don't know what's going on when things are moving at that speed. McCarthy moved in to make sure no more damage was caused.

I was beside myself. I had already made it farther than I ever thought I would. I had just gone above and beyond my expectations. I went into it hoping to knock him out, but I hadn't been able to stop Gilbert in such a fashion even though I'd dominated the match. The feeling was indescribable, almost like it wasn't even me. I ran up the side of the cage and stuck my face into the camera to give a shout out to everyone back home, "Hilo!" 2–0 in the UFC!

AFTER MY FIGHT I DECIDED to walk around the venue alone just to experience it all. A fan ran over to me and asked me to sign a program. I was honored to do it. It was the first time someone ever asked me for my autograph To think people cared about who I was overwhelmed me. I was thankful, and let him know it.

Once all the fights ended, the UFC told me I had to do the post-fight press conference with Tito Ortiz, who had been victorious as well. In that moment they could have asked me to do anything. Over at the press conference, another fighter who had won, Ricco Rodriguez, was sitting in my chair waiting to be interviewed. A big, hulking heavyweight, with an equally large personality, Rodriguez was someone I had known from my years competing in BJJ.

He was on the undercard that night and had defeated Belarusian Andrei Arlovski. He was not even supposed to be at the press conference, but there he was, center stage.

He had no idea he was even sitting in my chair but wanted to promote himself as much as possible. I was fine with it since I really liked him. Earlier in the night, he told me Thomas and me were going to have a war, but said I would "take him out." It was just a real funny thing to see him up there. Like was I supposed to tell him to get up? I had no idea what my responsibilities were, or what anyone was doing anywhere. I was just there to make a name for myself, and I guess Ricco was trying to do the same! There was no structure to anything; things just sort of happened.

When the press conference ended, I went back to the hotel, where people were partying at the bar. The after-parties always stink and have from the beginning, but you have to show your face and play the game, so I did. I like being with my friends and family after fights, not drinking with people I don't know. Fighting is very personal to me, and afterward, win or lose, I need the emotional support from people I am close to. Some guys love it, though, and occasionally you will come across one of the louder personalities within the MMA world.

On this night, I was standing near the hotel bar with Bob Cook, and out of nowhere some guy walks up behind me and bumps into my back, almost shoving me. With no idea who it was, I looked at Cook somewhat confused. He said to me with a half smile, knowing I would respond, "That was Phil Baroni."

I asked, "Was that an accident or did he just try to punk me?"

He could have lied to avoid a problem, but in typical Cook fashion, still smirking, he responded, "He tried to punk you."

One needs to realize this guy Baroni's nickname was "The New York Badass," and he walked around like he was the greatest thing since the wheel. He was one of the up-and-coming fighters out of New York, and he really fit the New York mold: stocky, big muscles, Italian, with jet-black hair. Exactly what you would expect a guy named Phil Baroni to look like. I was no stranger to having two fights in one night, even though it had been a while. He probably had me by about fifty pounds at the time, but it was of no concern to me.

I walked back over toward him and banged into his back. He turned around and I introduced myself, "Hey, I'm BJ Penn."

He just looked at me and started to smile. In less than thirty seconds I had just made my first friend from New York.

THREE-FIGHT DEAL

AS MUCH AS I HAD WANTED to find out what I was going to do with my life during the last five years, part of me still wanted to just be a kid. In less than a year, I had won the Mundials and competed twice in the UFC. I had become well known in certain circles and had established myself as both a great jujitsu fighter and a legitimate MMA contender. Not too bad for a Hilo boy just chasing after some dreams.

I returned to Hawaii after the fights to take a little time for myself. The fighting had not drained me in a serious way, nor had the training, but I did want to take a break from everything. I still liked seeing my friends, partying, and having a good time like anyone else. I missed the waterfalls, rivers, beaches, and the ocean, and now I even had some money too, which gave me the freedom to do what I wanted, or at least I thought it did.

When I first got back, I took the checks the UFC had given me and deposited them in a checking account at one of the local Hawaiian banks. I figured that was the best way to keep the money safe. It seemed like such an incredible amount, and I imagined all the things I could do with it. After a few days of it sitting there, my dad asked me what I had done with it. I told him I put it in the bank, which I thought was a responsible decision. He told me otherwise. As he saw it, the only thing I would do with money in the bank was spend it, and that is not how you earned money for your future. Right away he had me pull it out, saying that having my money sit in the bank was not going to make me any money. At the time I did not agree with him, but upon reflection, it was clearly the right decision.

My parents were not really big on giving us life lessons, or telling us how to do things. They pretty much took the position that we would all figure things out for ourselves. They'd help us when they could, but for the most part we would blaze our own path. Except when it came to money—that they would provide us guidance with.

Money was to be invested for the future, and not just your own. Just as their money helped to sustain us when we were growing up, they wanted us to view the money we made as something that could sustain our own lives—now and in the future. Even though I was still young, they were not going to let me waste the money I'd earned through hard work on traveling, partying, and having a good time. My winnings were the dividends on the investment they had made in my future. It was going to be reinvested wisely from day one, and there would be a little left over for spending—just enough so that I could reap some benefits from my accomplishments without going overboard.

Of course, I was still going to have a good time. Back in Hilo, I had become something of a celebrity, which is pretty much true for every fighter from a small town who finds himself winning. The first fight with Gilbert people had heard about, but the second against Thomas people had seen. For any guy my age, the fame could come in handy, especially with the girls. For what other reason do young guys want to become famous? As far as that investment went, clearly my stock had risen around Hilo.

Not surprisingly, my minor fame mattered most to girls in Hilo. Back in San Jose, I could say to a girl I met, "I'm with the UFC," and she might reply, "Oh, is that a school in California?" or maybe, "Is that a new start-up Web site?" It didn't go very far. Even the people in Honolulu didn't seem to care. One would think Hawaii would celebrate all of its homegrown celebrities, but I was viewed as an outer-island guy, not just then but even later on in my career. Back then, no one seemed to really care very much about the sport, so I had to be satisfied with the notoriety I received around Hilo, which I certainly was.

I HAD ABOUT FOUR MONTHS between fights, and the first two moved both too slowly and too fast. You never look forward to training camp because like any other job, love what you do or not, it is still work.

The UFC had offered me a fight at UFC 34 in Las Vegas, against the man I'd originally been scheduled to fight in my first match: Caol Uno. This would be the first of a three-fight contract, the first long-term deal I signed with the UFC. Uno had lost his fight to Pulver, but was coming off a victory against a very game Fabiano Iha, who, like me, had a solid background in jujitsu in addition to being a good striker. Uno and I had been on the same card in the Meadowlands, so the timing of it all made sense.

Coming into our first scheduled fight, Uno had been the likely favorite, but by now we were at least even up. And I was definitely getting paid more. We both knew the importance of this fight: Uno was trying to get back to the top, and I was still making my way. Even though I had wanted to face Pulver for the title, I knew it was still too early. The UFC needed to take its time building up the fights, and I had not earned that right just yet. In MMA, one shot, lucky or planned, can end any fight, and while my fight with Thomas was impressive, it did not mean I had reached number one contender status. Beating Uno would get me there, and if I won this fight, I'd get a title shot.

Preparing for Uno would be a little easier this time around. I had reached a level where I was coming into contact with more and more fighters at the events, and I was learning how other guys trained. While Cook and Mendez were basically running my training camp, I felt a strong need to be involved in how the camp was run. Though some guys preferred to be told what to do, I was not one of them. I had learned over the years through trial and error that only the fighter truly knows how he feels.

I was trying to keep things in perspective because my two fights to date had not been incredibly difficult, and I did not want to start thinking things would be easy. I had certainly expected them to be longer than one round! Uno had gone the distance with Pulver, the champ, making it important for me to prepare like it was a championship fight. In just that one fight, Uno had spent more than two times as long in the cage as I had spent in both fights together, so I needed to push myself extremely hard in preparation. At the same time, though, I had to wonder how ready he would be, since he'd been training and fighting battles year in and year out for a while now. Did Uno want this as badly as I did? We had been on a similar schedule, but I was definitely less worn.

Up until my training for Uno, I'd been quite lucky in one important way: I'd never sustained any serious injuries in either my fights or my training. Training was (and is) often a major source of injuries. Today you hear all the time how fighters break body parts, tear muscles, tendons, ligaments, incur sicknesses because they train nearly as hard as they fight. Back when I was practicing jujitsu, the training was not like this; it was all about technique, not power. Going the distance in a BJJ competition is nothing like an MMA fight. Even while they were wrestling in the gym, I noticed how guys got hurt a lot more frequently. Injuries for me had never really been a concern, until a couple of weeks before I met Uno.

The temperature in San Jose fluctuated a lot more than it did in Hilo. If it got down to around fifty degrees, it was really cold for a kid like me who rarely took off his flip-flops. One day the temperature must have been in the high forties, and when I got to the gym, I decided not to warm up and stretch like I normally did. I just started moving around on a track we used to warm up on, but because it was so cold, I started moving faster. After circling the track once, I decided to sprint to speed up the process, and at some point, I felt one of my quadriceps really tighten up on me in a way it never had before. I rubbed it, stretched it for a few seconds, but it still stayed very stiff, almost like it was cramping. I pushed on through training as if there were no problem, and it didn't seem to get any worse, so I figured it was something that would subside later in the day.

After the workout, though, it really stiffened up, so I began stretching it out. While standing, I did a standard quadriceps stretch by pulling my foot up behind me, bending my leg. As I did that, I just felt something pop inside my leg. It was one of the most painful things I had ever experienced, and I wasn't sure what was going on. I decided to lie down to rest it, and eventually the pain eased, but I did not see a doctor, or even a trainer, about it.

Knowing there was a problem but not thinking it was too serious, I decided to just keep on stretching every day before training. The stretching made the muscle feel better, even though it was limiting my movement and hurting me from time to time. The last thing I wanted to do was pull out of the fight with Uno, because I didn't know if or when I would get a chance like this again, plus I was young enough and strong enough to push through it, which was what I did.

Other than the nagging leg injury, training at AKA was as good as ever. My regular guys were there, and more guys were being brought in from the outside. My good friend Brian Johnston, who was an MMA fighter and a tremendous source of support for me, had contacts with so many fighters in the area. He had started his own clothing line called PAIN Inc., which sponsored fighters in the States and in Japan. He would supply us with partners from outside the gym, including guys more familiar with Uno than any of us were. It was a very good camp that helped me perfect what worked for me when it came to preparing myself. More and more, I felt the training was becoming a natural fit for me, just as it was for jujitsu.

THE FIGHTING COMMUNITY WAS anticipating my fight with Uno even more than it had my first two fights. It was UFC 34: High Voltage, on November 2, 2001, and it would be my first fight in Las Vegas, the fight capital of the world.

Though Las Vegas is often a very raucous place, remember it was still only a few short weeks after September 11, 2001, so Las Vegas was probably the quietest it had been in years. There were very few people traveling anywhere, let alone to "Sin City." People who came to see a fight were more likely planning to see the boxing match on Saturday night, which was between Zab Judah and Kostya Tszyu for the light-heavyweight title. The UFC was more or less piggybacking that event, probably a smart move considering the environment at the time. While my fight was supposed to be a battle, it seemed like it was still just people in the know who really cared.

The emptiness of Las Vegas made me feel like I was not supposed to be having a good time, so I just focused on the fight. I had a lot of friends in town who I could stay with and J-Sect, where I could train, so both of these kept me out of the casino. Like everyone else in the country, I was just trying to stay focused on my job. Since my job was to entertain people during this uniquely difficult time, I had to do the best I could in this fight. I did not feel any added pressure, or anything like that, but it seemed like everyone was trying to do the best they could for each other.

Fight night arrived like any other, but this time the environment seemed a little different from the previous events. Just walking downstairs through the casino, being around all the noises from the slot machines, gamblers, drinkers, smokers, and of course the fans, was exciting. Even the locker rooms had a more professional feel to them, with more guys having their own rooms instead of everyone piled into larger rooms with curtains. There were more fans too; some were saying there were close to ten thousand people in the arena.

On this card, I was not the co-main-event like I had been, even though this fight was arguably bigger than the last one. This time the bigger guys, and titleholders like Couture and Matt Hughes headlined the card. Even Ricco Rodriguez, who fought on the undercard during my last fight, was after me. I guess his plan of taking over the podium at my last event worked!

There was a lot more hype for this card than there had been for any of mine, and you could feel it. Couture and Pedro Rizzo had taken part in a war during their last fight, and this one promised to be the same.

You could sense the UFC was doing their best to build up this particular card. UFC 33 was their first fight in Las Vegas, and it had pretty much been a disaster. Mostly, it was too close in time to the tragedy in New York City, but what made matters worse was that all of the fights had been boring matches that went the distance. In addition, the event ran long, and most of the fans on pay-per-view did not even get to see the end of the final fight between Tito Ortiz and Vladimir Matyushenko. Because of all these problems, there was this sense the UFC needed us to perform better. That if our fights were not exciting enough, the UFC would no longer be around, and neither would the sport. This was something I never believed, as I have always thought this sport could never really fail, but given the circumstances, it was understandable why they saw things this way.

Even the announcers for the fight were there to add tension. For obvious reasons, Pulver was in the booth alongside Shamrock and

Mike Goldberg. Before the fight even began, Pulver was saying neither Uno nor I was as good as he was, and that he would be ready for either guy. Everything they talked about was geared to build up this event, and whatever would come after.

My relations with the Fertittas and White were still good at the time, but to them it was probably more about the success of the business than the martial arts. There were rumors of guys like Rizzo getting paid close to $200,000 per fight, which was a tremendous amount at the time. He and I were both contenders, and he had even lost. It was hard to hear things like that and not think of what I could make if I continued to win. In addition to the amount I was getting paid by the UFC for the fight, I started wearing some sponsors on my shorts for this fight, half out of a favor to Johnston and his PAIN Inc. and partially because he would give me a little something. And for this fight, I also decided to have my Web site, bjpenn.com, posted on the back of my shorts. There was a feeling among everyone that things were growing quickly—at the events and in the gyms, with the sponsors and out in the crowds. Everywhere you could see signs of it, but none of it really mattered if you didn't win fights.

In order to do my part, I needed to come out with energy and apply pressure on Uno. That is how you avoid boring fights, and it was the only thing I could control. Maybe I would get another knockout or pound him out on the ground. I wasn't sure how I was going to win, all I knew was that I would. It is a feeling I am sure most fighters have, knowing you will beat your opponent, going over it in your head hundreds of times, picturing it, but not really knowing which one of the results will actually take place. Uno had the experience and was a bit older, but I had height and reach on him—both of which I planned on using. A lot of times, Japanese fighters would come out a little more slowly than some of the American and Brazilian fighters did. They brought the calmness which comes from true martial arts into the cage; most people, however, did not.

This was taken in eighth grade, around the time I gave up soccer. (Photograph courtesy of BJ Penn)

Me (*left*) with one of my best friends from Hilo, Saul (*right*), on my front porch, the place where I used to scrap with my friends after school. (Photograph courtesy of BJ Penn)

Reagan (*left*), Jay Dee (*center*), and me (*right*). When we were growing up, my brothers and I were always looking for something to do. Sometimes trouble would have a way of finding us in the process. (Photograph courtesy of BJ Penn)

From the moment I arrived at Ralph Gracie's school to practice BJJ, Dave Camarillo and I were working together. He was a big reason why I was able to adjust to California life and learn quickly. This shot was taken back when we were grappling as purple belts and Dave had me on my back. (Photograph courtesy of BJ Penn)

Kevin Graham, trying to escape my full guard during training at Ralph Gracie's

This was taken right after my victory at the Mundials in 2000, when I became the first non-Brazilian to win gold in the black belt division. (Photograph by Marcelo Alonso)

I've done a lot of things since then, but winning at the world's best BJJ tournament is one of the accomplishments I'm most proud of. (Photograph by Marcelo Alonso)

In this shot, I'm with Shaolin (*left*) from the Nova União team. He's one of the best BJJ competitors out there, and he took home black belt gold in his weight class on the same day that I did. (Photograph courtesy of BJ Penn)

After winning the Mundials, I took some time off and went to France with Steve DaSilva (*left*) to teach BJJ. He was the person who came up with my nickname "Prodigy." (Photograph courtesy of BJ Penn)

Left to right): Jay Dee, me, Alex Oxendine, Casey Cruz, and Thomra Oxendine, at our Legends "gym," which my brothers and I started with Alex in his garage. Photograph courtesy of BJ Penn)

My second fight against Caol Uno was at UFC 41 in Atlantic City. This shot of Rudy Valentino (*right*), one of my trainers at the time, and me was taken on the boardwalk before the fight. (Photograph courtesy of BJ Penn)

At the weigh-in with Caol Uno (*left*) for UFC 41. The UFC was a lot different then, from the amount of press to the formality of the prefight events. (Photograph courtesy of BJ Penn)

UFC 41 postfight interview with Caol Uno (*right*). Matt Lindland (*left*) was sitting next to me (*center*). (Photograph courtesy of BJ Penn)

This shot was taken after my win over Duane Ludwig in K-1 Romanex in Japan. Fighting in Japan was unbelievable, but the fight culture there was much different from the UFC and the crowd was a lot more subdued. (Photograph by Scott Petersen, MMAWeekly.com)

Fighting Renzo Gracie (*left*) at K-1 Romanex in Hawaii was an amazing experience. I'd fought in Hawaii for the Rumble on the Rock, but I hadn't done it for K-1 and it was a great way to finish out my contract with them. (Photograph by Scott Petersen, MMAWeekly.com)

There was a lot of talk about the bad blood between the Gracie family and me during the lead up to the K-1 Romanex Hawaii fight, but once we were in the ring we were both motivated by the same thing: winning the fight. (Photograph by Scott Petersen, MMAWeekly.com)

I won the fight with Renzo Gracie (*left*) by unanimous decision. After the fight was over, Renzo and I hugged, the bad blood seeming to trickle away once we'd had a chance to settle the score. (Photograph by Scott Petersen, MMAWeekly.com)

Landing a punch during my second fight with Matt Hughes (*left*) at UFC 63.
(Photograph by Dave Contreras)

Battling it out with Joe Stevenson (*right*) at UFC 80. (Photograph by Lee
Whitehead, MMAWeekly.com)

After beating Joe Stevenson, I took home the UFC lightweight belt. I had held the welterweight belt, but this was the first time I'd had the lightweight belt. (Photograph by Lee Whitehead, MMAWeekly.com)

This shot was taken while I was teaching kids at my new MMA academy in Hilo. UFC fighter Shane Nelson (*lower right*) helped me out that day. (Photograph courtesy of BJ Penn)

Throughout everything, my family has been there for me. This shot was taken at my brother Jay Dee's wedding. (*Left to right*): Me; my brother Jay; my sister, Christina; my father, Jay Dee Sr.; Jodi; Jay Dee; my mother, Lorraine; my brother Reagan; my brother Kalani; and my cousin Greg. (Photograph courtesy of BJ Penn)

Hawaii is about a lot more than surfing, but it's hard to live here and not take part. (Photograph by Kaz Sano)

Often in our early UFC days, Matt Serra (*right*) and I were compared to each other because of our BJJ skills. Though we eventually competed inside the cage, we've remained friends. (Photograph courtesy of BJ Penn)

At home with Shea and Aeva. Fighting used to be the thing that made me happiest; now they are.

At the prefight press conference for UFC 94 with Georges St-Pierre (*left*). In all the years I'd been fighting professionally, I'd been around a lot of hype, but nothing even came close to what I experienced with this second St-Pierre fight. (Photograph by Ken Pishna, MMAWeekly.com)

Training with Jason Parillo (*right*) before my fight with Diego Sanchez, which was held in December 2009. (Photograph courtesy of RVCA)

Before my fight with Kenny Florian, I trained with Rudy Valentino (*left*) at RVCA. (Photograph courtesy of RVCA)

At the weigh-in for my fight with Diego Sanchez (*right*). (Photograph by Jeff Cain, MMAWeekly.com)

Toward the end of the fight, I opened up a sizable cut above his eye. I went on to win the fight in a TKO. (Photograph by Jeff Cain, MMAWeekly.com)

This is why I fight. (Photograph by Jeff Cain, MMAWeekly.com)

I no longer had any real nerves during the walk out to the Octagon, heading down that long walkway above the crowd toward the cage. I walked out to the cage second, and as I entered the Octagon, Uno was lying down in the center of it enacting some sort of prefight ritual that he did. When I saw him there, I thought to myself, *That's where you are going to end up after I hit you!* As the American fighter, I could sense I had the support of the people inside the MGM Arena; the question was, would it even matter?

Once we were both in the cage, the referee, Larry Landless, called us out to fight, and without hesitation, Uno came running across the cage and attempted a flying kick aimed at my head, which missed. So much for coming out slowly like other Japanese fighters. After he passed by me, I circled back to my left and attempted to take over the center of the Octagon. Uno tried moving toward the center as well, but I wasted no time at all as he moved toward me. I backed him up by throwing a right cross and a left hook, neither of which landed, but they did force him to cover up and move back toward the fence. Once he did that, I threw a big right uppercut which landed square on his face and knocked him onto his back and into the cage. I jumped right over him and started throwing punches with my right hand into his face.

As I stood over him throwing blows, Landless stepped in to separate us. Uno was out cold. The fight had lasted eleven seconds.

Because I was so excited, I just wanted to get back to the locker room with my team, and I ran out of the cage as fast as I could, only to be called back out for a postfight interview. I had not expected things to go so quickly or easily. I felt good in the cage, saw an opportunity, and capitalized on it. The best part was since it was all over so fast, my leg injury didn't hinder me at all.

In six months, I had gone from being a guy nobody in the fight world had ever heard of to 3–0 in the UFC, and the number one contender for the lightweight title. In less than one round I had eliminated two opponents who had been extremely difficult for the champion Pulver. People were starting to take notice of what I was doing, and it was hard for me not to think I was going to soon be the UFC champ. Immediately after the fight, I was congratulated by the rapper Everlast from the band House of Pain, and I was excited he would even take the time to recognize me. Soon after that, the boxer Zab Judah commented to the media that he liked my style and watching me fight. It was almost like an overload of things was happening all at once.

Though I didn't totally realize it at the time, I think the best part of it all was the lack of drama surrounding the entire fight scene. Even with all of these things I achieved later, the negative drama can make it all seem not worth it. But early on in my career, none of that stuff existed. After the Uno fight, there was not even a hint of it, which made all the things I had going for myself that much better.

As EXPECTED, THE NEXT FIGHT WOULD be the biggest of my life, and in many ways, it will always be. I was finally going to get my chance to fight for the UFC Lightweight Championship against Jens Pulver. The only problem was that Dana White wanted me to fight for it in two months at UFC 35 at the Mohegan Sun Casino in Connecticut. I really had no interest in fighting so soon, but White insisted that it had to happen this way. They wanted to build on the momentum from the last events, and with the bad economy at that time, he really needed the money.

At first, I was very hesitant, even though the Uno fight had been so short. It is not the length of the fight that matters, it is the training that beats you down, and I was not fully prepared to go right back into the gym and start all over for another eight to nine weeks. But just like White is now, he was the same way then. He called me up and said, "Come on, you gotta do this. You gotta do this! We need you, kid. This is your chance to get the belt." Over and over, he was beating that drum.

Finally, I told him, "Okay, I'll do it on one condition. You have to make me the main event."

He thought about it for a second and said, "Okay, fine. It's the main event."

I did not even really want to do it. I wanted the belt, and I wanted to fight Pulver, but part of me knew I was not necessarily in the best place to start this camp. Still I didn't know if I was going to get such a big chance again.

When I returned to AKA, the guys were ready to restart the training, and despite my needing a little time to relax, the guys told me to at least start running. Every time you prepare for a big fight, you look forward to taking a bit of downtime when it's over. Even in jujitsu, where the fights are not nearly as mentally taxing as in MMA, you give yourself a little break. Mendez and the other guys didn't think I should do that. They thought I needed to at least be doing something small, and then come in, ready to go after a few days. But I was at odds with them over this. In my mind, once I started working out, I was officially training, which defeats the purpose of a break in the first place. I was so burned out that I wanted to just not train at all at the time.

In addition to being hesitant about the training, I made the camp difficult in other ways. From being around the fights, I had met a lot of new guys, and I picked up a good deal of new things along the way, adding them to what I already knew. I was doing all of the same things I had done for the other three fights, but instead of replacing one thing with another, I just tacked on more. I used to do a light morning workout, a noon training, and maybe hit Legends, but by the time of the pre-Pulver camp, I had expanded this to nearly an entire day, every day. I also had Charuto, Tony DeSouza, and other guys come to AKA to prepare me.

For the first time in my life, I was overpreparing and pushing myself too far, yet I had no idea that this was happening. I thought I knew what was best for me, but in actuality I didn't really understand how to prepare perfectly for a training camp, especially since I had just come off of one.

As I approached the fight with Pulver, everything I did felt like suffering. I was slow in my sparring, and I became tired when I grappled. Meanwhile my leg had only become worse. It was not the type of injury that could withstand being hit, and it affected how I could push off, plant my feet, or shoot on someone. At some point during the camp, I went to see a massage therapist who recognized that there was something really wrong with the muscle in my quad. She told me it was bulging and that it felt like there was a ball inside my leg. It was not the type of injury that could be seen with the naked eye, but today, if you look at my leg, you'll see a dent about the size of a golf ball, which should give you an idea of how serious this really was. She was concerned I could have muscle atrophy if I didn't do something about it, but again, there wasn't much I felt I could do. This was my shot.

The closer we got to the fight, the worse I looked in camp. Coaches and friends were telling me I needed to push myself harder, that resting was not going to be the answer. No one wanted me to treat the situation like I was burned out, but I felt I was. I listened to what everyone said and pushed myself as far as I could go, hoping there would be some kind of break that would let me catch my breath. It never really happened.

This fight was also the first time that the hype was not coming from the fans, Dana White, or other fighters waiting to see a new guy—it was coming from Pulver himself. From the moment I beat Uno, he talked and talked about how he was a bigger challenge than Uno or Thomas, and that I needed to prepare for a war. He said other things just to get under my skin, little things, almost like he was testing me to get me off my game. Maybe he knew I had never dealt with this kind of stuff before, and the truth was, I hadn't. Other people would then be pumping me up, telling me Pulver didn't stand a chance. Deep down I'd always wanted to avenge John Lewis's loss to Pulver, since Lewis was still one of my boys. It was this back-and-forth—the mind game, the training, being able to handle it all—and I was not keeping up as well as I should have.

NEW YEAR'S 2002 ARRIVED VERY QUICKLY, and before I knew it, I was back on the road headed toward the East Coast to the Mohegan Sun Casino. This was my fourth different location in four fights. Part of me liked seeing new places, but there was nothing too exciting about Uncasville, Connecticut, that's for sure.

The UFC put us up in the Best Western Hotel, which was a few miles away from the venue. At the time the casino did not have a hotel, so we had to drive back and forth. Just being there felt like I was in an episode of *The X-Files*, caught in the middle of nowhere, stuck inside this huge forest where all the roads looked the same. Then the casino itself was no prize either. There was absolutely nothing to do at the place other than gamble. Everything closed really early, the only girls you would see were actually not girls at all, but more like someone's grandma, and the whole vibe of the place was just off. The UFC likes to have events at casinos—not because you can bet on the fights there because most of the time you cannot—but because the casino will buy up all the higher priced tickets and entice their high rollers to come gamble. For that reason alone, we all had to be worried if we would soon be getting a visit from Skully and Mulder.

The UFC also did a poor job of setting up our rooms. They put me directly across the hall from the guys in Pulver's camp like Tony Fryklund and Matt Hughes, all part of Team Miletich. At the time I had nothing against any of Miletich's guys since I hardly knew them, but I did not want to run into Pulver before the fight, or hear any of these guys shit talking. Seeing him at the weigh-in, and maybe in the lobby was enough. The place ended up being so uncomfortable that Mendez decided we were moving. We ended up getting a room at the Foxwoods Casino, which is about ten miles away, just to change the stale environment.

EVEN THOUGH I KNEW I DIDN'T have a great camp leading up to the fight, I was sure I was going to win. I had no idea how I was going to pull it off, but my expectation was no matter where the fight went, I would prove to be the better fighter. For whatever reason, the oddsmakers also believed I was going to win and had made me the favorite at nearly three to one, which was probably extra motivation for Pulver, which he didn't need.

The UFC used a charter bus to bring everyone over to the casino from the hotel. Once we got there, I was comfortable and focused. If there were any nerves, they were not over whether I could beat him. I was confident I could win; however, I wasn't so sure I was prepared to be a champion, to wear the belt and represent all that comes with it.

It was the main event of the night, and I had to watch every other fight come before me. There was definitely something more intense about going last, as if it now all rested on my shoulders, the anchor so to speak. When it was my time, I calmly headed out toward the Octagon and could feel the excitement in the building. I entered the cage wondering if this would be the last time, since I'd told myself I would retire after winning the belt. As the challenger, I had to wait for Pulver to make his way through the crowd. I waited in my corner with my guys outside the cage, and John McCarthy on the side of the Octagon. Next thing I knew, Pulver was in the cage and McCarthy was shouting his famed "Let's get it on!"

Pulver and I came across toward each other, and for the first time inside the Octagon, I started backing up. I immediately shot for his legs and tried to take the fight to the ground. Throughout the entire camp, this had been the plan, to avoid going toe-to-toe with him since he had been known to have knockout power in his left hand. After I was able to get him down, I stayed inside his guard for a while and tried to cause some damage. Neither one of us had much success from our respective positions. Eventually he was able to work himself free and get to his feet. I jumped on him while we were both standing and went for a guillotine choke, with my legs wrapped around his body. I was unable to get my forearm underneath his neck all the way for it to be effective, and this enabled him to walk me toward his corner and slam me down into the mat. What had started off as a fight I felt I was in control of had quickly turned into one where he had the edge.

We battled on the ground back and forth, and at one point McCarthy stood us up because there was no action. I ran across the ring to my corner after he did this because every time you were stood up in jujitsu you had to go to your corner. It was the first time I did something thoughtless like that inside the cage. I remember thinking, *What the fuck did you do that for? You just wasted energy.*

Once standing again, we started exchanging punches with just over a minute to go, and I felt I was getting the better of the exchange. I was even able to land a knee on him, but then all of a sudden I jumped guard again by wrapping my legs around his body and pulling him back down to the mat. There was really no reason for me to do it since I was having success standing up, but again, I had been told to be wary of standing with him and trading punches even though as a fighter, my instincts told me to do this. The round ended with him in my guard, on top of me. I had just lost my first round in the UFC, and in many ways, I'd let him have it.

As the second round began, I was immediately able to get takedowns and control the action. Pulver pressed me and backed me up, but he was not sprawling well enough to keep on his feet. Even though Pulver is known to be a striker, I had figured it would be tougher to get him down since he had worked with great wrestlers and was one himself. During the second round, I was able to dictate the pace and land shots on him. After battling on the ground for a while with me in his guard, we made it to our feet one more time, and I continued to be backed up.

Late in the round I shot on him again, took him down, only this time I was able to mount him completely. There was about 1:30 remaining, and I was doing my best to land some blows or get the submission. Pulver did a great job of preventing this from happening. He swung his legs up and tried to hook my arms, or at least slow me down as I was straddled across his chest. I went for an arm-bar submission, but he was able to roll out and escape. I still had him in control, and was then able to mount him one more time with less than a minute to go.

Finally, he tried bucking me off him, which brought us very close to the cage—so close that it limited my ability to pull off another submission. I kept trying to cause damage, and with about five seconds to go in the round, I finally went for the arm bar. I was in perfect position, and I wrapped my legs over his chest and head, pulled his arm free, and applied the submission. Just as I had locked it in, the horn sounded to end the round, and it looked as if he had tapped at exactly the same time. It was too close to call. Another three seconds and the match would probably have been over . . . but it wasn't.

At the very least I had evened up the fight, one round apiece, and except for a few mistakes in the first, I probably should have been winning both. Cook came out into the cage as I headed back to my corner and was yelling at McCarthy, "He tapped! He tapped!" McCarthy said the round had ended. There were still three rounds left, but I felt depleted physically. I had the energy to fight, but I hadn't fought this long in my previous three fights.

The third round and the fourth round came and went quickly. I was able to take him down, but he was able to maintain control, even reversing positions a few times and landing some punches from the bottom and the top. Pulver was really great at not going away, and apparently I was really bad at finishing fights. I hardly knew how to do it, or what it even meant. It seemed everything I was trying was lackluster, and he was able to take the advantage away at the end of every exchange. Eventually, I reached a point during the fight when I almost didn't know what to do.

Meanwhile Pulver pressed on. Whenever I gave him an opportunity, he took it and scored points with the judges. All the way into the fifth round we continued to stand in front of each other, with me throwing out mostly jabs and weak kicks and Pulver trying to counter with big left hands, which he occassionally landed. My corner was yelling at me to throw my hands and take the fight over, but I just couldn't do it. I knew I had to try something big to win the fight, but I was hesitant to let him connect a big left hand. These two impulses left me unsure of where to go. His power was not causing a lot of damage and I felt I could take it, but in the back of my mind I worried he would land that one big shot. It also didn't help that both my kicks and punches had very little on them. Maybe it was from the leg injury and my inability to really push off, or maybe I was just uncomfortable in the cage.

Down the stretch he was successful with his combinations, and he even shook off a kick that landed to his groin. McCarthy gave him a few seconds to recover, and for the last 30 seconds we just traded back and forth. I threw a weak kick at his head, which was met by a stronger one right back at me. I tried to attack him in the last few seconds, but he was prepared to answer. As I faded late, he remained ready to fight, and as I waited for the time to expire, he waited for the judges to award him his belt back, which was what they did. In what was a close fight decided by points, he won a majority decision, 48–45, 48–47, 47–47, according to the three judges, and I had just been handed my first UFC loss.

Back in the locker room Mendez was really emotional, and I was just in a fog. I couldn't believe I had fought such a lackluster fight. I had not felt like myself, and everything I'd done seemed hesitant and delayed. Mendez agreed. He was shouting at me, saying I had not been active enough, that I'd strayed from the game plan and fought poorly. Others could hear him going off at me, and Liddell's trainer, John Hackleman, jumped in and told Mendez, "He's just a kid man. Leave him alone." I knew what it must have looked like to others, and while I really was a kid, Mendez meant no harm by the whole thing.

Truth is, Mendez was right. I did look like shit. And regardless of anything, he was my coach, and that's what coaches do: they praise you when you are doing well, and give you hell when you are going wrong. I went wrong that night, and while there was some drama, the fact remains Mendez was like a father figure to me. He just wanted what was best for me, and the best from me. That night neither of us got what we wanted.

WHEN WE GOT BACK TO SAN JOSE, I had some real soul-searching to do. I knew before the camp had even started that I was not ready to be the champion and handle all the responsibilities that came with it. I was not sure if the blame should fall on AKA, me, some combination of both, or just something altogether unknown. Whatever it was, I used the situation as a reason to leave California and move back to Hawaii.

Jay Dee, along with his girlfriend, Jodi, were finished with school, and Reagan was tired of his job in San Jose. I was so depressed from the loss I just needed a change. The only positive thing to come from the fight was being able to give a major portion of my purse to the families of firemen who had died during the rescue effort at the World Trade Center disaster site. After all was said and done, and after paying out my cornermen, I had just enough money to get myself back to Hawaii.

Before I left, I told Mendez of my plans. He knew my head was not in a great place, and he could sense I wasn't the same person I'd been before the fight. Hawaii made sense for a lot of reasons, and with his blessing I moved. He told me then, and many times after, I was always welcome back and he would always be there for me.

It was upsetting to me how things had played out, but the parting was not bitter. There was enough blame to go around, but at the end of the day, I wasn't in any place to point fingers. There were too many voices coming from too many different people giving me way too much advice. California had been great to me, but I needed things to be simple again, and Hilo was the only place where that was possible.

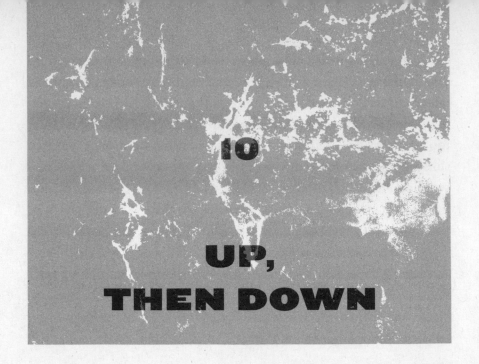

10

UP,
THEN DOWN

ONE OF THE BIGGEST DIFFERENCES between competing in jujitsu and MMA is the feeling you have
afterward. It is fair to say after I won the Mundials,
I was on top of the world, but the feeling I had after winning
inside the Octagon was something entirely different. Losing is
also different in both sports. After a jujitsu loss, as soon as your
hand is not raised, you start thinking about what you could have
done better and vow to come back stronger the next time. You
forget about those matches almost the moment one ends. This is
not true with MMA.

I struggled through my match with Pulver, and when it was
over I struggled with thoughts of having lost. I had no idea if that
would be my only shot, and if it was, I had just blown it. Unlike at
the Mundials in 2000, I had to confront the question of whether

I had given my all in the fight, and in the training leading up to it. Was I really prepared to even be a champion at the time? Because becoming a champion is as much a frame of mind outside of the ring, as it is what you're capable of doing inside of it.

Looking back now, I do not know if I was mature enough as a fighter to wear that belt. What could I have done differently? These were the questions that repeated themselves inside my head over and over, similar to the way I could never get jujitsu out of my head for all those years. With MMA, a loss proved to be something that ate at me. Fighters are known for having the highest highs and the lowest lows, and I was experiencing the latter.

Luckily I had good friends around to help me through it, but that could also be dangerous. I slipped into my old ways again, hanging out with my friends, drinking every night, and partying, just like I was doing before I left. Training every day, but making sure I was having a good time too. In some ways, it was the vacation I had wanted to take after the Uno fight; things were more on my terms, not those of a team or coach. I was not wasting away, though, and I never stopped training. I was twenty-three, and at that time in my life, I never needed motivation to train since it was still so much fun.

The UFC was not going to allow me too much time to sit on the sidelines and do nothing. Even if I had wanted to really kick back and relax, the opportunity was not going to last very long. I still had one more fight in my three-fight contract, so it was just a matter of time before I'd see who I would be facing.

More importantly, I now had to figure out how I was going to train going forward. There was no more of the old regimen, no more "noon" practice, Legends jujitsu, West Valley wrestling, or Garth Taylor. I used to follow Mendez, Cook, and Shamrock, but now it was entirely up to me to put together a regimen that worked since I was the only experienced MMA fighter in town.

I welcomed the opportunity to design my own training program, and on some level I had attempted to do that for the fight with Pulver. The lack of training partners could be a problem, but in truth, as long as I had Jay Dee, Reagan, and Charuto to work with, I'd be okay. Charuto was now preparing for his first MMA fight a couple months down the road, Reagan had great grappling skills, and Jay Dee could compete with practically anyone, anywhere. There were also some other fighters around Hilo, like Wesley "Cabbage" Correira, who I had known since I was about fourteen years old. Things were not terrible, but I would still need more partners, so I began looking around.

The first trainer I found was a local guy named Adrian Silva. Silva was a well-known boxing trainer and a real big guy, like one of those three-hundred-pound Hawaiians you see in a movie backhanding people to the floor. He was known for developing punching power in his fighters, and since I didn't need a lot of ground work, he seemed like a solution, at least in the short term. Silva was someone I could use to keep me focused while at home, but he was not necessarily the guy you'd pick to coach you through an MMA fight. He helped me develop some serious power in my hands, especially my jabs.

In addition to Silva, I decided to continue bringing Bob Cook to my fights as my lead cornerman. I needed Cook's experience, because while Silva helped me develop strengths, it was Cook who had the experience in MMA to help me win a fight in the last round, especially with his loud unmistakable voice shouting instructions. No matter how loud the fans in an arena are, they can never be loud enough to stop a fighter from hearing "Crazy Bob."

I trained over at Silva's gym since he had a ring, and used the mats at the school with Charuto, but we did not have a proper training facility in the area. As luck would have it, there was a local promoter who had recently put on a fight at the Neal Blaisdell Center in Honolulu. It was a pretty big event at the time, featuring guys like Wesley "Cabbage" Correira, Yves Edwards, Duane Ludwig, and Robbie Lawler. One of the guys who worked at the event handling the pyrotechnics somehow got ownership of the cage they had been using. After the fight, he reached out to Jay Dee and asked him if he wanted it. Why wouldn't we want a cage to train in? Of course, Jay Dee said yes, and next thing I knew we had a cage.

As I was assembling a new group to work with, the UFC found an opponent for me, a guy by the name of Paul Creighton. Creighton was training in BJJ under Renzo Gracie and was known to be a good grappler. He was 2–0 in his short MMA career but had not yet competed in the UFC. However, his record was largely irrelevant since I had received a shot at the title when I was only 3–0 in the UFC. In other words, this sport was still in its infancy, so you really never knew how good someone was based on their record.

In the early days, any opponent could be a problem, especially if you didn't know a lot about the guy. Not everyone felt the same way, though. Ricco Rodriguez, who always had something interesting to say, told me I had been offered an easy fight to help me get back to the top. Maybe he was right, I didn't know, but a fight was a fight, and anything could happen.

Dana White and I had been discussing opponents during the time that I moved back to Hawaii, and finally he settled on this one. It was a fight both Creighton and I accepted on short notice, possibly because the UFC needed to bulk up the event they were planning.

Ricco was probably right: if I had won the title, I highly doubt I would have faced an opponent most people had not heard of, but did that mean I had to fight him in a town no one had heard of either? UFC 37: High Impact, May 10, 2002, in Bossier City, Louisiana. From Atlantic City, New Jersey, to the Meadowlands just outside New York City, over to Las Vegas, then the Mohegan Sun, and now Bossier City, Louisiana, just outside of Shreveport. Just outside . . . Shreveport! Talk about a company on the rise! Nothing against Shreveport, since everyone there seemed nice, but Honolulu was hosting events nearly as large. It seemed like every time I had to fight, the city was more obscure than the last, but no matter, a cage was a cage regardless of its location. I think the only thing that could have surprised me more than Shreveport itself would have been if there was a direct flight there from Hilo.

As the Creighton fight approached, I worked on my takedown defense all the time, having as many people as possible try to take me down. In BJJ I didn't mind being taken down, and often ending up on my back by choice, since I was very effective from there. I never really trained hard to avoid such a position, but with Creighton it was the one area I continually worked on because it was most likely going to be his strongest position. I wanted to keep this fight standing the entire time. The wrestling had helped me tremendously in this respect, but I knew Creighton only had one chance, and it would not be on his feet, so the game plan was to keep it standing.

Going into the fight, it would have been natural for me to be nervous, knowing as I did if I lost, it would set me back, but I didn't feel the nerves at all. A lot of times when I faced pressure situations, or a new experience, I had shown emotion. This time was a lot different because I had been so down about losing my last fight all I really wanted was a chance to hit someone new. Besides, even though Creighton had nothing to lose, this was his first fight in the UFC. I am sure he was more worried about me than I was about him.

I was still working out the kinks in my training, but I didn't think this would be a problem in a three round fight. Lucky for me Rodriguez was right on the money. The fight with Creighton was not a difficult one, as he was overmatched. He was a lot smaller than me, and these days would probably compete at fly or bantamweight. Sometime in the second round I was able to mount him, and the referee stopped the match due to strikes. Creighton was a game opponent, as are most lightweights who make it in the UFC, but it was not his time. The fight was exactly what I needed to get back to winning.

At least, I could begin putting my last loss behind me.

WHEN I GOT BACK TO HAWAII, my goal was to keep building a new camp and training regimen to prepare myself for a shot at the title. I was still behind the times when it came to training on my own, not knowing exactly what I needed. Even when I was with AKA, we never really knew exactly what had to be done to prepare. Everything was just a guess, assuming if we pushed forward and worked ourselves until we could no longer stand, we were doing the right thing.

As for another shot with Pulver, that could not happen fast enough. Unfortunately, it was not going to happen anytime soon. Pulver was in contract negotiations with the UFC, and like many before him (and certainly many more after him), he felt he was not getting fairly paid. He was probably right, since no one ever seemed to be, except those few fighters the ownership seemed to want to make stars.

There would always be that one guy the Fertittas and White would give a lot of money to, like a Rizzo, or later on a Liddell, based on what they thought he was worth. But what did they know? The Fertittas were jujitsu white belts and White was an aerobic boxing instructor; should they be judges of which guy will be a star? So Pulver decided things were not fair, and his manager advised him to take his show on the road, which is what he did, heading off to fight in Japan. He would not fight in the UFC again for a long time, which meant our rematch would have to be somewhere else, some other time. Wherever or whenever, fighting him was always on my mind.

Coincidentally, the UFC was also in the process of offering me a new three-fight contract. Jay Dee was negotiating the details with them, but our expectations were not very high. The first contract had never really mattered to me, and it was for the most part pretty low, even by UFC standards. As I have always said, I did not really deserve much, but seeing as they considered me one of their best, maybe I deserved more than I got. I remember for my first fight my dad thought the pay was so low I might as well just fight for a dollar, and he told them that. "Why even give us a thousand? A legal contract is a dollar. The offer is so insulting I would rather see him fight for free!" Looking back on it, the flight to New Jersey, the hotel room, food, and bringing my team out there probably cost more than what they'd paid me to fight.

Right from the start of the new contract, I got the sense dealing with these guys was going to be difficult. Although the UFC was growing, they always framed things as if they were losing money. Maybe they were, maybe they weren't, but if they made money it was because we were always told, "You have to put on a show!" In those days, White was not the cocky and smiley guy he is today. He didn't really know what he was doing, and everything seemed to overwhelm him.

For this new contract, he seemed determined to hold the line. Beyond that, he always acted like now was "not the time," and that "down the road," if we did this or that for him, we would be rewarded. My father seemed to know better than we did from the get-go. He viewed White as a clueless guy playing a game with other people's money, and not even a shadow of the businessman he would eventually be considered. I trusted White to do right by us because he often made us believe that this rising UFC tide would lift all boats. While all of our boats would, in fact, eventually rise, White was showing off his yacht while other people were still paddling surfboards. The new contract eventually got signed, and it was a one-year deal starting from the day of the next fight. It would pay to fight/win, $15K/15, $20K/20, $25K/25. The real question was, if Pulver had vacated the belt, would any of these fights be for the title?

The UFC had an answer to this question. They decided to hold a tournament among the four best lightweight fighters which would take place over two events. Essentially the four semifinalists were myself, Caol Uno, Din Thomas, and Matt Serra. I had beaten the first two, and I knew something about Serra. Another guy training under Renzo Gracie out of New York, he was considered by many to be the best BJJ practitioner on the East Coast. In 1999, when I lost my match to Tererê, Serra had finished one spot below me in the next division up.

When I found out the tournament was the way for me to get the belt, I didn't want to do it. By process of elimination, I would end up fighting at least one person I'd already faced, and I had no interest at all in fighting those guys—or Matt Serra, for that matter. No disrespect to him, but it just seemed like a waste of time to repeat what I had just done. Would the winner really even be the champion? I didn't think so, but it was my job, so I didn't have much choice.

In September of 2002, the UFC offered me Serra in an effort to keep things fresh. Serra would almost certainly be a challenge. He was 5–1 at the time of the fight, and in many ways he could easily have been undefeated if not for the fact that he was caught by a Shonie Carter spinning backfist in his first UFC. He had been winning that fight before it happened, and it was more a move of desperation on Carter's part, but a great strike nevertheless. Winning this fight for either of us would almost mean more to the jujitsu world than it would the MMA world. Serra was East Coast, and I represented the West. There was a period of time before we even fought in the UFC when people discussed the two of us facing off in jujitsu, but it never happened. Now we could settle all scores.

To say my preparation for Serra was dumb would be an understatement. Initially I worked my jujitsu with Charuto and sparred with anyone willing, like Correira and other local guys. As we got closer to the fight, maybe about five weeks out, I devised a plan with Silva and my brothers which to this day seems more ridiculous every time I think about it. The plan was to spar one round for five minutes the first week. The second week, we would go two rounds. The third week, hold your breath . . . three rounds! The last week, three rounds again! It was our genius idea if we built up toward the fight, we would be primed and ready to go. Never realizing the first two weeks were a joke, or that maybe we should do three rounds for five weeks, and push ourselves to the maximum. It was just a weak method.

Adding to the terrible training, my diet was not very good. Not that it ever was, since I had never been focused on eating foods to enhance my performance. The school where we trained was located right behind Verna's, which is a Hilo hot spot for burgers, ribs, things with cheese where you would never expect it, saimin, and anything that could tip the scale toward a heart attack. Verna's was a place you went to be happy when you wanted to be happy while eating—not exactly a good place to lose weight. Still it was my first stop every day after working out. Being from jujitsu, I simply didn't know about the role a diet played in training. I'd learned technique, and if you were fat and out of shape, you could still perform.

One of the good things about the camp, though, was Silva. Even if he was not really schooled in MMA, he was working on my punching power and my stand-up all the time, just like Mendez had done. That pretty much became my plan for Serra. I figured I was stronger on my hands, so why even bother going to the ground if I didn't have to? It wasn't that I was worried about his jujitsu; I just felt strong standing. Since he had already been knocked out once, I figured why not go for two?

The Serra fight was scheduled for September 27, 2002, as part of UFC 39: The Warriors Return. And return we would, back to Uncasville, Connecticut, to the Mohegan Sun Casino. It was at least two flights for me, but a short drive for Serra from Long Island, New York. Suddenly Bossier City, Louisiana, seemed like a really good place.

• • •

THE DAY BEFORE THE FIGHT, I knew Serra was ready to go because we had a really intense stare-down at the weigh-ins. Normally those things don't matter too much, but sometimes you can look into a guy's eyes and figure out if he really wants to be there. I knew Serra saw a huge opportunity, and he would do his best to put it all on the line.

Even with the strange training camp, I was in a good place mentally. Despite not wanting to be in a tournament, I knew I'd be fighting a very good opponent who I had not faced yet. I told myself I was going to let this fight come to me, meaning I didn't want to force what was not there, and I wanted to focus on what I trained to do. If I did that I should be able to finish my opponent. I had spent hours upon hours having guys grab my legs, trying to take me down, knowing that was what Serra needed to do.

Fight night arrived, and I had the opportunity to be in the locker room with Rodriguez, Cabbage, Baroni, and some other guys. This time I was not the final fight of the night, as it was Rodriguez's turn. The UFC was trying to push its East Coast guys, which included Serra and Baroni as well. Uno and Thomas fought before we did, so I had the chance to see who I would fight if I won. It would be Uno, who won a three-round unanimous decision over Din Thomas.

The walk out to the Octagon had become something I was used to by now, to the point where I didn't even notice it. I walked second and entered the cage with Serra already waiting there. Big John once again did the honors of alerting us to the start of the fight, and once again yelled, "Let's get it on!"

Both Serra and I raced to the center of the Octagon, and immediately I was able to control it. Serra went for a single-leg, trying to grab hold and push me to the fence, but I jumped up and kneed him with my other leg. He continued to try to control me by pushing me against the cage while looking for the takedown, as I expected. I kept my balance nearly every time he went for it and tried to throw punches anywhere I could as he drove forward. Eventually we separated and were both on our feet. Serra lunged for my left leg again, but I threw a lower right-hand uppercut to his face which landed. He still held on to the leg, though. We separated and again moved around the ring in a circle.

With about two minutes to go in the round, we started to exchange again, and I landed a right hand that knocked him down. He again was able to hang on to my leg, but I had him in a place where I thought I could finish him. Serra did a great job of holding on to my leg to avoid the punches I was throwing, and eventually got back up and pushed me against the cage. He was not going to go away easily, but I had assumed he would not. Unlike my pre-Pulver days, I no longer went into a fight thinking I was going to drop my opponent in the first round. I had learned to be more patient. The round ended with neither of us doing much more.

At the start of the second, I came out and threw a kick to his body, but slipped and fell to the mat. I jumped up quickly, but he was all over me and went for a guillotine choke. He was unable to get it, but then transitioned into a nice takedown where I fell to my back with him in my guard. After a few seconds I was able to slip out, get back to my feet, and press him into the cage. We were exchanging knees to the body the entire time. After jockeying for position, Serra threw some elbows that landed while pressing my back to the fence, playing to his strengths well. We separated and circled each other in the center of the Octagon.

We stood toe-to-toe when all of a sudden he threw an overhand right that landed at the same time as I kneed him in the stomach. We separated, stared at each other, and both waved toward each other as if to say, *Come on, let's fight!* He smartly lunged at my right leg, grabbed it, and threw another right hand that landed, all in one motion. He was doing a great job of keeping me off balance, and his confidence was growing. He went for the leg again, grabbed on, but I threw some punches to his face that stunned him a little. He held the leg tight and pushed me back against the cage.

I was unable to get comfortable throughout the second half of the round. By the last minute, we had both spent a lot of energy, so we pushed each other up against the cage. The round came to an end.

Back in my corner, I was exhausted. I had my legs up, and I didn't even want to go out for the third round. My corner was shouting directions at me, mostly Cook telling me to "Turn it up, BJ! Turn up the striking!" Despite what Cook and Silva were telling me, all I was thinking was, *I cannot let this guy take me down no matter what. Do not go down. If he gets me down I will lose.* Striking, or no striking, I just wanted to remain standing.

When the third round began I took a deep breath and promised myself I would not quit. I came out and landed a jab and a kick early. Serra took another shot at my leg, but missed. He was standing farther back this round than he had been in round two, so shooting was a bit harder. I could tell he was also very tired. I was definitely more active at the start of round three.

Time and time again Serra was going for the takedown, but he couldn't get it. He was a world-class grappler, but I refused to let him get the takedown. The round was much more lackluster than the previous two, but even though Serra was taking shots at my legs, I was landing the only shots of significance. I connected with a few jabs, and some head shots whenever he put his head down in an effort to get a takedown.

With one minute to go, it was anyone's fight, even though I was slightly in the lead. If someone could just land one shot, one takedown, that was who would win. Serra threw a soft leg kick that had no effect, and then missed with another aimed at my head. I returned with a kick right back that landed on his leg, then a counterpunch, and another kick. The horn sounded with both of us standing with our hands on our hips and our heads down. It had not been a great fight for either of us. He knew he hadn't done enough to win, and I knew I'd looked like shit. In the end, I came away with the unanimous decision from both judges.

• • •

EARLIER IN THE NIGHT on the undercard, another one of Cook's guys had been fighting—an up-and-coming welterweight named Sean Sherk. I had known Sherk pretty well because of Cook, and we had hung out together a decent amount. He was definitely a really tough, strong guy, with a lot of ability. He had beaten a much bigger fighter named Benji Radach. Sherk, who stands about five eight, gave up a few inches in height to Radach, and some pounds as well, but was able to throw an elbow that cut Radach and stopped the fight early. He was one of Cook's prize guys who was making a move up the ladder.

Not long after the fight, Dana White called to congratulate me and to talk to me about the other guys on the card, especially Uno, who I would soon have to fight. During the conversation, he also mentioned Sherk.

"Cook's promoting Sherk," Dana said.

"Yeah, I know," I responded.

"Well, did you also know that he's thinking of moving Sherk down from welterweight?"

"I hadn't heard that."

"Yeah, well, Cook says he can bring down Sherk because Sherk can beat you."

"Are you sure?" I asked.

"Without a doubt" was his response.

It was weird hearing this from Dana because I was surprised Cook would tell him such a thing. At the time, despite the contract negotiations, Dana and I were still friends. I did not look at him like the hard-to-trust businessman he is now, but more like someone I could talk to. Lo and behold, though, I approached Cook about the statement, and he didn't deny it.

A few months before my fight with Uno, I pulled Cook aside.

"Did you tell Dana you want to bring Sherk down because you think he can beat me?"

He was a man about it, and without missing a beat said, "I did. It is what it is. I will still corner you for Uno if you want me to."

But it was too late. That was officially the end of my relationship with AKA. I had no hard feelings toward Cook, though. He was trying to make his way in California, and I was doing the same in Hawaii. It had become a relationship which no longer made sense. If I'd stayed in San Jose, I'm sure he would have remained by my side. At the end of the day, though, he proved himself to be an honest guy in a sport where honesty is sometimes hard to find. So many other people I know would have denied saying what Dana White reported to me, but Cook did not even hesitate. The guys at AKA were no longer my trainers and cornermen, but they would always be my friends. Friends I could trust.

THE UFC GAVE ME ABOUT FIVE months to prepare for the next Uno fight, and I would need them because with Cook gone, I had to find another cornerman. There were a couple of things I'd be looking for, namely someone who understood striking, and hopefully someone who could help with the ring fatigue I was experiencing. Considering how hard I was working out, there was no reason for it to be happening. It was certainly not a lack of training or the hours put into it. I worked out as hard, if not harder than most anyone I knew. I was incredibly hungry to win, never needed any motivation to train, and even though I was not on the best diet all the time, the amount of work I was putting in should have overshadowed that.

I have always been labeled as a guy who does not train hard, someone who sits back on the island taking it easy, thinking my natural abilities can carry me through. This belief could not be further from the truth. I worked hard from the first day I started doing this, probably too hard. The concept of overtraining and understanding your body is very real. This is why when I returned to Hawaii after the Pulver fight, I was searching for a way to perfect the science of physical training. For whatever reason, my body had not been responding correctly as far back as the Pulver fight. Whether it was my mental state in the ring, or that I overexerted myself, I couldn't say, but it certainly wasn't due to a lack of training.

Down at the rec center there were some older guys who practiced different martial arts a few days a week. I decided to check it out, and see if, in addition to my brother, Charuto, and the people at the BJJ school, someone over there could help me train. I met a guy named Rudy Valentino who I had heard about when I was growing up. He had trained in kickboxing, karate, muay thai, self-defense, judo, and had grappled as well. If there was a martial art to train in, there was a chance he had worked at it. I introduced myself, but he was aware of who I was already. We talked about what I was looking for, and then he asked me an important question:

"Why did you come to me?"

I replied, "I don't know. I'll tell you when I do."

Little did I know that Rudy was familiar with me not only because of the UFC, but because there were other fighters who came to him looking to kick my ass. At some point before I left Hilo for California, my friends and I had gotten into a street fight, and one of the guys we fought was badly injured. I can honestly say, it was not me who put the hurt on the kid, but for whatever reason, probably because I was well known now, I had become the target of some other people. They blamed me for the kid's injuries. It didn't make sense to me, but it did to them, which is all that mattered.

The uncle of the injured kid wanted to teach me a lesson, so he went out and found these three guys from around the world who could teach it. One of the guys was an Israeli Special Forces fighter trained in Krav Maga, which is the Israeli system of self-defense. The second was a martial artist from somewhere in Africa, and the last guy was this older Indonesian guy who carried a big stick with him, literally.

Rudy told them, "He trains over by Dairy Queen, behind Verna's, at another school." They went looking, but I wasn't there.

They stayed in Hawaii for nearly three months waiting for me to come back. I had no idea of the magnitude of the situation, although someone had mentioned to me some people were looking for me back home. This did not stop me from coming back; I wasn't going to turn down a fight, especially when falsely accused and in my hometown. Three guys were not coming to Hilo and kicking my ass. That was not going to happen.

It sounds humorous in retrospect, but it was upsetting at the time. Street fights were what made you tough; they were how you earned your stripes. You did not want to hear about someone getting seriously injured in one. I have never been in a street fight from which my opponent did not walk away. Most of the time, especially once I learned submissions, I would get a guy's back and just choke him out. It was more about sending a message that if you want trouble I can be your trouble, but you never want to be responsible for hurting someone permanently, not in a street fight, or even a professional fight. To this day, when I fight in a ring or a cage, I immediately go over and help an opponent up, if I have to.

As for Rudy, he accepted me as a student with open arms, and I unfortunately had to let Silva go. Boxing was too one-dimensional when it came to MMA. You needed a boxing coach, but you needed a martial arts coach even more. I had also learned in San Jose that if you overload yourself with guys, ideas, and methods, you become the a practitioner of many things but a master of none.

With a new team in place, I prepared for Uno, confident I would beat him again. Even though I had not been excited about the tournament, at least I was going to have another shot at the title. Training with Rudy was great from the get-go, with him helping to perfect my hands and my legs and rounding out my skills. The tools he brought to the table were similar to those of Javier Mendez, and that was a good thing because Mendez was a great coach. I was lucky to find him. Rudy didn't allow me to train as poorly as I had for Serra. There was no more one-round-the-first-week, three-rounds-the-last-week nonsense. It was a five-round fight, so we trained for five rounds, maybe more, every week.

Preparing for Uno was strange, though, because after suffering a KO loss to me, he surely had a lot more motivation than I did; I just figured it wouldn't be a tough fight. It is quite possible that the quick fight we had the first time hurt me the second time. When the fight finally arrived, I was viewed as the champion and he as the challenger.

ONCE AGAIN, BACK ACROSS THE UNITED STATES for UFC 41: Onslaught, at Boardwalk Hall in Atlantic City. Onslaught! Would it be one? I have always wondered if Dana White has a book called *The English Dictionary of Tough Sounding Words,* and before every event, they just flip it open and point to one. "Looks like *onslaught*!"

I'd had success in New Jersey, so despite the long trip, at least the other two times had been good experiences. New Jersey was working for me, though this time I would be there with a completely new team, except for Jay Dee. Charuto and Rudy would be my corners in my first fight without anyone from AKA. I wondered what it would be like without Cook shouting instructions, but I had confidence we would get the job done.

The fight was scheduled for February 28, 2003, and we left Hawaii about a week before. We flew to Los Angeles and then straight into Philadelphia, where we were picked up by a limosine and taken to one of the Trump properties in Atlantic City. It was freezing when we landed, quite possibly the coldest day I had ever experienced. It was snowing and the ground was already covered. During the limo ride we all just stared out the window. Forget Hawaii, now New Jersey was the nicest place!

The Boardwalk Hall was a cold place, probably because of the temperature outside, and because it had these tremendously high ceilings, which made it hard to heat. It seemed big enough to hold two MGM Grand Garden Arenas. Even though this was a title fight, we were not the last fight. Rodriguez was defending his belt against up-and-comer Tim Sylvia, and even Frank Mir's bout against Tank Abbott came afterward. I never understood why they scheduled nontitle fights, regardless of weights, after a match for a belt, but such was the case.

When it was finally time to fight, I walked out to the Octagon after Uno. He was waiting for me inside the Octagon, looking confident and ready. I wanted it to be over quickly, like the last one.

Once again Big John McCarthy was the referee. He checked to see if we were good to go and began the fight. As soon as it started, Uno came out looking to touch gloves, which is a MMA way of shaking hands. It was a good move because it slowed down my race to get across the stage and enabled him to set himself. This would help him avoid taking a quick shot.

I wanted to think Uno had a different game plan for this fight, but I had no idea what the last one was, so it may have been the same. From the outset, it looked like he was going to be moving a lot, side to side, always changing his positions, so I could not get set. He was able to take me down pretty quickly, but I got right back to my feet and followed up with a right hand that knocked him down. I got ahold of him, and was draped on his back with my legs wrapped around him. He escaped, but on two consecutive occasions I picked him up and slammed him to the mat, hard; both times I was able to get control of his body, once on his back, the other from the side.

Even though I was in control and able to get him onto the ground more than once, I was not effective enough from those positions. He was even able to land some shots as I was trying to gain even greater control. The round ended, though, and while I was dominant, I should have applied more punishment than I had.

Round two was different. Again I came out looking to land punches, and threw a big overhand right up the middle with a few other punches. It sent him back to the cage. I kept the pressure on by pushing him against the cage, looking for the takedown. Uno was able to turn me around and get my back toward the cage, then pull me to the ground. It was a solid reversal.

Uno felt strong from the get-go and was using his power to maintain good positions, even when I had him in trouble. He was constantly circling to avoid letting me set up anything. His plan was to slow me down by kicking my front leg. Every time I got set, he was already moving to a new position. Throw a kick and then move, throw a kick, move. Somewhere around his tenth kick in the round, I lunged and threw a punch in his face that landed. We then locked up, but he was able to score another takedown. I got up in a hurry, but he kept the pressure on, throwing punches and taking me back down again. The second time he fell into my half guard, one leg between my legs and the other on the outside. His punches were not landing from this position, and I was able to escape back to my feet.

As the round came to a close, I threw a straight right and an up-percut, both connecting, but not nearly enough to steal the round. I landed some solid shots in the round, but compared to his pressure, it was sure to be 1–1 on the scorecards.

In the corner after round two, I could feel my body was tired. It should not have been, but it was. I felt a half step slow, and that is all it takes in a sport decided by a split second. Coming out to the third round, I wanted to try to control him, but he again started off moving side to side and had a lot of energy. He immediately charged me, wrapped his arms around my body, and pulled me back toward the ground. The punches I threw that landed did not cause enough damage. He maneuvered around them, and found himself in good positions most of the time. The body lock was the third time in the fight he had pulled me down with the same move. That had never happened to me before.

Again he was in my half guard, landing some decent shots as I tried to scramble back to my feet. Eventually I was able to, but it seemed the entire third round was going in circles. Later in the round I got back to my feet, was able to grab control of his body, and take him down. As we both went to the mat, he wrapped his legs around my head in a scissor position. That was not going to have much effect on me, but it was enough to slow me up for a moment. I escaped and was able to outwrestle him and get around to his back again, where I controlled his body. I had a dominant position, but I was unable to cause a lot of damage as he held on to my arms. He really was overpowering me from the start of the fight, which was something I rarely experienced in the cage.

It was a close round, but one I had probably lost. I was not damaged, but he scored a lot of points with his kicks. In my corner, I was not even hearing much of what they were telling me other than to throw my combinations. I was completely exhausted, as much as I had ever been in a fight. I didn't want to even get up off the chair, but I summoned as much energy as I could and prepared for the last two rounds, both of which I knew I had to win.

Uno immediately came out and stuck to his game plan, landing an inside leg kick that almost made me slip and fall. I was not on the most stable of footings at this point, and his kicks were effective. From that point on, I just dug deep and went on adrenaline. I could not lose this fight.

It was a battle in the center of the Octagon. Uno threw some more kicks, and then I threw a right hand to his face. I moved in for a sweep by grabbing his body and tripping him to the mat. I was now in his half guard but had little in the tank. He then reversed to his back, where I controlled him. I noticed his eye started bleeding when I had his back, probably from the right hand I landed. I continued to control him from the back, throwing my heels into his abdomen whenever I could, but then Uno was able to turn over into my guard.

He was now as tired as I was, and eventually I got free. I landed a jab, as he did another kick. I landed another right up the middle, grabbed his body, and slammed him down. In the process I landed a left hand. He was starting to bleed a lot more, maybe even from the nose.

At the end of the round I lunged at him, grabbed his body, and threw him down again to end the round. I had won that round decisively.

The fifth and final round was still anyone's fight. Whichever one of us took this round would win the lightweight belt. My corner was telling me to throw "right left, right left" as soon as Uno stopped in front of me. If I had fumes in the tank, that was a lot.

The horn sounded, and Referee McCarthy brought us back to the center. To no one's surprise, Uno came out and went for a kick, but I landed an immediate left and right on him a couple of times. He tried for the takedown, but his power had waned.

At this point Uno had stopped moving side to side as much, more or less staying in front of me. I landed a few shots to his face, and it was apparent he was bleeding from his nose now in addition to the area above his left eye. I went in for a takedown, but was too weakened to get it. From the looks of things, we were both tired, but my face was unscathed. I was a lot more exhausted than hurt.

With about two minutes to go, he pushed me against the cage, but I stepped out to the side and landed a shot square into the middle of his face. It hurt him. I then backed away and we both moved to the middle. He came at me, but I was able to take him down and get his back again. I figure-four-locked his body to control him, but Uno was able to turn over into my guard. I got right back to my feet, knowing ground control was enough to win a close round.

At one minute remaining, Uno landed a nice kick, and then tied me up going for the takedown, but neither of us was able to do much. When there were only thirty seconds left we stood toe-to-toe in the middle of the cage. I landed a right hand, and then another with two seconds left.

The last round was mine, it had to be.

With both of us completely exhausted, McCarthy brought us back to the center of the ring for the decision. The judges made the announcement. The first judge scored it 48–47, Penn. The second 48–47, Uno. The final judge, 48–48. A split decision. The look on Uno's face was one of relief and on mine one of disgust. Yes, it was a close fight, one where we both had our moments, but I did not think it was the correct call, and neither did Lorenzo Fertitta.

Back in the locker room, I was sick to my stomach physically and disgusted mentally, when Fertitta came in and said, "You won that fight, no question. You're the champion." He then told me he was going to send me the belt because I deserved it, but he never did, and I did not care. A win is not a win if it doesn't happen legitimately. Fertitta was not suggesting he was going to award me the belt, just that I had deserved it. It was just a kind gesture.

After the fight, the UFC was unsure of what to do with the lightweight division, so they did something that would have a lasting effect on me: they did away with it altogether. From now on there would be no lightweight fights, let alone a champion. Only welter, middle, light heavy, and heavy. All at once my options were limited. What I had hoped would be a night to clarify things had only made them foggier.

11

JUST
SCRAP

WHEN I FIRST ENTERED THE UFC, I told myself I just wanted to be there for one fight. Then I followed that up with just wanting to win the belt. It seemed now I was going to have to find a new goal since the first one had not been enough, the second was not going to happen, and I still had the drive to fight. The UFC still wanted me to fight for them, and I had no plans to leave, so it was just a question of who my opponent could be.

After the Uno match, the first conversation I had with Dana White was about fighting a welterweight named Robbie Lawler, a fighter he loved. White saw Lawler as one of his future champions, a guy he had watched fight at a Shogun event in Hawaii.

"Would you fight him?" he asked me.

"Yeah, let's do it. I'm ready," I told him. I was always ready to fight whoever they put in front of me; even though Lawler was bigger, he was no different. I figured there were a lot of ways I could beat him at the time, and I kept a jujitsu mind-set, that size did not matter.

For whatever reason, White must have had second thoughts after our conversation because he changed his mind pretty quickly. Perhaps he realized there was no reason to burn two of his younger, up-and-coming fighters in a match against each other, especially since Lawler had just come off a loss. Either way, White said he would think about it awhile longer and come up with a good match for me.

In the meantime, I was focused on doing two things. The first was letting my body rest. I'd had four fights in a little more than a year's time, and I felt like I was always training for one. It's one thing to be doing your daily workouts and finding new ways to train, but preparing to fight someone is different. The intensity that builds inside of me as I focus on another fighter takes a lot out of me mentally. Ordinarily I could go for a five-mile jog and think about nothing of significance, but if I have a fight coming up, it would be the only thing on my mind. Same workout, different mind-set. I wanted to have a few months to not really think about ripping someone's head off.

During this period, I started asking myself questions about whether I really wanted to continue fighting at all. I even considered going back to school, but knew I would sit there daydreaming about fighting the whole time, just like I had at West Valley. I contemplated opening my own jujitsu school, but then I knew if I was in there all the time training, I'd also want to be fighting. The only thing that made sense was to use the rest I was enjoying and channel my energy toward fighting when I had to.

Throughout this downtime, I was still looking for more effective ways to train and trying to get my diet right. Against Uno I had been physically outmatched, which should never have happened. I wanted to figure out what I could do differently. This was the second thing I focused on. Since returning to Hawaii, I'd tried so many different things, none of which really seemed to work for me inside the cage. It was time to limit outside influences because no one in Hilo, or really in Hawaii, understood MMA like I did. No one had trained like me, met the people I met, or even been in fights on the level I had. In a sense, I focused more on becoming my own coach.

While the UFC was looking for someone for me to fight, one thought I had was to find Pulver and take him on somewhere else. He had been in and out of a few organizations since we fought, and it was not uncommon for a fighter, even one in the UFC, to go fight somewhere else in between UFC fights. Back then contracts were not as limiting as the ones today, and fighters floated between organizations, chasing the biggest payday and/or the best opportunity. The only problem with this fight, though, was that Pulver was no longer considered the best fighter in the world at our weight class, and when it seemed like it could happen, he always wanted too much money. After beating me, he had a few lackluster fights, unable to finish anyone, and in his last fight was knocked out by Duane Ludwig in the first round. This was not making me look any better, nor was it increasing Pulver's ability to demand more money, but I still wanted another crack at him. I was considered by many others to be the best lightweight in the world, but I didn't have a belt to show for it.

However much I wanted a fight with Pulver, it didn't make sense to anyone else. The fight that did make sense was against Takanori Gomi, who, depending on who you talked to, was either the best in the world or second to me. Since I entered the UFC and won my first two fights, Jay Dee and I had been talking to White all the time about bringing the best lightweight fighters into the company. When I arrived, Din Thomas had not fought in the UFC, neither had Ludwig, or countless other guys who were in other organizations like Shooto and Vale Tudo Japan. The UFC's new ownership still did not have great contacts in the fight world, especially at my weight class. We told them to bring in Gomi for a fight against me, and that this would help bring more fighters over if the two best were here. But we were unable to convince them, and whether it was Gomi or someone else, we were always told the guys we wanted to fight were already under contract elsewhere.

After realizing the UFC was not going to be active in finding me opponents, we figured we should try to bring Gomi to Hawaii ourselves. Jay Dee had started his own fight organization called Rumble on the Rock (ROTR), which had already put on two shows and was nearing its third in August. Since the UFC didn't seem to be in any rush to find me an opponent, a fight with ROTR just made sense. We contacted White and told him of our intentions, and he supported us. My contract with the UFC didn't seem to be an issue with him as long as the contract would be fulfilled, and of course, it would be. We then contacted Gomi's people and they were happy to do it. He still had an upcoming fight in August with Joachim Hansen, but would take the fight with us on October 10, 2003, in Honolulu.

SOMETIME IN MAY, I TRAVELED BACK to Las Vegas to spend some time hanging out with Troy Mandaloniz while working out with the guys at Nova União at Lewis's school, since it had been a while for me. Competitive jujitsu had fallen out of my life so quickly, and the world of MMA had taken over.

After a couple of weeks there camped up at Mandaloniz's place, I went up to San Luis Obispo, California, to help Chuck Liddell prepare for his June 6 fight with Randy Couture at the Thomas and Mack Center. I spent a couple of weeks at Liddell's house and then drove with him to the fight in Las Vegas. Unfortunately for Liddell he lost his fight, but in the end would do all right for himself. It was a funny thing to see Couture fighting on the main card, while Pedro Rizzo, a guy who made as much in one of his fights as I had made in all my fights combined, was in the first fight of the undercard. Money well spent.

During my time in Las Vegas, I heard about this seminar going on in Portland, Oregon, with John Hackleman, Couture, and other fighters. Hackleman had been training Liddell at the time, but was also preparing Matt Lindland for his next fight. I wanted to be a part of the seminar, so I told some of the guys I could teach the jujitsu part of it in addition to the striking, wrestling, and whatever else they were doing. They were all fine with it, so I went up there and spent a couple of weeks living at Couture's with his wife, Trisha, and their newborn son, Caden.

I used to spend the entire day at these seminars just taking in everything that was being taught. I would teach the things I knew and then listen to what every other fighter and trainer had to say. Then I'd spend hours practicing the moves over and over. Just like years earlier at Ralph's school, I was becoming addicted to martial arts. I was taking all that I had learned, and was going to be able to apply it in my fight with Gomi, and anyone else going forward.

The same was true for the training sessions with the Team Quest guys, who were Couture and Lindland's team. Guys like Nate Marquardt were there training with up-and-comers Chris Leben and Ed Herman, and they would really go at it full speed, which I liked. There were days when guys would go toe-to-toe, and bodies would hit the floor as if it was a real fight.

This is how you prepare for a fight.

For me, the best memories were working out with Couture, who was a lot bigger than me. For a smaller guy, I was able to give him some fits when we grappled. At this point in my training, I had become quite skilled at putting people in arm bars and triangles, and it was no different with Couture. One of the times we were grappling, I nearly had him in an arm bar, and he barely escaped. He realized that he couldn't top my BJJ skills so he tickled me in defense. It was a joke, and he knew I was not going to let go, so he figured let's see if this will work.

Couture was such a competitor, even in practice, and it was fun for me to be able to frustrate him. During that same session, he was trying to hold me down on the mat, but I kept escaping. You could see him start to take things a bit more seriously after it became difficult to control me. Couture is such a fierce competitor that even during training he can take things very seriously. You have to respect a man who takes training to heart the way he does and looks at everything as a challenge to overcome. There's a reason for his success, and a lot of it has to do with his intensity. But I do admit seeing him get all worked up like that made me feel good because I must have been doing the right things. It is fair to say each of us learned a lot from the other.

I WOULD ALSO GO TOE-TO-TOE with Lindland—full-contact sparring, which was good preparation for Gomi. We beat the crap out of each other, which is a strange way to form a friendship, but that's how it was done with fighters. You could earn the respect of guys you trained with by dropping a guy to the floor, or choking him out. It was all about being able to help and teach each other, and no one was more into forming friends that way than I was.

After a summer of trying to perfect my training and, of course, having a good time, I began training full speed for Gomi. Rudy and I had really started clicking, and going into the fight, I felt unstoppable. I was getting the same kind of support I had received back in AKA from my teammates, but in truth, it really didn't matter. I felt so good I'd stopped caring what other people thought of me. All I wanted was to get back in the cage. It would be nearly eight months by the time I fought Gomi—a lot longer than I had wanted.

I had believed the fight between me and Gomi would truly decide who the best lightweight fighter in the world was, and most people who I knew did as well. Even without a belt on the line, that was motivation enough. Plus, this was a huge event for Jay Dee, and for ROTR in general. It was exciting to help my brother grow this thing, and most importantly, to be able to fight in front of the Hawaiian people in Honolulu. Those earlier ROTR events were small compared to this one, so it was really an opportunity. In many ways it was bigger than fighting for a belt because it was like fighting for my family and on behalf of those in Hawaii who had supported me. It was a chance to prove Hawaii was the toughest place in the world. A credit to Gomi, though; this was a big fight for him too and he took it in my backyard.

When I first started training for fights, I always found out as much about my opponent as possible, get my hands on tapes, study his moves, and try to have my partners emulate those moves as much as possible. For Gomi, though, there was a lot less of that. It all stemmed from how confident I was feeling. The rebirth seemed to come out of nowhere, and it gave me a tremendous amount of drive and desire.

Around this time, a phrase that referred to this mind-set, almost a way of being when it came to fighting, became popular: "just scrap." It was no longer about doing the jujitsu, preparing for an opponent's hands (which Gomi certainly had), or anything else. "Just scrap" was how I would approach this fight. A time of near-perfect comfort, being in the place where I had first fought, and now culminating in this chance to fight for everyone including myself. Taking all that I had learned over the years, and no longer worrying about what my opponant could do to me, and just going for broke. The same way I never worried about the biggest guy at the party, the toughest guy at the beach, or in the streets, it was just going to be a full-on brawl. It was not going to be about one thing I had learned, or fifty things, it was just a scrap. Once this attitude sank in, mentally, I could not be beaten.

Meanwhile, Gomi could be beaten, and right before this fight he had lost to Joachim Hansen, his first loss. It was a fight that went the distance, and he lost on majority decision, but it was close. He was not going to come into this fight anything less than fully prepared because in no way was he prepared to accept back-to-back losses after starting 14–0.

October 10, 2003, was the day of the fight, and it came quickly. The media started picking up on the event because it was going to take place in downtown Honolulu, unlike the previous ROTR events. The Honolulu media were still partial to their stars, and to events that took place in the city, or elsewhere on Oahu. Thus the fight was hard to ignore, not only because it was local but because we had sold so many tickets at the Neal S. Blaisdell Center arena. This was the first time all of the people in my family who were living in Hawaii would be able to see me fight live. Not just my immediate family, but my aunts, uncles, cousins, and people who were like family too. Dana White even showed up, as he was looking forward to seeing a fight of this magnitude. Yet even with all of this going on, I was in a very good place. I remember sleeping comfortably for hours that day and woke up almost forgetting that I had to fight in a couple of hours. I was that relaxed and confident.

When the time came for me to fight, I walked out of the locker room with a feeling of invincibility. There was a long path to the cage just like there had been in the UFC fights. I had the guys in my camp behind me, minus Charuto, who had fought earlier in the night. When I got to the end of the path, I stopped for a second and looked around at the people in the crowd, almost checking to see if they were as ready as I was. As I entered the cage, I saw another familiar face: Alex Oxendine had been hired to be the announcer, and having one more of my people with me, calling out my name, introducing, made this feel even more like a family thing. He announced this fight as being "for the MMA lightweight championship of the world," even without a belt, since we were the two best. Once he was done, we were both ready to claim that title.

I immediately came across the cage as quickly as possible, went for a double-leg takedown, and ended up driving Gomi into the cage. We both fell to the mat, and I was on top of him right away, in his half guard. He held on to my arms, trying to minimize my ability to hit him with fists or elbows. I dropped my chest down onto his and started lunging my right shoulder into his face. This forced him to loosen up on my arms. From there I got my leg out of half guard and mounted him completely. It was a bad spot for Gomi to be in so quickly. I planned to end this thing fast as I had with my earlier fights. He tried turning away from the mount to avoid punishment, which put me right on his back, a very familiar and comfortable spot for me to work.

Gomi tried to stand up with me draped on top of him, but I had my legs around him, and my feet hooked in between his legs. The whole time I was throwing punches into the side of his head and under his arms into his chin, as he was down on all fours. There were few places for him to go. I started throwing more and more shots and tried to use my legs to spread out his legs so he would be flat on the canvas. Again he tried to stand with me on his back, but we went right back on the ground. He eventually turned to the side and I rolled off the side of his body onto the mat, with him in my full guard. He threw some punches, but nothing really connected.

On my back, I kept my legs around his body, and my feet as high up toward his neck as possible, which limited his mobility and set him up for different submissions. He did a good job of keeping my feet down toward his lower back, remaining in a decent position to land strikes. However, I was able to pull out of my guard and get to my feet. I wasted no time and landed a left hook near his head, and went straight into another takedown, driving him into the cage and the mat. There was about a minute to go in the round.

I was in the full mount again, and then right back on his back, throwing punches and elbows to the side of his head. He was starting to bleed from his nose and his mouth. This is what I had wanted to do to someone for months, and whether it was Gomi or anyone else, this was how it would be. I started looking for the rear naked choke by sliding my forearm under his neck, but he prevented this from happening by grabbing my arms and head. Whenever he gave me a chance, I threw more shots into his head and face. Eventually the time expired, and he escaped.

Gomi was in surprisingly good shape and quite calm after the round. Possibly no more winded than I was, but I had dominated him the entire round, never taking any real punishment. My coaches were more than satisfied with my performance.

In the second round, the referee had to put his hand on my chest to stop me from coming across the cage before it began. He sent me back to my corner, then called us out. We both came out firing. Gomi threw a right hand, and I landed a knee into his chest, similar to the one that had dropped Thomas. I countered his punches with a right hand of my own, which was followed by a left of his that connected.

Moments like these were why I became a fighter; these toe-to-toe exchanges were why I wanted to fight Gomi, and why I still fight today.

Gomi was determined to keep it standing, and he started out using his jab immediately, landing it more frequently. I started to time it, countered with a left hook that put him on the mat. I rushed him to take advantage, but he was able to push me off and take control. He pushed me onto my back and fell into my guard again. Now he was throwing punches and elbows, more and more of them, but most either missed or were not landing solidly against my head.

Then, for whatever reason, most likely because of the blood, Gomi asked the referee to have his mouth guard cleaned. Once he did this, the referee stood us up. I assume Gomi had no interest in fighting from the ground position, even though in the past he was very effective doing so. He had given up a good situation, maybe thinking he could beat me on his feet. After we started up again, he came out and threw a big right hand that missed, followed by a left hook that landed. Then we both tried to clinch each other by securing our hands on the back of the other's neck. I then took my right hand off and started throwing punch after punch into the side of his face. We split apart, and now I was getting the better of the exchanges. The round was nearly dead even.

Gomi tried to jump toward me and get his hands around my head for a standing guillotine choke, but that was not going to happen. We traded more jabs, grabbed onto each other, and back down to the mat we went. Both of us were starting to slow down as we went to the ground. This round had been a full-on war.

We got back to our feet and were now both throwing our hands wildly at each other, both of us losing our footing slightly as a result of the fatigue. Nearing the last thirty seconds of the round, I knew it was anyone's to win still, so I shot on him somewhat lamely, but was still able to push him up against the cage. I was hunched over trying to get my arms around his legs as he tried to keep his hands under my arms to prevent a takedown. With about five seconds left on the clock, I was able to pull him down to the mat, possibly giving myself the edge in what had been a great round.

WE BOTH PULLED OURSELVES OFF the mat slowly. I got myself across the cage and Valentino led me to my seat. Gomi could hardly stand up and was bleeding more heavily out of his mouth and nose. I was in bad shape, but he was in worse.

In the corner, I was advised to keep doing what I was doing. Valentino told me I was winning the fight and just to keep the pressure on, so that's what I did. The third and final round was here, and I knew he had to finish me off to win. I was not going to let that happen.

From the sound of the opening bell, I took the center of the cage and started throwing jabs. I missed with a big right hand, and then he started throwing punches back. We were both missing more than hitting, neither of us keeping our hands up. I slipped a punch and shot in for the takedown, getting him onto his back. He tried again to get me in a guillotine choke from his back, but that was not going to stop me at this point. I escaped, got control of him, and again transitioned onto his back, where he attempted once more to stand up with me on his back. I put my legs around him in a figure four in an attempt to slow his breathing. Meanwhile he tried to stop me from punching him—to no real effect. I got him back to the ground and this time he had taken too much of a beating to stay up with me all over him.

I was beating on him from every angle. He had no choice but to go down. With my back to the mat and me pulling him down from behind, I threw a few more shots at his head. With my legs wrapped around his body, I slipped my left forearm underneath his neck and secured the choke with my right arm. He tapped almost immediately. Oxendine came in from behind to grab me, and I almost threw a punch at him I was so confused from the fight.

That was the moment when I realized that I was now, for the first time, considered the best lightweight fighter in the world.

After the fight, Phil Baroni approached me with the microphone, as he was helping us do some of the commentary. Baroni and I were very close at the time, and he came to Hawaii to help us out. After he congratulated me, I took the microphone from his hands, and doing something I rarely did, I spoke to the audience. I was not someone who ever had a lot to say, but it was important to me to say something to the Hawaiian people. Echoing the thoughts of guys like Steve DaSilva, I told them what I believed.

"Thank you, Phil. Proof of what I've been saying all along. Hawaii has the best fighters in the world! We grow up fighting. It's all we do! I want to thank everyone for coming out and supporting. That's it. I don't talk much, but thanks for coming out."

It was a big moment for me, not just winning the fight, but getting the opportunity to speak to those who'd supported me in so many ways. It was a real first for me—I had the stage to myself to say what I wanted, and people were really listening. For someone who is as emotional as me, it meant a lot. This entire night was proof of why I loved fighting, and it gave me even more reasons to push forward.

● ● ●

WHITE CONGRATULATED ME on a great fight. He had always had confidence that I would be the best in the world; it was just unfortunate it didn't happen in the UFC. He had promised to be in touch when he got back to Las Vegas, as I still had one more fight on my contract. We both had no idea who I'd be fighting, and even less of an idea of what was to come. The only person I could think of who I wanted to fight was Sean Sherk, the welter-weight Bob Cook and AKA thought could take me on. Sherk had lost to the UFC welterweight champion Matt Hughes earlier in the year, but was still 18–1 and one of the better fighters in the organization.

I called White and said, "I want to fight Sherk at one seventy."

"Yeah? Really?!" He sounded surprised and excited. I reminded him of the history with Sherk, and let him know that I wanted the opportunity to prove AKA wrong about him. White told me he loved the idea, but he was having problems with Sherk's manage-ment, which at the time was probably an everyday occurence for him. He countered with, "If you want to fight at welterweight, how about fighting Matt Hughes? We don't have anyone for him right now, so maybe you can be that guy?"

I told him, "Perfect! That's the only reason I wanted to fight Sherk in the first place—so I could get to Hughes."

"You got it," said White.

Now all he had to do was clear it with Hughes, which was easy. Hughes was not going to back down from anyone, especially me. After all, his smaller teammate Pulver had taken me the distance and won.

It was almost like a dream come true. Things with the UFC had looked so bleak just a matter of months ago, but this opportu-nity put me square in the middle of it all once again. I didn't think Hughes had a chance against me at the time, and that for him I was a bad matchup. Granted, Hughes was the bigger fighter, who had defended his title five times after winning it in dramatic fashion, but the matchup did not work in his favor. He was an accomplished wrestler and very strong for his size, but on the ground I figured I could submit him, and on the feet I was not worried about his striking.

The fight was scheduled as part of UFC 46: Supernatural, on January 31, 2004, at the Mandalay Bay Events Center. The card was loaded, with Couture taking on Vitor Belfort, and others like Charuto, Georges St-Pierre, Serra, and Frank Mir fighting too. The sport was really starting to pick up steam, and the UFC were expecting this card to be huge. Pulling off a victory here would place me at the center of the MMA world, no question.

I did not need motivation to start training for this fight, and I went about it exactly the same way I had for Gomi. I traveled up to Oregon to stay with Couture for a while, and this time it was even more necessary, considering Hughes's wrestling background. There were no better training partners if you had to face a wrestler than the guys at Team Quest. After working with them for a couple weeks, I was even more confident I would win. The guys there, with their all-American collegiate wrestling backgrounds, Matt Lindland with his Olympic silver medal in Greco-Roman, and all the others who were just starting to get involved, it was the best place I could be.

From there I flew to Hilo and continued with what I had been doing before the Gomi fight. Again, no real game plan was being formed because in my mind I could not lose. No matter what I was working on, it was clicking for me. Having been defending takedowns continually since the Serra fight, and now working with wrestlers, I was not even concerned with Hughes's big weapon up until that point, the power slam. That was the one move that was consistently hurting other fighters, and the one that essentially helped him capture the belt when he knocked out Carlos Newton with it. Even that was not really a concern because I could not see him getting me in that position. The whole time during training, I could not figure what he could possibly do to me to win.

I traveled to Las Vegas a week before the fight, and by this time it had become a very comfortable place for me. Although Hughes was a better-known and celebrated champion who had won his title in Las Vegas, there had been many Hawaiians living in the city for quite some time. For the first time in my career outside of Hawaii, people were really starting to take notice of me, and fighters in general. Fans were showing up at the casino days before for autographs, the weigh-ins had people waiting to get in, the entire vibe was different. It was Superbowl weekend in Las Vegas, which always brought a lot of people to the city, but I just had a sense this thing was taking off. The card was packed with stars, more than a lot of other cards that came afterward because back then there were only about five events a year. We were the secondary fight behind the light heavyweight bout between Couture and Belfort, but that was always the case with the lower weights.

I weighed in at 170 pounds on the dot, which was mandatory for a title fight. In nontitle matches you can often "float a pound" and weigh 171, but not in this fight. Hughes also checked in at 170, but as a wrestler, he had been cutting weight for years in order to get down to the required number. In all likelihood Hughes would show up on the night of the fight close to ten pounds heavier, if not more. For me, being 170 pounds probably meant I was overweight, which was not a problem for me.

In the locker room I was comfortable, but I had nervous anticipation of the fight. Not the kind of nerves where you are worried about something bad, but about waiting to achieve something great. I just kept thinking, *Let's go. Let's go. Let's do this,* as I paced around the locker room.

I was already waiting inside the cage when Hughes entered. It seemed the audience was split right down the middle. I was the underdog in the sports book, but hearing the voices of the fans there you wouldn't have known it. Over ten thousand people were there, and they seemed evenly divided on who they wanted to win. Ring announcer Bruce Buffer began saying our names to the crowd, and as he called out my opponent's name, Hughes was pacing back and forth across his side of the cage, as if the Octagon belonged to him. I just stood there, focused on him, ready to go. Referee Mario Yamasaki brought us together to the middle of the cage, explained the rules, sent us back to our corners, and we were ready to go.

I came right across the cage to take control, avoiding a Hughes jab and countering with a left hook. He closed in on me, and I threw another left and a short knee that landed. We locked up for a second in the middle of the cage, and right then I realized that his strength wouldn't be as big a factor as I'd trained for. Often, when two guys collide, you can get a feel for where the fight is going. From that moment I knew his power would not be a problem.

We danced around the cage, latched onto each other, both throwing some good knees to the midsection until we broke apart. He tried to bait me with head fakes, hoping I would throw a punch he could counter, but I didn't fall for it. He then threw his own right hand, but I countered with a straight right of my own and a left hook that knocked him toward the cage. He came in again trying to land a punch, but slightly lost his balance when he went to grab me, either slipping or feeling the effects from the left hook. He went down to the mat and immediately spun around with his feet toward me, getting himself into good position from his back.

As a wrestler, Hughes should have been less comfortable on his back, but in actuality he was well rounded enough that this position wasn't a problem for him. The Miletich guys were all well rounded and could fight anywhere. I fell into his full guard while we both jostled for control. He tried to grab my right arm in an attempt at control, or maybe moving toward a submission, but the moment he went for it, I rolled around and got a hold of his back. You can teach a wrestler submissions, but that was a natural transition for a jujitsu fighter. I remained there for only a second or two, and immediately gave up the position so I could get back on top of him. I did not want to roll around with him; I wanted to throw punches and try to finish the fight. Once on top again, I began throwing big right hands at his face as he tried to push me away. We were only one minute into the round, but already I was doing whatever I wanted.

While I was in his guard, he caught me with a nice inside elbow across the side of my face, but it was not enough to shake me. I stayed in control of his body by controlling his legs and feet with my hands. I could hear some fans start to chant my name, "BJ! BJ! BJ!" I pulled myself out of his guard, forcing my way somewhere in between side control and his half guard. We stayed in this position for a little while as things started to slow down. The whole time I was just trying to position myself to land punches. Eventually I pulled his legs over from his side and was practically sitting on his chest, tugging at them, trying to maneuver myself into a better position, but he used his strength to remain in a decent position.

Finally, with only about a minute left in the first round, I got back to my feet, controlling his legs with him lying on his back. I lunged in and landed a short left jab into his face, waiting for a chance to pounce. Seconds later, with his left foot in my hands, I pushed his legs to the right and came down with a huge right hand that landed flush across the left side of his face (breaking my hand in the process). It was timed perfectly, and I knew it had rocked him. I could feel his body go limp for a second, and now he was fighting on instinct. When you take a big blow, you are often just moving without even knowing what you are doing, just following the training. The punch placed me on the right side of his body, next to him on the mat, and then I moved over top of him into full mount. It all happened in about five seconds. He was in a really bad stop.

Without hesitation and with me on top of him, he rolled over and gave up his back, almost in defense to avoid taking more shots to the face. I wrapped my legs around his body, and he was now on all fours. I was on top of him almost like I was riding a mule, throwing punches to the side of his face. I brought my left arm across his body and pulled my elbow back across the side of his head, which also hurt him. Eventually he collapsed to the mat, both of us going down together. In a move of desperation, he tried to grab my foot, but it was not to be. I pulled him farther down into my grasp with my back on the mat, rolling him to the side a bit. Like I'd done with Gomi, I slipped my left arm under his neck and secured the choke hold with my right arm. With twenty-three seconds left to go in the round, he tapped my arm. As ringside announcer Mike Goldberg liked to say, it was "all over."

In a state of disbelief, I stood up, not even knowing what to do. I turned and saw Hughes on his knees, upset that he had just lost. I went over and kissed him right on his face, and his blood ended up on mine. I walked away, licking off the blood, which tastes like metal, or iron. My team rushed me and tackled me toward the cage. Cabbage picked me up and put me on his shoulders, parading me around the ring. I started smacking and punching myself in the face. I was beside myself. I had just moved up in weight and won the Welterweight Championship of the World. I then went over to Hughes to thank him and wish him well.

"I never underestimated you!" he said to me. It had been said before, even by announcer Joe Rogan during the fight, that Hughes sometimes did not take fights seriously or train very hard. I guess he was responding to those rumors.

In Hughes's corner was Lorenzo Fertitta, consoling him in his defeat, and it also seemed to me Dana White was not very happy that I had just knocked off Hughes. Part of me believed they liked having their all-American wrestler as a poster boy for the sport. You could see it in their eyes: the plan had not been for me to win, friends or not. Whatever the case, it was time to make a new poster.

Finally, the moment had come, made official when ring announcer Bruce Buffer was proclaiming me as the winner:

"And new UFC welterweight champion of the world . . . B . . . J . . . Penn!" Mario Yamasaki had my hand raised as White strapped the belt across my waist. In less than a split second I went from an ear-to-ear grin to torrential tears of joy. I could not comprehend what was going on. My emotions were all over the place. It was the most joy I'd ever felt, greater than winning the Mundials, or anything else before it. My entire family had witnessed it live. All the faith they had in me, the tools they provided, the countless hours of training I put in, the moving, traveling, the flying, the sleepless nights and endless days wondering what my life would be like, and any other question I ever had, all of it was answered inside that cage.

I told myself I would take the best care possible of the belt, like I never had anything else in my life. I would never let it out of my sight.

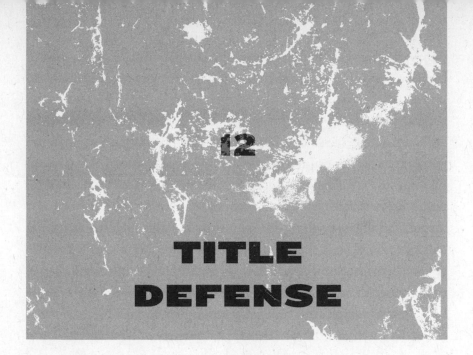

12

TITLE DEFENSE

HE NIGHT OF THE HUGHES FIGHT I had one of the best times of my life, as I remember it. Just as it was for a lot of others who have won major championships, it was time to celebrate, and I did, with many of my closest friends. I no longer had anything to worry about or think about accomplishing: it was a total relief. But all parties end sooner than you want them to, and this one came to a close faster than I had hoped.

I have had a lot of differences with the UFC over the years, but the first started the day they did away with the lightweight division. During the time when I was resting and they were searching for an opponent for me, I began talking about my options if nothing came to pass with them. I had never really thought about leaving the company until their inability to find me an opponent made the concept very real. And so I opened myself to the idea of fighting somewhere else, like Japan. Coincidentally, the weekend of the Hughes fight a man named Mak Takano approached Jay Dee about this very possibility.

Not wanting to miss an opportunity, Takano approached Jay Dee in the concourse of the Mandalay Bay immediately after the event. He was a recruiter for K-1, a well-known martial arts organization that had helped popularize kickboxing, kung fu, karate, and other, similar arts. They were trying to grow their own MMA division called K-1 Romanex, and Takano was there to make me an offer. Right from the get-go our ears perked up because Takano was talking about money in a way the UFC had never talked. On top of that, Takano seemed to have a true passion for the martial arts. At the very least, we had someone who could help us out if the UFC was unable to find opponents for me, which they had been somewhat reluctant to do before Hughes. Knowing as I did that a lot of great lightweights were in Japan made K-1 Romanex a real option.

Takano had come in at just the right time, somehow aware that I had a three-fight deal with the UFC and that the bout with Hughes was the last. He made it his business to be in town just so he could introduce himself and make his offer of $187,500. It was a bold effort by someone who clearly admired what I brought to the table. The only problem, we thought, was the UFC had a contractual right to counter any offer he made. At the very least, if the offer was high enough, I was going to get paid considerably more than I was making.

The day after the fight, I was in McCarran Airport in Las Vegas, heading back to Hawaii, completely spent. If you have ever been in the Vegas airport on a Sunday, you know the feeling, but now add a fight on top of that. For the first time I was being recognized in public, though I was probably not in the best shape to be shaking hands or signing autographs. On the way to the gate, I ran into the UFC announcer Joe Rogan, who I knew by name but wasn't really acquainted with. He congratulated me, and the next thing I knew, we were talking about fighting.

Eventually Rogan asked who I wanted to fight next, and if the UFC had someone in mind. Knowing that K-1 had made this big offer, I just told him, "I think I might go fight in K-1." Jay Dee and I didn't think this was going to be a problem since White had been willing to let me fight in ROTR against Gomi and had allowed Liddell to fight twice in Pride, another competing organization from Japan. After all, Liddell was very close to White and one of the UFC's rising stars, so there was no reason for me to think I couldn't try my hand over there as well, have someone else pay me some money, and help popularize the sport.

The conversation seemed really innocent, and certainly I had nothing to hide, but by the time I landed in Hawaii, my phone was filled with messages from Jay Dee and Dana White. Apparently Rogan called White to tell him of my intentions, and White was not happy about it. He left some of his typical profanity-laced messages on my phone, and then called again to do the same. When I took the call, I could tell that he wasn't freaking out, but was wondering how the new UFC champion could even be considering such an offer. I had no idea it was such a big deal, or anything that would bother him.

It seemed that the UFC had not only just lost a champion in Hughes but had suffered a second setback when Couture, who was under contract to them, lost his belt to Belfort in a fight that ended because of an accident. Belfort threw a punch which for the most part missed, but the edge of his glove sliced Couture's eyelid, almost like a paper cutter. From White's perspective, he had to do everything in his power to keep the boat sailing straight. I told him not to worry, that we merely spoke with Takano, and I was not about to do anything to hurt the UFC. At the same time, though, I didn't see what the big deal was: my traveling to other organizations with the UFC belt on my waist was a chance to make the UFC look good. I guess they were taking the opposite view—that if I lost a fight in Japan, the UFC would look bad. In any case, I was more than happy to put K-1 on hold and negotiate a new contract with the UFC.

This was easier said than done. As soon as the UFC realized I was considering other options, they came to me with a new contract, and quite frankly, it was laughable. I had made "25 and 25" against Hughes, which in and of itself was not a lot of money. Not to say that $50,000 is a bad thing, but when you're fighting for a championship in an event of this size, you would expect a little more, to say nothing of the risk. The thing is, I didn't even question it. Hughes was making close to double what I did, and the total event payout was $540,000, which meant on average fighters made $33,750, and I know most of the lower-level guys were not getting paid anywhere near this. Had Hughes won, he would have received "50 and 50," which means the average payout would have been $36,875, and I'd have made $25,000, a lot less than the average.

In other words, there were quite a few guys making a decent amount of money, and while I was not going broke, I thought I should be making Hughes-like money. I had a signed contract and never said one word about renegotiating. I fought for what I signed for. Now I was the champion, and we came to the table with a very realistic offer. We wanted somewhere in the vicinity of $50,000; $45,000, maybe even $40,000, would have sufficed. Dana White started at $28,000, and then made the bold move to go all the way up to $30,000. Hughes would still be getting more money than me, and he couldn't beat me. Was I supposed to be satisfied with this?

The way they saw it, the company always increased the payout by increments, not by big jumps. From twenty-five to thirty was normal, and in their eyes, the real opportunity for me was how they'd still be promoting me. This in turn would bring me more money through advertising on my shorts, T-shirts, or anything else I wanted. In other words, *they* wanted to pay me less money so I could go out and sell myself to *others* for more.

Knowing I had this possibility with K-1 did not motivate them to increase their offer. We were not even discussing future opponents, or anything of that nature, just money. It was frustrating because I was not the type of guy who wanted to deal with these things. K-1 was offering me $187,500 per fight—*five times* what the UFC was offering—and I was still willing to stay with them for one-third of that amount. This was when the relationship took a turn for the worse, and my view of White changed drastically. From that point on, I knew when it came to money, we couldn't trust him to treat us right. Did I like him at the dinner table? Sure. But at the negotiating table? Not at all. The pressure to perform and safeguard other people's money had changed him, even though he was constantly bragging to anyone willing to listen about how "big this thing was going to be." Things between us would never be the same.

A FUNNY THING HAPPENED DURING THESE negotiations, which in many ways would change the UFC forever. The UFC lawyers had apparently not understood the contract they themselves had written, and this was going to be a problem. We had let a local Hilo attorney look over the contract and during the negotiations we were still in contact with him. He picked up on something none of us—Jay Dee, the UFC, nor I—had realized and it changed the nature of the negotiations. The UFC had written their contract in a way that bound me to them for one year, or three fights, whichever came first, beginning on the day of my first fight. That date was September 27, 2002, the night I fought Serra, and therefore the year had expired on that same day in 2003. I had only fought Serra and Uno under their contract in that time period. Hughes was my third fight under the contract, but in some ways Hughes had nothing to do with the deal since I fought him on January 31, 2004—four months *after* the contract expired.

Had we noticed beforehand the contract had expired, maybe

we'd have tried to negotiate before the fight. If we had done that, the UFC would probably have locked us in for a smaller deal. Maybe they were aware of this and assumed that after I lost to Hughes they could cut me loose altogether. Truth is, they really had no idea. In fact, what they thought they had was what's called a "sixty-day matching clause," wherein they could match anyone else's offer starting from whichever came first—the year or the final fight. Now, as it turned out, both the year and the sixty days from September 27, 2003, had expired. The Hughes fight took place only because of a separate "bout agreement" I had signed. That agreement was in and of itself a completely different deal, which did oblige me to fight him under the terms of my signed contract but did not bind me to that contract in a way that changed the terms. All it basically did was get me paid under those terms, and nothing more. If I had won the title under the terms of the original contract, I would have been bound to fight for the UFC under an automatic extension. The bout agreement contained no such language.

After a whole lot of back-and-forth with the UFC, things deteriorated to the point where I heard from the UFC that if I fought in another organization, they would strip me of the title. It was complete nonsense again, and just another way to keep me with them for low pay. It too was not going to work because nowhere in the contract did it say that if I didn't defend the title, I'd be stripped of it. Again, since they never thought I was going to be wearing the welterweight belt, it had been of no real concern to them. Whatever tool they could use to threaten me—*other than simply paying me what their former champion was making*—they tried to use. It was unbelievable.

Every day I just sat around my house wondering why in the world they wouldn't ante up the money, which was nothing to them. They'd probably end up losing more money fighting me in negotiations than they would just paying me. But for White it was about more than that. As a guy who'd never actually fought anyone in his life, he considered these negotiations his fights, and he was not going to lie down. The UFC started making it public how I'd be stripped of my title, going the public relations route rather than the legal one. A common tactic for someone who has no real case based on the words in a contract.

There was a small break in communication between the two sides after this move, and by now word of what was going on had spread in the MMA community. I started doing some interviews for MMA Web sites, and on one of their radio programs I said, "I'm looking for Dana White! If anyone knows where he is, tell him I want to talk to him. I want to work this thing out, so have him call me." He got wind of this, and then the organization decided to contact me through one of his people. A UFC attorney named Kirk Hendrick called me up and offered me their version of a "deal." I mean, knowing how they operated, you prepared yourself for the worst and the best—the worst possible deal from a monetary standpoint, and the best in terms of comedic value. They did not let me down on either end.

Sensing that I wanted back in, Hendrick said the only way this situation could now be resolved was if I came to the next scheduled event, walked into the Octagon with the belt, publicly apologized to White, and left the belt in the cage. Did White think he was Vince McMahon? Was this the WWE? He needed a public apology from a fighter just so he could then tell people he was right? That apology would be an acknowledgment that I had done something wrong, but the only thing I was guilty of was asking to be treated fairly. There was no way in the world I was ever going to do it. At this point, if I did enter the cage with White standing inside of it, the only thing that'd be left on the floor would be him.

Eventually the UFC did strip me of my belt, which forced me to enter into a lawsuit against them. I found a local law firm in Las Vegas, and they filed a complaint in July of 2004, alleging that the UFC had wrongfully stripped me of the title and that they had breached my contract. I also requested "injunctive relief," which would basically stop Zuffa from holding a welterweight title match for my belt, which they were planning to do between Georges St-Pierre and Matt Hughes.

This whole experience was not easy for me because of all the emotions involved. I still liked White—when we spoke, or ran into each other, it was all smiles and laughs. Separating myself from this personal aspect has always been somewhat difficult for me, but when they made it about business, I had to do so as well. Working for and with Zuffa/UFC has made me a different person, as it did my entire family. I knew I had to have my guard up not only inside the cage but outside of it as well—indeed, more so outside!

When it was finally official I was going to fight in Japan, White called me up and told me his true feelings.

"You motherfucker! You're fucking done! You'll never fight in the UFC again! You're finished. You're scorched earth, mother-fucker. Scorched earth. Don't call me crying saying you want to come back because you're fucking done!" And on and on and on, like a true professional—even going so far as to tell me I would never see my face again in a UFC video, promotion, or anything else. He also planned on removing my fight with Hughes from the UFC 46: Supernatural DVD so no one would even know who I was.

"It doesn't have to be this way," I told him. "You know it wouldn't take that much to make this work."

But he just kept yelling.

THE ROMANEX CARD HAD A LOT of big names on it, guys I had watched for years. I got the sense they were trying to do some big things with guys like Josh Barnett, Don Frye, Lyoto Machida, Gary Goodrich, Ganki Sudo, and Royler Gracie. If you followed the sport, these were guys you either knew or were going to know. I didn't leave the UFC for the minor leagues. There were a lot more fighters in Japan than in the United States.

Takano made the transition happen in a hurry, and while I

definitely missed fighting in the UFC, it was good to know I was wanted elsewhere. From the beginning Takano told us about some of his ideas, how I would be marketed in a big way, that the fans in Japan respected the fighters differently than the U.S. fans did, and that I could become a star there. Even though I knew I was leaving something behind, I looked forward to what could happen in the future.

The first order of business was a matchup with Ludwig, the guy who knocked Pulver out and had also beaten the highly regarded Genki Sudo. It did not seem very hard to make this happen. I wanted to fight a guy who mattered, and with Ludwig they had one for me. In essence, this would be a title fight with no belt on the line. The irony of the Ludwig fight was we both decided we would fight at welterweight, not lightweight, because it was easier not to cut, and we were both comfortable there. The only issue I had with this fight was Ludwig was not Japanese, and when I had signed on to do this, I had expressed a desire to go up against the best Japanese fighters and not just the best guys in Japan. Because martial arts were huge in Japan, and jujitsu a creation of the Japanese, I wanted to prove myself to these people, against their fighters. I was fine with Ludwig as an opponent, but going forward, he was not the reason I was there.

About fifteen thousand people showed up for my fight with Ludwig in Saitama, Japan, but compared to the raucous UFC crowd, the audience was pretty mellow and much older. There was not a whole lot of yelling and screaming; it was more like a bunch of people coming to watch a respected art. Quiet, reserved, clapping at the right times, as if they had been watching this sport their entire lives. I respected their take on it, but as an American, I preferred our more intense style; it suited my personality better.

Just before the fight, I felt completely calm. Ludwig was the taller fighter, maybe even a little bigger, but I felt like in that moment I was the best fighter in the world in any division. Things were still just clicking for me, and while training, I'd felt I could do no wrong. Despite the loss, the draw, the battle with the UFC, something was keeping me incredibly motivated. It would be my first MMA fight in a ring in years, since the time when Ralph Gracie set me up with that random kickboxer. From a small gym to a huge arena, yet oddly enough, I'd been more nervous back then.

When the fight began, I came out of my corner and shot on him immediately, tackling him right to the ground, onto his back. I was in his half guard, and from the beginning, I was throwing heavy punches into his body, face, and head, as well as some hammer fists, which is when you pound a guy with the back of your fist. He was able to hold me off for a while, but soon I passed his half guard and had him fully mounted.

Unable to buck me off, he had to start throwing some punches of his own from the bottom, hoping to knock me off. This only left him wide open for more shots to the face. He tried to resist, but I was now holding his right arm and punching him. I then grabbed ahold of that same arm with my right hand and pulled it across his face, setting him up for an arm triangle choke. With his arm secured by my shoulder, I threw my body off his torso to his side, had my other arm under his head, and secured the choke. He tapped out 1:45 into the first round.

It is often said a good fighter has the ability to adapt and change on the fly. You have to give Zuffa some credit when it came to the lawsuit because they did just that. Previously they had argued in as many ways as they could why I needed to remain with the UFC, and under contract. It was pretty basic stuff, nothing that would necessarily convince a judge to side in their favor, but then they went in another direction.

In October 2004, the UFC decided rather than argue about which one of us was in the right regarding our deal, they'd argue about the actual value of being a UFC champion. From the day the Fertittas took over the company, White had always proclaimed the

UFC to be either the best organization in the world or the eventual best. Holding the UFC belt, as White would lead you to believe in any conversation you had with him, meant you were the best in the world. Their new legal claim, however, contradicted this completely, instead stating that a UFC belt was actually irrelevant when it came to assessing its value in the world of MMA. A champion in the UFC might be the best in the world, maybe not the best, but the belt did not confer any status. To win the belt and take it somewhere else, to defend it on another stage, was viewed by the UFC as both illegal and irrelevant. "Why go to Japan with the belt around your waist if it means nothing at all?" is essentially what they were asking.

Unlike boxing, where a fight promoter organizes an event for two opponents to battle for the WBC, WBA, or IBF title, and the organization (the WBC, WBA, etc.) is separate from the promoter, the UFC was both the promoter *and* the organization in which a fighter could win a belt. This meant that the only person who could possibly hold a UFC belt was someone who was under contract with the UFC. Hence "best in the world" was no longer a concept that applied.

This argument didn't seem to be far-fetched, and in some ways it made sense, but it was an argument that had never been made before. Prior to my suit against them, I was completely unaware of this line of reasoning. Everything they had ever said, ever implied, ever marketed when it came to their organization was that you could win a "world championship." They were not just telling me this when we negotiated; it was the product being sold to the fans, media, and all of the athletes who competed. However, from this point on, the message changed. To them, the UFC was *still the best in the world,* but it really mattered only to them, which, of course, was all that really mattered in the first place.

In court proceedings, the judge sided with the UFC—they could hold their championship bout—but the decision acknowledged that questions remained regarding whether they had practiced fraud in their marketing, advertising, contracts, and wherever else they claimed to hold "world championship" fights. There was also a question of whether there could be two titleholders at one time, and what would happen regarding my belt. In other words, they had not so much won the case as they had created a way out for themselves. The match between St-Pierre and Hughes took place on October 22, 2004, and Hughes won, making him the champ again.

But everyone knew who the real champ was.

WITH THE UFC TRYING THEIR BEST to take away my belt, I just continued to find fights that mattered. Real fans of the sport knew what the UFC had claimed, and knew that the belt did not matter if I was not wearing it. Seeing Matt Hughes become the champion again was a joke, so I just looked for more solid opponents anywhere I could find them. The next guy we found was Rodrigo Gracie for Rumble on the Rock 6 back in Hawaii on November 11, 2004.

The Gracie name had only become more prominent as MMA grew, and for me, it would be the first time I had the chance to face a member of the famed family either as a jujitsu fighter or an MMA fighter. It was no secret that Nova União and the Gracies were not fans of each other, so at the very least, it was an opportunity to promote the fight based on that rivalry, even though I had no issues to speak of with Rodrigo. In fact, I never had issues with any of them; it was always their side having an issue with me. At this point of my life, fighting was strictly business.

Rodrigo was a middleweight fighter—185-pound limit—and he also had a few inches on me in height, but none of that really mattered. We both just wanted to be part of a big match, and at the time he was undefeated at 5–0 and I was essentially the world champion. A lot of people had been asking how I would fare against someone with a jujitsu background as good as mine, limiting my ground advantage. All of these things aside, it was really just an opportunity to put on a big show in Honolulu, even bigger than the one with Gomi, so I was more than happy to be a part of it.

At this time I was still training hard, but due to my success, I was able to bring guys in to help me train. Prior to this, I just went as hard as I could against anyone I could find. For this fight I brought in a few extra guys, namely Thales Leites from Nova União and Mike Pyle, who was a great coach. Leites had a big frame, probably very close to Rodrigo's size, and after working with him on the ground for a couple weeks, I knew Rodrigo was not going to be a problem.

ROTR events meant a lot to me because it was Jay Dee's baby, and so a family affair. For this event he went all out, bringing hula dancers into the arena, having the entire place covered with such Hawaiian paraphernalia as tiki torches, all just to add to the excitement. The event was so big locally we sold more tickets at the Blaisdell Center than Elvis Presley had for his final show. Sadly, the fight with Rodrigo was somewhat uneventful from the get go. Truth is, he seemed a bit scared, or at least intimidated by the whole experience. While he was an undefeated fighter, he had not yet fought someone of my level, and he was also fighting in front of all my fans. For three rounds, I basically put him on his back and pounded on him. He had wanted to make this a jujitsu ground fight, but I was not going to jeopardize a fight by putting myself in the one place where he could possibly win. So round and round, round after round, it was just takedown after takedown with me going after him. Even as the bigger fighter, he was backing up more than he was moving forward.

Following three uneventful rounds, I was awarded the unanimous decision. It was not the fight I expected, but it was the one I got. I commend Rodrigo for stepping into the cage against a tough opponent, but I felt he really was not trying to win the fight as much as he was attempting to just get through it. The only reason it bothered me is here I was fighting in Hawaii, wanting to put on a great show for our people, and yet it was just one of those lackluster fights, which can sometimes happen in MMA if one guy does not want to fight for blood.

ACCORDING TO K-1, MY NEXT FIGHT would be on March 26, 2005, again in Saitama, as part of their first "Hero's" event. Literally, it could be against anyone, not even someone in my weight class, and as it turned out, this was the case. K-1 told me a little more than two weeks before the fight I would face off against Lyoto Machida, an up-and-coming karate fighter. It is how K-1 did it back then; you didn't know your opponent until the last couple of days, which I guess helped make for exciting fights.

Machida was a much bigger fighter, and I had heard they wanted to use me to make a name for him. I guess K-1, or his management, figured beating me would put him on the map. I didn't give a shit what they thought. I was going to throw overhand rights all day long and make him pay for wanting to fight me. Winning and losing mattered, but it was more about putting on great fights for the fans and proving myself to the Japanese audience.

Machida came into this fight weighing close to 225 pounds, since it was rumored he wanted to fight in the heavyweight division. I came in around 180 or so, but I can't be sure because the weigh-in was hardly relevant, since we were basically fighting open weight. Even though he had the size, I knew deep down I was going to win: when I sign on the line to fight, I sign to win.

As I stared across the ring, his corner was like a mirror image of mine, him standing there with his two brothers, me with mine. We should have just had a brawl, for it could have been one for the ages, but instead it was just the two of us. From the get-go, I just attacked him, throwing big right hooks and overhand rights. He was nimble enough to get out of the way, but I was just going to stay on this guy for as long as I could and not let him get comfortable. His signature move was to throw kicks, and a left hand at the same time to catch guys coming in. I was prepared for that. A lot of times when a guy throws a kick, it is an opportunity to throw a punch, so his punch is more like a defensive maneuver rather than something that can cause a lot of damage.

I shot in for the first takedown, pressed him against the ropes, but he used his size to turn me around and get me on the ropes. That was the one area where he had a clear advantage in that he was so much bigger than me. I sensed his goal would be to tire me out with his weight. He threw a lot of knees into my legs as well to slow me down. Every time I threw a right hand, I tried to get on top of him, right in his face, and control his body, but the size was definitely a factor. I was clearly the more aggressive fighter from the start, but then again that could be expected when you face a karate fighter, a martial art that relies on distance and counter-strikes. Whenever I did get in on him, he would tie me up, and then try to throw short punches and elbows on the break. When he wasn't doing that, it was all about keeping distance. I was the complete opposite; we both played to each other's strengths and weaknesses.

At one point in the first round, we were pressed into the corner with him trying to break out with a quick flurry, but I attacked and landed an overhand right that sent him backward. He tried to counter with a kick, but I landed another overhand right. He had yet to land a shot of significance, while I had landed quite a few. He did keep the pressure on my body by throwing knees into my legs, but not enough to cause noticeable damage.

We moved around the ring and eventually started throwing wild punches, both of us, with one of his left uppercuts connecting on my face, but not causing a lot of damage since he was moving backward. From there, I was able to get the first takedown after he missed with an attempted trip. We both wrestled for position with me on top, neither of us landing many blows. He knew his best option from the bottom was making sure I could not get free for a submission attempt, and Machida wanted to be anywhere but on his back. The round ended, and I thought I'd clearly won.

When the second began, he tried using a lot of fakes, the same ones which have thrown a lot of UFC fighters off their games. They didn't have much of an effect. We both threw punches but nothing landed, and again he tried to hold me into the corner to wear me down. Holding a big man up during a fight can be more tiring than being punched, or having a guy lie on top of you. At this point keeping his weight on me was his best option because that also slowed the fight down. As the round went on, he connected with more shots, but none of them were landing flush. When he tried to throw one of his favorite moves, a spinning back kick, I saw it coming and delivered an overhand right that sent him into the ropes. I pounced on him immediately, but the ropes held him up and essentially saved him. The missed takedown was the difference in the fight.

Going into the third, I figured it was close, probably at one round apiece. I was growing really tired at this point. He seemed tired too, but was probably in a better place because of his size. He came out a lot more active than I did. I landed a decent jab, and eventually went for a takedown, but he was quick enough to get up. None of his punches or kicks to this point of the match had caused any real damage; it was still just a matter of being grinded on by his size. I saw all his fakes, and most of his punches coming the entire time. He landed some solid leg kicks in the third, but more for points than damage. At one point when I was on my back, he jumped up for a stomp, which glanced off the back of my head.

I did not have a lot in the tank at this point, and I was looking for one big shot in the hope of taking him out. More than halfway through the round, he was definitely in the lead. With a minute to go, he held me against the ropes, throwing knees, again tiring me out. Then he went for a takedown on the break, knowing any points this late in the match could decide the whole thing. The round ended, and I was as tired as I had ever been in a fight.

The entire fight hinged on the second round and whoever won that. Once the announcer called out his name, I knew it had been him. All three judges scored the victory for Lyoto. I was not surprised by the decision, but it was the first time I had lost by unanimous decision. Still, I was not devastated like I had been versus Pulver, where I knew I should have won, but like any other fight, I was emotional and down. Lyoto is a great fighter and I had been looking to test myself against the best, but this doesn't mean I was comfortable with the loss. It was not the type of thing which was going to sit with me for ages, but still it was not easy to let go.

Inside the ring I had sustained little to no damage, but physically I was exhausted. When Rudy, Reagan, and Jay Dee walked me back to the locker room, they had to take me around underneath the stadium bleachers. I was so completely spent I had to sit down on the floor right there, and I couldn't make it back to the locker room. Valentino told me I had to get back, so they picked me up and pretty much carried me. Having to hold up Machida's weight the entire fight was exhausting since he had at least forty, maybe fifty pounds on me. It was not a problem during the fight, but it sure was afterward.

As for Machida, I knew how good he was, but I didn't realize he'd briefly be considered the best in the world just a few years later, viewed by some as unbeatable. I thought he was more than beatable, and truth be told, I landed at least as many, if not more, powerful shots than he did. I often hear things like "Machida is not the same fighter now" or "he has developed his skills since then." I don't believe any of that matters. Machida is a karate fighter first, and if you go back and watch his fight against me, or even his previous fight against Sam Greco, he fought the same way then as he does today. The reason he has walked through the UFC and won the light heavyweight championship is guys are either impatient, or too scared to take him on.

I have seen countless fighters get picked apart by Machida because they either do not know what they are doing or are scared to get hit. Feeling intimidated inside a ring or a cage does not generate the type of energy that is going to help you, but rather will ultimately lead to a loss. Fighters try to keep their distance from Machida to avoid his strikes rather than getting up in his face and limiting his karate skills, especially his kicks. Karate is all about that, closing the distance fast, and it is what Machida does well.

To take nothing away from Machida, he's a great fighter, but I haven't seen him beat anyone in his division who I consider to be an amazing fighter in his prime. This does not mean Machida is not a great champion because he is, but I gave up at least five inches in height and a ton of weight to this guy, and landed as many big shots and went the distance. I do not think a fight with Machida today would be much different than it was then; one that could go either way. When it comes to the way I fight, I do not think size is especially relevant.

Machida would be my last opponent in Japan, and while I had some success there, it was not reason enough to stay. Japan had been an amazing place, and the fans were both so respectful and knowledgeable that it made me want to stay. But things didn't work out that way. Ironically, I yearned to be back in the UFC when it was almost cool to not be in the UFC. Most of the best fighters seemed to be guys who were in Japan, and it was clearly a bigger sporting event there. The fights were regularly shown on local television, and were not viewed negatively. I still had one more fight in my K-1 contract, but it looked like it might take place in Hawaii— against whom I did not know.

MEANWHILE, I CONTINUED TO PRESS my case against the UFC, but things were not going anywhere. It seemed the law firm I was using had no real interest in pursuing the matter, since any time anyone from my family contacted them, they never seemed to have any information for us and would continually say they would get back to us. They never did, so we sought new counsel.

In 2005, we found a new firm, and in the beginning it seemed like we were getting the same treatment we had at the last firm. Once again we had to ask the same question—why was nothing getting done?—as I sat and watched event after event take place. Couture had already won back his belt, Hughes was the champ again, and I was taking fights in Japan, but still considered myself the real UFC champ.

After we bothered the people at the firm enough times, they finally told us they were on the case. They passed it off to their newest attorney, who had just joined the firm a month earlier. His name was Raffi Nahabedian, a licensed lawyer from California, who had recently relocated to Las Vegas. Nahabedian had more of a big-city mentality, and even though Las Vegas may be a big city in terms of the size and number of its buildings and its population, in reality, it was a very small town and things can move slowly. At the very least Nahabedian was a willing advocate, someone we could depend on to fight for us and stay in touch too.

Soon after Nahabedian got up to speed, the summer of 2005, depositions were taken from both sides. Having inherited a lawsuit that had been going on for some time, Nahabedian believed depositions were the way to get to the bottom of all the bullshit and finally put the UFC on the line: you can't lie your way through a deposition while under oath. White was not the only UFC person there; other UFC employees were also called to speak on the specifics of the case. It was a hard thing to watch and listen to. These were people I had known a long time up there trying to make me look bad in an effort to take away my belt. I argued that the case against me defamed my character, but these guys were trying to make the case that I had no character to defame, that no one knew who I was, or even cared, and while I may have been well known in the MMA world, they tried to say that people really didn't care who BJ Penn was.

Fortunately for us, things went very well during the depositions. We felt confident things were moving in our direction and were pleased with the result: we were going back to court.

IT IS OFTEN SAID FIGHTERS HAVE the highest highs and the lowest lows—you've even heard me say it already—and this is not just an aspect of the fighting game. It also has to do with the partying and the lifestyle you lead as a fighter. I can't speak about all fighters, but when you're training for months on end, when your fight is over, win, lose, or draw, the first thing you want is to eat some type of unhealthy food followed by a beer . . . or ten. It's no different for me, as a guy who always likes to live life to the fullest. Unfortunately, sometimes when you're living that life, and not being the model citizen people hope you are, you can get yourself into trouble.

As much as I have always wanted to be the best at what I do, the accolades and notoriety that go along with this can be hard to escape, and there are times when it goes to your head, when you think you can do whatever you want, whenever you want, because you believe you've earned it. At the same time you can become a target for others who see you as some kind of a prize, as someone who, if pushed, will make a bad decision they can capitalize on. I have been this kind of target, most notably in May of 2005 right after another ROTR in Honolulu.

The event was really big for us, and this time I didn't have to fight in it. I had friends like Leites, Vitor Ribeiro, Ricco Rodriguez, Charuto, and others in the event, and most of them were victorious. Overall it was a really good night, and after the fights we all went out to party at a club in Honolulu. I didn't have a fight scheduled, so I was having a good time like anyone else. Nobody was getting rowdy inside the club, and I was there with a girl I was dating at the time. While leaving with friends and driving away from the club, I saw Reagan being pounded by not one but several guys outside the club entrance, so I immediately had my friend stop the car and ran to help him. I jumped in to pull the guys off of him. Before I knew it, another guy comes in and blindsides me on the side of my head; it was just like a mob of people throwing hands.

Eventually the cops showed up, and we tried to leave, had our friend pull his car up right in front of the club. One of the cops decided to open his mouth for no reason and say, "Get out of here!"

My friend looked at the cop and said, "We were just getting mobbed!" I followed up with, "Me too!" We started walking to the car.

Another officer heard us talking to the cop, and just before we got into the car he yells out, "Just get the fuck out of here."

Not completely sober, I turned to him and yelled, "Fuck you." Which was a bad call because even when you're right, when it comes to cursing at a police officer, you will end up paying a price.

From there I tried to get into the backseat of the car as my girlfriend was entering from the other side. Once inside, I was pulling on the door to shut it, but it wouldn't close. I was looking at my girlfriend, and pulling on the door, wondering why it wouldn't close. At that moment I realized that the cop was standing there preventing the door from shutting. Next thing I knew, he maced me in the face, filling up the rest of the car with the stuff too. He then shut the car door, trapping everyone inside. None of us could see a thing.

I jumped out of the car, and all hell broke loose. Everyone was in the street again, hardly able to see, and we had people grabbing onto us. Covering my stinging eyes, I pushed some people off me, one of whom was a cop. He grabbed at me, and I just thought I needed to get away from this mess. It was a melee, so I just tried to get away from it all, and took off up the street. Within a second someone had tackled me from behind and dragged me to the ground. I landed on my elbows in the street, and they got completely torn up. I tried to escape my assailant's grasp and get up off the ground, crawling, not even to fight, but just to run. Suddenly I couldn't move and I felt myself being handcuffed, facedown in the street, with my eyes still burning like hell. From there, they threw me in the back of the police car and hauled me over to the police station. Within a minute we went from having words with a few police officers to being maced and jailed. And here I'd thought I could go out and party because I had no fights scheduled.

Next I found myself locked up overnight, which wouldn't have been so bad had they stuck me in a room with another person, but they didn't. I am claustrophobic, and this cell had no windows and a solid door. They stuck food through on a tray in the door, and I put my hand in there so they wouldn't close it. I kept asking them to just leave the tray door open so I could put my arm out, so at least I would feel like I had some freedom. They just laughed at me. Literally, they could have put anyone in there, even a wild animal— something to fight, or someone to talk to, it didn't matter. There is just nothing worse for me than being alone in a room I can't get out of. There were other people stuck in other cells screaming to get out, and the officers would just laugh. I guess this is the price you pay for doing something mindless and stupid, which is why talking back to the police, even if you are right, is a bad call.

The next day they let me out with a summons, and ultimately I was given a year of probation, a fitting end to what would be a personal low point for me.

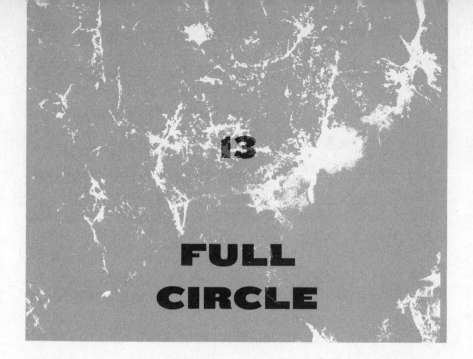

13

FULL CIRCLE

AMID THE PROBLEMS I WAS HAVING with the UFC
and the lawsuit I had gotten myself into, I had one more
fight remaining on my K-1 contract with the possibility
of extending it. I was 1–1 at this point, and awaiting my next opponent, hoping it would be one of the well-known Japanese fighters.
At the time K-1 was still trying to grow its MMA brand in Japan,
competing against larger organizations like Pride Fighting Championships, so they tried getting creative with the promotion. As a
result, I wouldn't get the type of opponent I had hoped for when I
signed with them, but at the very least, I'd get to fight in Honolulu.
In an effort to expand the MMA brand globally, K-1 had decided
it was going to hold my third fight locally, but this time against the
very well-known Renzo Gracie.

Once again, it was my family who had found Renzo as an

opponent, knowing it would create excitement for the event not only across Hawaii, but in the MMA world as well. MMA was on the brink of taking off, so fights with big names helped push it in the right direction. Renzo was about ten years older than me and had taken his lumps in previous fights, but he had fought so infrequently it almost seemed like he'd retired. The opportunity to fight me must have been too good to pass up, considering the family history and their dislike of me. Or maybe it was the money? Whatever it was, it would be his first fight in over a year and a half.

Since there was no chance a guy Renzo's age and size was going to cut to welterweight, I agreed to fight middleweight. Putting on weight has never really been a problem for me, but fighting at 185 pounds is not something I like to do. In order to carry the weight, I did a lot of sparring, grappling, and other gym training, but I was not doing a lot of cardio because it would cause me to lose weight. Even as far as dieting went, I watched what I ate on some level, but the training was not nearly as refined and defined as it would be years later.

Right off the bat, people were talking about the bad blood between the Gracie family and me. I played along with it to help K-1's promotional strategy, and all of the interviews about the fight were about me leaving his brother's school, and how a "lesson" was going to be taught to me. For Renzo, I did my regular training, but this time I brought in a few guys to work specifically for me, most particularly Dave Camarillo, who was now with AKA in San Jose. Even though it had seemed like Dave would remain with Ralph his entire life, it didn't exactly work out that way, and now here he was cornering me against the Gracie family. It must have been an emotional situation for him too. The camp was a good one, though; and in addition to Rudy, my brothers, and Dave, I had Troy Mandaloniz, a friend from Hilo who I often stayed with in Las Vegas.

The fight took place in Aloha Stadium on July 29, 2005, as part of K-1's World Grand Prix Hawaii. Aloha Stadium is an enormous place, known as the site of the National Football League's Pro Bowl. While it was nowhere near sold out, it was a cool feeling to be competing in a place of this size. This was clearly the biggest MMA event to date that was held in Hawaii.

After all the words were spoken and the calling of our names was out of the way, it was time to fight. Whether or not Renzo truly wanted to stand and trade with me was immediately apparent. The fight began, and he looked as if he was going to keep this thing on the feet, but then, after a moment or two, he went straight for the takedown, which he got, and then fell into my guard. From the moment the first round began until its end, Renzo stayed on top of me, trying to pass my guard, rubbing the top of his head into my face, doing anything to try to win the round from the top position.

Some fighters don't like being on their backs, and expend a lot of energy trying to get up, but I was fine in this position. Jujitsu teaches patience, since you spend so much time doing very little, just jockeying for position. I was fine with Renzo "laying and praying." Though you could sense the intensity of it, it was clear that doing so little and pulling out a round by just having advantage was not going to be enough. It was not why Renzo had taken this fight, nor the Gracies. While on my back, I could hear the family in his corner shouting, "For the family! For the family, Renzo!" Over and over, this is all I heard when he had me down, as if this fight meant more to them than it did to the two of us. Though Renzo was a well-known Gracie, and as far as I am concerned, the best MMA competitor of them all, he didn't seem to carry the weight of the family into this fight. Like me, it just seemed he wanted to perform at his best, and that was all. Maybe the words "for the family" did motivate him, but for two guys fighting inside a ring, it would have little effect on the outcome.

Since Renzo had control from the top, I did what I could from the bottom, using my heels to kick him in the back and on the side of his body. Nothing extremely effective, more to be a pest. If you can get a guy to change his position by catching him right with a kick like that, you could force him into a mistake that ends the fight. I didn't expect the heels to cause any real damage. The round ended in an uneventful way, in that same position with him in my guard. Renzo one, Penn nothing.

The second round began and again I was looking to stand and fight. I knew it was only a matter of time before Renzo tried to pull off the same attack. He threw some leg kicks, which were very solid, but it was all just a setup to stay away from my hands and get it to the ground. I did not consider Renzo to be superior to me on the ground in any way, but the difference on the feet was a lot greater than on the mat. I started landing some shots at him that definitely hurt, and every time I did, he immediately tried to tie up my arms or get me against the ropes. When he did throw punches, usually a counterstrike, he did so with his head down, as if he wanted to avoid taking hits but at the same time couldn't see the target. He'd throw a left hook over and over, which either missed or was ineffective. For a guy who really wanted to KO me, a hook with his lead hand was not going to do it, especially since no one had ever knocked me out.

By the end of the second round, I could sense Renzo slowing down, but at the same time I was not exactly speeding up. I definitely felt I was in better shape than he was, even with the weight. When the bell finally sounded I had taken round two, landing the only punches that mattered and stopping him from getting it to the ground: 1–1.

Round three began much like two, with me trying to throw punches and Renzo pushing me against the ropes. If he'd wanted a chance to win this on the ground, he would get it because I took him down with a sweep and immediately brought it to the mat. I was on top of him in his half guard, applying as much pressure as possible. Punches, elbow strikes, covering the mouth to stop breathing, whatever I could do to set him up for a submission. As much as getting a knockout would be nice, the idea of submitting a Gracie would actually be epic. From his half guard, he was unable to do any real damage. This was a reversal of round one, but since we were both more tired, there were more opportunities to land strikes, which I did. Nothing heavy on the face, but body shots and some head shots too.

After grinding out the fight for nearly three minutes from the top, with about a minute to go, I got up to my feet looking to land a big punch, similar to the one where I broke my hand on Hughes's face. After missing with a big shot, I was back on top of him, in the same position. All he could do was defend. With little time left in the fight, I finally mounted him completely. With me ready to rain down blows and end this thing, the bell sounded and the fight was over.

The two of us were both spent. We hugged each other, showing our mutual respect and appreciation. Bad blood always trickles away after two guys have a chance to settle the score. Even though for me it was never about that feud stuff, it was nice to put it all behind us, at least in that moment. Once we were standing, our two camps greeted each other, shook hands, and were cordial, but it seemed most of his guys just walked right past me. They seemed to know Bruce Buffer was about to announce they had lost to me again, and they weren't handling it well. I won a unanimous decision, just like I had over Rodrigo—although there was a big difference between the two, since Renzo had been there to fight. He was tough, was there to perform for himself, it seemed, and landed some nice shots, whereas Rodrigo was ineffective and seemed like he was overmatched. Given Renzo's age and how little he was competing, he fought more than admirably.

When I hear about the supposed conflict between myself and the Gracies, it hardly even moves me, yet for whatever reason, it seems to pop up all the time. For years, journalists, fans, fighters, and others have asked me how it began, and what my thoughts are on it. Truth be told, I have no thoughts on it, and I have no animosity at all. That something like this should have gone on for over a decade seems more embarrassing to me than anything else. I also assume it's more about one man, Ralph, than it is about the entire Gracie family. Surely family sticks together, and few understand the concept better than me, but for them to dislike me based on the actions I took as a teenager seems crazy.

The way I see it, Ralph Gracie, Renzo Gracie, or any other Gracie is no better or worse than any other competitor in the world of MMA, especially when it comes to training, changing teams, and things of that nature. When I showed up at Ralph's gym in the late 1990s, he helped me tremendously, but I was a kid. I had no desire to stab anyone in the back when I left; I just wanted to explore the martial arts world that was out there. It was Ralph who decided to push my entire family away. Ironically, when Georges St-Pierre was preparing to fight me, he trained with Renzo Gracie. Then St-Pierre was set to fight Renzo's student Matt Serra afterward. Of course, Renzo told him he couldn't train him because Serra was his long-time student, which is completely understandable. Only because of the circumstances did it play out like that, but it was Renzo *allowing* him to leave, maybe on good terms, maybe bad, I don't know. If the fighter *chooses* to leave, it's a whole other story.

I know of other fighters who are taken in by camps, and given opportunities to train and learn free of charge, or with a lot of help from the school. Maybe it's because the fighter is poor, or coming out of a bad situation, there are many reasons, but it happens that a camp provides him with a great opportunity. In one case I know of, a fighter left a Gracie school after being nurtured to greatness, taking the next best opportunity that came along without regard for those who'd brought him to this point. With me it was nothing of the sort. I was not someone who needed help; I was a kid who was choosing martial arts as a career, paying his own way, working tirelessly, trying to learn as much as I could at a young age.

I have nothing but respect for most of the Gracies and view the whole bad-blood issue as theirs not mine. When I think about mixed martial arts, especially jujitsu, I look at them as trailblazers, a group of people who, more than anyone else, helped bring the sport I love to the masses. For all the UFC's talk about it being the sport they made huge, to me, it all starts and ends with the Gracies.

Mixed martial arts is a sport which could not fail. Others like to say it was sinking, and was about to vanish. I do not believe that for a second. It was a sport that could not fail, and while the time line may have been changed by one event or another, it was and is a can't-miss thing. The Gracies are the spark that created the inevitable flame.

WITH MY K-1 CONTRACT FINALLY UP and no other obligations to them, I had only one more fight in front of me: BJ Penn vs Zuffa. The case with the UFC had lasted throughout my K-1 deal, which was well over a year, and there was no end in sight.

Eventually, the UFC filed a motion for summary judgment against me. Now, I am no lawyer, but you learn the legal game pretty quickly when your career is on the line. The motion against me in particular was an effort by Zuffa to get the judge, and the judge alone, to decide the case on its merits. In other words, they wanted to avoid a trial. It was a last-ditch effort to get the case thrown out, and it didn't work. The judge ruled that my case would be heard by judge and jury within a few months. My lawyer and Zuffa's lawyers argued their respective positions about the motion. The judge listened to the arguments on both sides, but instead of issuing his opinion right then and there, he decided to wait and deliberate.

For the UFC, it probably came as a surprise the judge didn't rule in their favor. Still, when we stepped out of the courtroom, everyone was gathered around, chatting, and in some ways acting like no conflict even existed. White and I were talking as if we had no friction between us, Lorenzo and Fertitta were nearby acting the same way. It was a strange situation.

In the meantime, I had no plan at all, for the first time in a long time. The UFC, though, they were doing just fine, and the lawsuit with me became more of a sideshow for them. They had bigger things on their plate. In January of 2005, they'd launched a reality television show called *The Ultimate Fighter,* which was helping to bring MMA into the mainstream. *TUF,* as it's called, was your standard reality competition show where a bunch of people, in this case fighters, lived in a house together, dealing with your typical reality-show nonsense, except these guys had the chance to beat the crap out of each other in the end.

The first two coaches of the show would be light heavyweights Randy Couture and Chuck Liddell. It was strange for me because I had fought alongside these guys, had known them very well, trained with them, partied with them, traveled with them, and talked to them about life, and now they were becoming the superstars of the sport while I sat on the sidelines. I didn't want to stay in Hawaii and teach while I was on top of my game, feeling great about the sport. I was a little envious of what was going on, and I wanted to be a part of it. As a member of the generation that was helping to propel the sport to new heights, I wanted in on the action.

Nahabedian felt confident the facts of the lawsuit were in our favor, and in a court of law, we would come away victorious. The only problem was even if I won, the chances of me ending up back in the UFC were slim to none, and in the end all I really wanted was to fight in the UFC again. A victory would mean I was right, and maybe they'd have to pay me the punitive damages I was asking for, but if I lost, I'd get absolutely nothing. Either way, my relationship with the UFC would be severely jeopardized.

One day I was talking to Nahabedian about the situation, and he asked me point-blank: "What do you want out of all this?"

I did not even hesitate.

"I want back in the UFC. I don't care how you do it, just get it done. K-1 made me some money, but they didn't give me what I wanted. Just get me back in so I can get my belt back."

With that said, Nahabedian put the wheels in motion and worked toward accomplishing what I wanted. Forget the court cases, forget the money, forget everything else because at the end of the day, I simply wanted to compete against the best guys, fight at any weight class, and prove to myself just how good I could be. As my attorney, Nahabedian did not fight me on this at all, even though he knew that I had an opportunity to beat Zuffa in a court of law. While it could have been a nice little notch on his own belt, he agreed that I was making the right decision.

Soon thereafter, Nahabedian reached out to one of the attorneys for Zuffa with whom he had established a good relationship and explained my desire. It was a delicate situation because on some level, the UFC probably knew it held most of the cards. Still, if they lost the case, there was no way they'd take me back. White's "scorched earth" threat would become a reality. Nahabedian's counterpart on Zuffa's side passed the word up the chain that this thing needed to be settled now.

Instead of dragging it out any longer, both sides decided maybe mediation was the best solution. If we could just hammer this thing out and come to an agreement, it would all be over with. And so in the middle of November of 2005, both sides sat at the table and tried to put the case to rest.

We met at a neutral law office in Las Vegas. I came with my lawyer, father, and brother Jay Dee, and Zuffa was there with their lawyers, Dana White, and Lorenzo Fertitta. It was not a very contentious situation because both sides realized that reconciliation was the best thing for everyone. We both made our cases again, and everyone had something to say. It was almost pointless for everyone to be there when it was really about two people. At one point White even said, "If he wants back in, I'll let him back in."

Finally, someone had the idea to just let me and White hash this out ourselves, or at least try to. They stuck the two of us in a room. I had no problem with this plan because while I knew deep down White was just trying to get one over on me, I didn't really care. He had what I wanted, and for the most part he wanted me to have it. I think we both knew that as far as my contract was concerned, and the other legal nonsense surrounding it, I had a very legitimate case. Once we started talking, White told me how big this thing was getting, how I was wasting my time being anywhere else but in the UFC, and how I could be a superstar. I believed what he had to say, even if it was naive of me to do so. History is usually a very good predictor of things to come.

When the two of us emerged from the room, we had reached an agreement which would bring me back to the UFC. I would have the chance to fight against the best welterweights, which is all I sought. White and the UFC got what they wanted and were able to put the whole situation behind them. My father was not exactly happy with this decision because he wanted to put it to the UFC and see them squirm, especially knowing we could win this case There were comments made about whether our case should go forward anyway, but White said, "He shook my hand and made a deal."

I replied, "He's right; I did. A deal is a deal. I gave him my word." With those words, it was just a matter of waiting to see who I would fight next, and when.

I went home to Hawaii after the mediation, but I was immediately called back by White for UFC 56; they wanted to make a big announcement about my return during the November 19 show. It was not only me, though; the UFC was rolling out all sorts of things that night, and in many ways White's laundry list of news overshadowed the announcement of my return.

First was the announcement of Liddell vs Couture III, which most people saw coming. They followed this up with the return of former heavyweight champion Frank Mir, who had been out of the UFC since injuring himself in a motorcycle accident. From there the news grew as the new coaches for the *Ultimate Fighter* TV show, featuring Tito Ortiz vs. his longtime rival Ken Shamrock, were announced. Finally, there was me, waiting for White to announce my return to a packed house at the MGM Grand Garden Arena, and I was as nervous about this moment as I had been about any of my fights.

Standing alone in the back of the arena underneath the bleachers, I could feel the excitement in the room. Even though I had agreed to do this, I started asking myself if I'd made the right decision, and if this was what I truly wanted. The whole thing was more like a circus or some TV drama than a bunch of fights. It had not been that long since I was fighting with the UFC, but it seemed like a different place entirely. But at that point it was too late to go back.

As I waited for the announcement, I walked past Sean Sherk and Georges St-Pierre, who were about to fight as part of the event. The fans were going crazy as Ortiz and Shamrock faced off in the cage in typical pro wrestling style. Finally, White got to the last big surprise and called me out to the Octagon for my reintroduction to the UFC. The crowd erupted as I stepped into the Octagon, and I knew I had made the right choice. I was back home.

With the formalities taken care of, I settled into my front-row seat to watch St-Pierre and Sherk battle it out. In all likelihood I would be facing one of these two guys next, since both of them were on track to fight Hughes in the near future. I was not sure if I was going to jump up and get Hughes immediately or if they would make me climb my way back.

As it turned out, St-Pierre dispatched Sherk in convincing fashion. Although Sherk was fighting out of his natural weight class, St-Pierre put on an exhibition and pretty much walked right through him. Sherk was beat up, most likely had a broken nose, and was stopped in his tracks for the first time in his career. I still harbored some animosity toward Sherk because of what had happened years earlier, and on his way back to the locker room, I overheard him say to his coaches, "I couldn't hold him. The guy had Vaseline all over his legs."

The first thing that came to my mind was, *Shut the fuck up, Sherk. You just got your ass kicked. Quit crying.* I had no love for him, so I was more than willing to view his complaints as those of a guy who had lost. Little did I know I would one day sympathize with his experience.

ALMOST IMMEDIATELY AFTER ST-PIERRE WON, I learned from Jay Dee that the UFC was going to match me up against him. Hughes had defeated Joe Riggs earlier in the night, but it looked as if the plan was to have the winner of our fight take on Hughes. St-Pierre had done very well against Hughes in his first match, and after beating Sherk, he got down on his knees in the Octagon and begged the UFC to give him a title shot. He had done everything in his power to earn a shot, and he deserved one. We both knew we could beat Hughes, but the UFC was happier making us fight for the opportunity. I was just excited to be back.

When I went home to start my training, it was obvious people were much more excited about my fighting in the UFC than they had been about K-1. The sport had grown quickly in the short period of time that I had been out of the UFC. *The Ultimate Fighter* had brought in new fans, creating something of a division between people who were fans of the show and people who were longtime supporters of the UFC. Suddenly these little-known guys were television stars, while the Evan Tanners, Matt Lindland, and Pat Miletiches of the world were being less promoted and found themselves pushed to the back.

But there was no denying that the sport's popularity was accelerating. White even called me up to talk about it, and for the first time in a while, we were about to speak casually and comfortably.

"Dude," he said, "this thing is fucking out of control. It's huge! I went to SeaWorld last week, and I couldn't even walk through the crowd!" He was calling to tell me how big I was going to be, but at the same time letting me know how big he was becoming too.

That was one of the stranger things about White and the UFC— how he had made himself the star of the show. In truth, I never saw it coming when I first met the guy. Since our first meeting, there have been about three versions of him I've encountered. At the beginning, he was something of a jokester and was fun to be around, with no ego to speak of. The second version showed up when he was no longer managing fighters but running the UFC. He was still your friend, someone you liked to talk to and party with, but you knew in the back of your mind if he could get one over on you, he would. Then came the third version, the one I was now going to have to deal with for the rest of my career, the famous Dana White. The one who is always loud, outgoing, aggressive, in your face, and loves the spotlight, to the point where he made himself the face of a sport and a television show. I did not dislike the old versions of him, and on some days, he was still the white belt John Lewis was training, but after the mediation and the legal battles, it was clear things were different in every possible way.

The hype for the St-Pierre fight was bigger than any I had been involved with, and right away it was obvious that the Internet was fueling much of it. Fans were in the chat rooms talking about who would win as if it was for the title. On the whole, I was pleased that the fans received me positively; even among St-Pierre's fans, there was not a lot of negativity, just excitement. Reading what they had to say about the fight was motivation for me, and I couldn't wait to match up with St-Pierre, a guy who I liked and had tremendous respect for as a fighter.

I started training for St-Pierre as soon as I knew he would be my opponent. I had my regular guys—my brothers, Valentino, and those around Hilo—but I also brought in Josh Thomson and Josh Koscheck, since Thomson had the fluid striking similar to St-Pierre, and Koscheck the wrestling and the size. Plus, I had Lindland training with me since he had all of these things in one package—the size, the striking, and the wrestling. As it would turn out, using Lindland as my main training partner was flat out stupid because he was a southpaw, and St-Pierre was right-handed. I didn't even realize until after the fight that as good as Lindland was, he was probably the wrong guy for this opponent. Still, Lindland had so much knowledge and overall ability he just seemed like the right guy at the time.

I trained a long time for this fight since I was so pumped to be back. We were scheduled to meet on March 4, 2006, as part of UFC 58: USA vs. Canada, which was a card built around the theme of all Canadians on one side with the Americans on the other. As if this was somehow going to be a huge selling point, the rivalry between the States and their neighbor to the north. We were not the main event on the card, but the fans were really fired up, and it showed. It was almost like my first fight in Vegas all over again, and in some ways, it was overwhelming. Media requests, interviews, the UFC, legal issues, people everywhere saying to do this thing, or another thing.

The fight arrived pretty quickly with the help of the drama. I had been asked hundreds of questions beforehand, standard stuff like "Do you have a specific game plan for this fight?" or "Do you think his size will be a factor?" The standard questions every interviewer asks over and over, no matter who it is. I knew St-Pierre was a very good athlete and had a lot of power. You could see it just by looking at him, but those were not concerns. On the feet, I knew I had better hands, and on the ground, I didn't think he could hurt me. It wasn't that I was being evasive with reporters. In truth, I had no "game plan"; I was fine going where he wanted to take the fight.

The match was not as exciting as I had hoped it would be from the outset. I came out aggressive and tried to land punches to his face. I was able to do so right from the start, and landed a solid shot across his face, which resulted in heavy blood flow from his nose. From the beginning of the first round I knew I could handle him on our feet, and by the end of the round, he looked like he had been through a couple of rounds already. For much of the next two rounds there was not a lot of action. St-Pierre did a great job of getting ahold of my legs and executing successful takedowns. The only problem was he was unable to land any shots of significance when he was in my guard. I tried to use my legs for submissions, but he did a good job of fighting me off. Back and forth we went like this for rounds two and three, with me never again having a real opportunity to stand with him and actually fight in the center of the Octagon, something I desperately wanted to do. Instead, he used his size to hold me down, and hope the judges viewed his control efforts as worthy of a win.

I knew when the fight was over it was going to be close. St-Pierre landed some good kicks throughout the match, and I knew the takedowns would weigh heavily on the judges' minds even if he hadn't caused much damage from the top position. The only time he landed much was when I had the omoplata on his arm, but I was in better shape than he was from that position. It was too close to call, though, and I could understand it going either way.

When Bruce Buffer announced that I had lost by split decision, I was devastated. Yes, I knew it was close, but I thought it was a close win for me. If you just looked at the two of us, I was completely unscathed, and he was a bloody mess. Granted, that does not tell you everything about a fight, but other than the leg kicks he landed and his tiring me out, I was fine. It was just one of those things where he scored points while I scored damage, and the points were enough.

In many ways what bothered me most was not the loss itself, but how it would end the likelihood of my getting to fight Hughes again. My last loss to Machida was just a fight, a big challenge against a bigger man, but for nothing other than the pride of winning. This loss was in the cage, my first fight back after believing for sure I could not be stopped in the UFC. Now I had not only lost to their number-one-ranked contender, but I was also further away from fighting Hughes than I had been before.

Afer the fight, I hit the town and partied, not like I had won, but just because I was fine and happy to be back. St-Pierre went to the hospital. Soon thereafter, I started wondering why I had tired myself out before the third round of a fight I had trained so hard for. It should not have been that way considering how much time I'd put in. I began to question the general state of my training. Figuring out the right way to fine tune myself for fights was never more urgent to me than it was after this fight. At least with Machida and Renzo, I could understand it, since I'd had to carry the extra weight, but with St-Pierre, even though I was not down to my normal fighting weight of 155 pounds, I had at least cut it back to 170 for this match. It had not been a difficult cut, but at the same time I was going full speed during my training, or at least what I believed full speed to be.

On the other hand, it could have been something else. Maybe it was the partying during the periods when I was not training for a fight, or my poor diet in between. The two seem to go hand in hand quite often. I was still having a good time in between my fights, especially since I was back in the UFC and living the life of a young guy with the world at his fingertips. The notoriety was almost as exciting as the fighting itself. While I didn't think that the fame had affected my performance in the St-Pierre fight, maintaining the balance between these two forces was becoming more difficult.

14

OPPORTUNITY AWAITS

ABOUT FIVE MONTHS PASSED after the St-Pierre fight, and I became the odd man out in the welterweight division. It was a matter of waiting to see who the UFC wanted to pair me up against in my next fight, but at the time they hadn't offered anyone I wanted. There was no one other than Hughes, possibly Sherk, and maybe St-Pierre again, who interested me.

St-Pierre himself was scheduled to fight Hughes at UFC 63 on September 23, 2006, and yet I still didn't have an opponent. Then came news of St-Pierre injuring his groin during training less than a month before the scheduled fight. My camp let the UFC know that I would take the fight if he could not. There was no time to think it over, the fight was too close, and every day we remained ignorant of the situation was a day wasted. In all likelihood, if I didn't replace St-Pierre, the UFC would have to scramble to replace the match altogether, and considering that this was an event outside of Las Vegas, it was going to be a problem.

Since I just wanted to fight Hughes, I didn't care about the short window to train. I let them know they needed to hurry, though, because two weeks would be too short even for me. They agreed I was the answer, and I accepted the fight. A Penn vs. Hughes fight was sure to sell tickets and pay-per-views.

For this training camp, if I could even call it one, I brought no one in. It was too close to the event to even begin making calls, and so I used what I had—Rudy, DeSouza, and whoever else was around Hilo training. I was taking the fight very seriously, but it never crossed my mind that I needed more time to train. If that were the case, I never would have taken the fight.

Not long after accepting, it seemed I was flying out to California. Considering I head out to these cards almost a week in advance, I probably trained seriously for about twelve days. Knowing the UFC could call at any minute, I'd been working out, just not as hard as I would have been had Hughes been scheduled months in advance. There were still those nights where the bar was going to be open, and there was a chance I'd be in there.

I knew Hughes was going to be pumped up since he had vocalized his desire to fight me before the St-Pierre fight, and he clearly wanted to avenge his last loss. Plus, he had to be bothered by what I had repeatedly been saying since I beat him, which even he would have to admit was understandable. Anytime anyone asked me about Hughes, the belt, or anything else, I would say the same thing: "He knows who the real champion is." With the belt around his waist now, I am sure he had grown tired of hearing this. All of this said, the animosity brewing was more about buzz than anything else. He was as big a superstar as you could become in the UFC, having coached on the second season of their reality show, and having been so successful. I respected Hughes as a fighter and as a person. There are cases when guys really do not like each other, but

Hughes and I had been around this thing for a long time; we could tell the difference between bad blood and hype.

When the two of us finally entered the cage, Hughes started walking back and forth, staring at me as if I had just beat up his family. He always had this look on his face as if I had just done something so bad that a fight was the only way to fix it. I started to mirror his walk, letting him know I was not intimidated. Once he saw me following him, he seemed to get flustered and stopped. It was an odd beginning to what would be one of the strangest fights of my career.

As soon as the fight got under way, Hughes tried to take me down, which was clearly going to be his plan the entire match. He had claimed he wanted to KO someone since he was known primarily as a wrestler, and I welcomed the chance to stand the entire fight and trade punches. Initially, that is what happened—until I dropped him with a right hand. He immediately grabbed onto my leg and buried his head leaving only the back of his head so I couldn't hit him again—a good strategy for anyone who is on the ground with nowhere to go. He forced me to sprawl into a split, with his arms wrapped around my lead leg, trying to gain composure. He was able to get back to his feet, but the same thing happened again. Whenever we were face-to-face in the middle of the cage, I landed punches at will. Hughes's game just was not designed around boxing; he had a grappler's body and a grappler's skill set.

Getting the best of him, I landed a three-punch combo to his face that left him smiling, as if to say, *I can handle that.* Usually a smile like that really means, *I've got a problem.* After the smile, with its false message, I yelled, "Come on, let's go!" This was just what I wanted: the sooner it was over the better. Moments later we got caught up in another exchange, and unfortunately for both of us, my left thumb ended up in his right eye, which resulted in him asking Referee McCarthy for a time-out, which, assuming the referee noticed the mishap, is perfectly allowable.

It wasn't the break in the match that bothered me, it was the timing, because at the moment I accidentally caught him in the eye, he had left himself wide open for a big punch. I had just blocked his jab with a jab of my own, sending his right hand over my head. I was set to unload on him with my own right. So not only did the time-out give Hughes a chance to gather himself, but I missed a big chance to connect a solid punch. At the very least, he was okay, which was good because you don't want to see a fight of this magnitude end so early and by accident. When it resumed, there was about one minute remaining, and Hughes again tried to score points by getting me to the ground. Again he could not do it.

When the second round began I felt fine, and was ready for more of the same. Hughes came out and shot on my leg immediately, but I sprawled with one leg and kept myself in good position. Eventually he was able to finally get the takedown, and fall into my guard near the fence. After trying to get a better position, he remained in my full guard and then attempted some elbow strikes. I remember the first one he tried to land—it missed and ended up hitting the mat, but he threw it so hard I remember thinking, *Man, this guy is really trying to kill me!* He threw it harder than I had ever seen anyone throw an elbow, and he let out a big sound, almost like a roar, when he threw it. I thought, *He must be really pissed for all the stuff I was saying about him.* Strange to be having these thoughts in the cage, but I was. I can admit now whatever he wanted to dish out was probably well deserved.

Hughes stayed in top position for a while, and kept throwing these vicious elbows. On one attempt, he missed completely, which enabled me to slip out from underneath him to my right side and climb around to get his back. He leaned forward as I was coming around and I felt what can only be described as a click near my rib cage, as if one rib had just slipped over the top of another. Now I was on his back and wondering, *What the hell was that?* It didn't quite hurt yet, but I knew it was not normal. I knew I had to finish the fight immediately because while whatever happened was not holding me back in the moment, it was definitely a problem. Had it not happened, I would have been content to pepper his face a little, bloodying him up and just demoralizing him a bit. But I had to end it now. I threw maybe one or two punches, but was more concerned with just getting the choke in. In all my other fights, I would beat on a guy until he gave me the chance to choke him, but this time I needed it to end fast.

I went to throw my leg over his arm in order to trap it, but he spun inside toward me, which helped him avoid the choke as the round ended. The entire time I was going for these submissions, I felt no pain in my side because you can just block these things out in the heat of battle. When I stood up, though, it was a different story. I knew there was something wrong with my side, and at the same time I was completely exhausted from attempting the submissions. I could hardly walk back to the corner. This is what less than three weeks of training can do to you. Yet as tired as I was, I felt no one was going to stop me. I was going to win this. It was destiny.

I pulled myself out of the corner to start the third round, but this time it was a completely different dance. He was moving circles around me, and I was just looking for the one punch to end it. It was Hughes, though, who found his range and was landing effective shots on me from the feet for the first time in either of our fights. Literally, I was standing in front of him letting him throw kicks and punches, and most of them were landing solidly. After he landed a good number of punches, I had to drop to my knees. Hughes came to the ground with me, a bad move at most other times, considering how well he was doing, but he could sense I had little left in the tank. Even Hughes's corner was yelling at him to stand back up, but he stayed on the ground.

Eventually he was able to move from my full guard into my half guard, and he started throwing punches and elbows into my rib cage. I had to take my left hand and reach across my body to try to stop him; the pain was excruciating. My right arm was trapped above my head, so I couldn't use it, but I had to avoid the body shots. He eventually got side control, and from there tucked my left arm between his legs, securing me in the crucifix position. Hughes just kept pounding on me, but a lot of his shots were not landing as solidly as they could have.

At the same time Hughes was yelling, "Jesus Christ, John, stop the fucking fight!" Eventually McCarthy listened to him, which was the right call.

I stayed on the ground, unable to move, knowing there was something wrong. It was more than being just tired; something was wrong within the core of my body. As it turned out, a broken rib had ripped my diaphragm, severely affecting my ability to breathe and ending the fight early. I would have liked six weeks to two months to prepare for Hughes, but no amount of training could have prepared me for getting hurt. After that, my entire body just fell apart. I would later hear announcer Mike Goldberg and Randy Couture comment how it was about "cardio," but they were wrong; as the UFC doctor later confirmed, it was the broken rib which did me in. Credit to Hughes, though, for all I know, maybe he landed something that broke the rib.

After it was over, Matt Hughes got up and circled me as I sat there in the middle of the Octagon, waiting for my corner to help me up. He had avenged his loss and redeemed himself as a great champion. This time he was the one who'd go out on the town to party. I would be taken to the hospital. Dana White and the Fertittas never looked happier putting a belt around a fighter's waist than they did right then. Hughes probably got a raise after beating me, and if he did, I'm sure it didn't take a lawsuit to make it happen.

It's bad enough losing a fight; not being able to get yourself off the canvas or being forced to go to the hospital is even worse. If a fighter is clearly injured, the UFC sends in one of their doctors. If the injury is bad enough, the fighter is sent to the hospital.

There've been times when so many fighters on a card were injured that they couldn't find enough hospitals to send them to. And

I've heard crazy stories, like the one about Nick Diaz and Joe Riggs fighting in the hospital after they had just fought in the cage.

The hospital just made everything worse. The doctors wouldn't listen to me when I told them what was wrong, and from the second I got there, I wanted out. When I finally got back to the hotel, I was incredibly upset. First I'd lost to a guy I should have beaten, and then I had to go to the hospital. Someone offered me a cheeseburger, and I refused it. If you know me well, refusing a cheeseburger is a sign I'm in a really bad place. This was clearly the worst night of my life.

Eventually, I had an MRI and they discovered two cracked ribs, and other problems. At the very least, I was going to have a lot of time to recover, but truth was, I had no idea what I was recovering *for*. I had just lost to the top two guys in the welterweight division, and there was no other opponent out there who made sense for me.

FOR THE FIRST TIME IN YEARS, I had no idea what I was going to do. All I could think was that there was no real reason to keep fighting. Even though I loved it, and I felt like I was still on top of my game, I didn't want to be the type of fighter who just hangs on, fighting a bunch of nobodies just to get a paycheck. I was still in serious pain and it hurt when I coughed, which prevented me from having a good time with my friends or considering doing any type of real training.

In order to get myself out of my own head, I decided to corner Tony DeSouza for his fight with Dustin Hazelett at the Seminole Hard Rock Hotel in South Florida on October 10, 2006. I arrived a few days early because the fight was part of the Ortiz vs. Shamrock card; as the final fight between coaches from the reality show, I wanted to avoid the crowds. It seemed as if these guys, who I'd known for a long time, were becoming bigger stars while I was just fading away. As I walked around, seeing the UFC employees and the other fighters on the card, I felt like I didn't belong. I had no idea who half of the guys on the card were, and the entire thing just seemed strange.

While I'd been taking on these welterweights, the UFC had decided to bring back the lightweight division, but I was too preoccupied with having lost a chance to recapture the welterweight belt to pay attention to this. The lightweight title was vacant, however, and it seemed the UFC was trying to make Sherk, who was scheduled to fight Kenny Florian for the title in just a couple of days, the champion. I had wanted to fight Sherk, but he wasn't someone I needed to fight, and Florian was not even on my radar.

I was hanging out with DeSouza in one of the UFC offices when Dana White came in and saw me. He smiled and said, "Hey, congratulations!"

"For what?"

"Your brother didn't tell you?" asked White.

"I was on the plane all day, and I haven't spoken with him," I said.

"You got your wish, buddy. You're the new coach," White informed me.

"Coach for what?"

"*The Ultimate Fighter!*" he replied.

"Really?"

White laughed. "And guess who the other coach is."

I replied, "I have no idea. Who?" For the life of me, I couldn't think who it could be.

"Jens Pulver."

"What? Who said this? What's going on here?"

White looked like he was having the best time telling me this. "I can't believe your brother didn't tell you. Well, this is your chance, kid. This is the fight you want, but you have to go to lightweight."

"Don't worry about that, I'll start cutting right now." And I needed to. Ever since the injury, I'd weighed about 180 pounds and was a fat piece of waste. Fighters like me add weight very quickly when not training.

So there I was, stewing about having no idea what I was going to do, and out of nowhere I get the opportunity to kick the ass of the person whose ass I wanted to kick more than anyone else's on the planet. Talk about life being unpredictable. I was finally going to fight Pulver, and maybe even win back some self-respect like all these other coaches on the reality show had done. It was a perfect example of why you should never dwell on the negative, because something positive could be waiting right around the corner. My wish had been granted.

IN LATE JANUARY OF 2007, I went out to Las Vegas to start recording season five of *The Ultimate Fighter,* and at the same time I started to prepare myself mentally for a fight with Jens Pulver. I knew what the show was all about, and I expected it to be pretty easy. After all, how hard could it be to teach guys how to fight? It was something I'd been doing for a long time since I've always liked sharing what I know. My plan was to just get through this thing, fight Jens, and then figure out what to do next.

The interesting thing about season five was how the UFC had two lightweights, me and Pulver, as coaches, and all the contestants on the show were lightweights as well. Almost four years had passed since the UFC's last lightweight fight, and in that time I had fought guys from lightweight to heavyweight. Truth was, I had no real desire to go back to lightweight, but the chance to fight Pulver was too big an opportunity—even more of an enticement than being on the show.

As was always the case on the show, the coach could bring his team to help train the contestants. Reagan, Rudy, and DeSouza all joined me, so at the very least these guys were going to get some first-class jujitsu training. It was an exciting time for all of us; even Reagan, who usually does a great job of keeping his emotions in check, was excited. We all learned a thing or two about television, especially how the producers of the show create conflict and resolution just through careful editing. It's called reality television, but in many ways, it was more scripted than real. The only real thing taking place was my desire to beat Pulver.

The UFC hyped the show by building up the rematch between the two of us, which would take place when the season ended. The first thing the viewing audience witnessed was the two of us picking teams. It was quite the telling moment, and one that worked in my favor, but in a lot of ways it was a total accident.

Dana White and the producers placed all the contestants in a large group inside the UFC training center where they film the fighting and training. Jens and I stood in the room, waiting to pick fighters for our respective teams. The contestants were all standing together in one large group, awaiting selection. The first thing I did, I looked over at some of the guys and asked, "If any of you here know for a complete fact that you want to be on my team and give me one hundred percent, and want nothing to do with Jens Pulver's team, raise your hand."

Most of the guys in the group raised their hands, and it became an extremely uncomfortable situation. It made Pulver look bad. The strange part was I wasn't looking to embarrass him on TV. I was simply looking for one, maybe two guys who really did want to train with me and work their tails off in order to be the best. I never thought the majority of the guys were going to raise their hands, and probably only did it because I had been in the UFC limelight more recently than Pulver. The whole episode was sort of like a happy accident, but as much as I didn't care for Pulver, doing it didn't make me feel good. Right off the bat, I'd raised the tension between us.

After White stepped in and resolved the dispute about which fighters would go to which camp, we started picking one at a time. My first pick was Gray Maynard, a wrestler from Michigan State who I already knew. When Charuto was going to fight Frank Trigg at an earlier UFC, I went looking for top-notch wrestlers who were interested in MMA, and ended up finding Maynard. He came out to Hawaii and ended up training more with me than he did Charuto, so I knew how good his wrestling background was. However, I didn't think Maynard was the best fighter of the group. I took him out of loyalty and friendship. In my heart, I knew Nate Diaz, younger brother of MMA fighter Nick Diaz and a student of Cesar Gracie in Northern California, was the most talented guy on the show. Winning was important to me, but friendship came first. Pulver picked Diaz.

From the moment the show started, I was really into it, and it was harder than I had expected. At first, I figured it would be an easy thing to train guys, watch them improve, and hope for the best. This was not the case. I got very emotionally involved, and I really wanted to win this thing. Training the guys on my team mattered because it was a reflection of who I was and what I could do. I wanted to win the show and turn the tide in my direction before my match with Pulver, so when guys were slacking off or not listening to me, they had to be dealt with. No one more than Andy Wang, a Taiwanese-born Brazilian jujitsu fighter who resided in Los Angeles.

Wang was a perfect example of what not to do when you're training to be a fighter as opposed to wanting to be a star on television. He had fought a few times in Hawaii, and although he was not tremendously successful, he was skilled in BJJ. He worked as hard as the rest of the guys, but when it came time for him to fight against Brandon Melendez from Pulver's team, everything changed.

Melendez was more of a striker, someone who wanted to stand on his feet, and Wang clearly was more skilled on the ground. We told him to take this guy down, and either finish him with punches or go for the submission. When the fight started, he did everything but what we told him to. He decided to stand in front of Melendez and try to punch it out with him. Clearly a poor strategy, but what bothered me more was how he had no interest in listening to me.

What in the world did he want to be on my team for if he intended to stand there and punch? Pulver was the striker; why did he raise his hand? Ignoring us as we shouted at him to take his opponent down, Wang lost to Melendez. After the fight, he apologized over and over, saying he should have listened and the next time he would take his guy down and not screw us over. We gave him another chance, figuring he wouldn't make the same mistake twice.

Things always change, though, when the boss is around, and when White and the show's producers came into the gym, Wang would immediately start telling them what they wanted to hear, things like "I did that for you guys!" and "I want to put on a show for the fans" and "If that's what you guys want, I'll do it!" He wasn't doing this quietly when none of us were within earshot around either; he did it right in front of us, and he didn't seem to care!

I was fed up with his act and told him he was off the team, that none of us wanted him around anymore. Wang was the first fighter to be kicked off *The Ultimate Fighter* by the coaches, and maybe he'll be the last. All I know is the other guys on the team wanted to win, and myself, and the other coaches, we really cared about their success and worked hard to make them better. Of course, this did not stop the hate mail from coming in, as many of his fans, especially a few who were of Chinese descent, were upset that I kicked the only Chinese fighter ever off the show. It was just amazing to read the feedback from his defenders, and the assumptions people make from watching a reality television show. All I can say is, reality television is only a notch more real than the movies.

The rest of the guys trained hard, and even though both of the finalists came from Pulver's camp, I was happy with the way my team trained and learned. At the same time I was becoming more and more frustrated with Pulver. Being around him all the time was just too strange an experience for me. Wrestlers like Pulver were used to fighting their best friends just to be the champion.

Whether you want to win a collegiate championship or an Olympic gold medal, you must beat your teammates. All top-level wrestlers I have ever worked with operate in this way. This was very different from the martial arts, and no matter how hard I tried, it felt foreign. For Pulver, it was easy to be around me, act friendly, then go out there and try to break my nose. He's an easy guy to like, and I knew becoming his friend would only make things harder when it came time to fight him.

DURING THE LEAD-UP TO MY FIGHT with Pulver, I became more introspective, seeing my place in life differently than I had before. Never before had I been active in politics, concerned about social injustices, or anything even remotely like that. The only stand I had ever taken when it came to right and wrong was defending someone who had been picked on, or fighting the person I believed was the bully of the bunch. When it came to political issues, though, that was not really my thing. Whatever the reason, my mind started pulling me in a different direction. I was nearly twenty-eight years old when I started to have feelings about Hawaii, about how I was being viewed as a Hawaiian, and the people of Hawaii in general. It was not the first time I thought about who I was, where I came from, or what I could do for others, but it all started to crystallize inside my head in a different way.

I am fully Hawaiian, having been born in Hawaii, but in truth, I am not of completely Hawaiian blood. My mother's ancestry is Hawaiian but also Korean, and my father is what we Hawaiians call haole, which for the most part means foreigner but normally just means white. While I was born and raised in Hawaii, my roots do not run as deep as the original Hawaiians. After fighting St-Pierre, I started to question who I was, but even more, to wonder what I could do for Hawaii.

Over 70 percent of the prison population of Hawaii is native Hawaiian, who represent less than 30 percent of the people. No

Hawaiian people are represented on television in a significant way, and it is equally rare to see a musician, actor, or celebrity representing the state. Hawaiians rarely see their own kind becoming famous, and I'd noticed that whether I was in downtown Hilo, on Maui, or in Honolulu, I wasn't seeing many pure Hawaiians at all, which really left me wondering, *Where have they all gone?* I thought about high school, and how I had to choose between Spanish and Japanese for my language elective. Why not Hawaiian? There was a gradual buildup of such thoughts inside my head, leading me to something.

There is an area of Hawaii on the Big Island called Kohala, located in the northwest, and I had never spent any meaningful time there. My knowledge of the area was limited, to say the least, but I started to wonder, *Maybe that's where the Hawaiians are?* One day Rudy and I decided to take a ride up there to check it out, maybe see if the Hawaiians really were there since they didn't seem to be anywhere else. Turned out that, not only were the "real Hawaiians" missing from Kohala as well, but the place was completely filled with tourists! For some reason, this bothered me. When I arrived home that night I was lying in my bed trying to get some sleep, but I couldn't do it. I kept thinking about Hawaii's history, where the people went, and how there could be such sadness among so many people in such a wonderful place. I got out of bed and started searching the Internet for information about Hawaii and its native people. From that point on, I knew I was going to do more.

After going over it many times in my head, I decided to change my entrance song for my fight against Pulver. This was something I'd experimented with when I'd fought Hughes the second time, walking out to a song called "Hawaii '78," which is the year of my birth. Against Pulver, I also came out to that song but added another titled "E Ala Ē," also Hawaiian, and sung by an artist named Israel Kamakawiwo'ole. Both of these songs are rather mellow and seem to contrast with the mood surrounding fights, but they have profound meanings that serve a motivational purpose; they are songs about the Hawaiian people.

In addition to the music, I took another, more drastic step, deciding to print the words *Hawaiian Unity* on the front of the shirt I would wear as I walked out against Pulver. It was not a decision I took lightly, and I only came to it after a lot of discussion with my parents, especially with my mother, who was concerned that making a statement like this would reflect negatively on me. I finally decided I was going to wear it, regardless of the backlash. I wanted to be someone Hawaiians could be proud of, and look upon as their own. If I could do my small part to put a smile on the face of a few people back home, it would be worth it. More worth it than just throwing another sponsor across my chest, or coming out to heavy-metal music. It was the least I could do.

WHEN I STARTED TRAINING FOR PULVER, I knew something had to be different, so I reached out to Tony Aponte, a nutritionist and conditioning coach living in the Seattle area. I had met him years before through a friend, and at that time Aponte volunteered to help me. It had taken a long time, but I was now finally willing to listen.

I called him and told him straight up, "I am sick and tired of being sick and tired. I am losing to guys I should be destroying, and I need to make a change." I knew the problem was not the amount I was training, and as far as sparring and grappling went, that was all I did. Something was not adding up for me like it was for other guys. I had spent years trying to define and refine the way I trained, from inventing my own methods, to working with CrossFit—everything others had tried, I tried. Nothing seemed to work. I knew on some level that having to fight heavier opponents made me keep some of the cardio work on the side, but it had to be something else. This was my first lightweight fight in years, and I was finally going to turn over my conditioning to a professional.

The first thing Aponte told me was I had to change my lifestyle. I knew he was right. It was time to cut out all of the bad foods, especially the fast food, but it was more than that. It was not enough to make weight and train like an animal. I had to look at food like fuel, and like a car, the higher the grade, the better the machine would run. Aponte promised me that losing the weight and getting back down to 155 pounds after years of being at least 170 was not going to be a problem, and he was right. Within a couple of weeks of working alongside him in Hawaii, I could already see and feel the changes in my body. I started looking more like I did in my late teenage years and early twenties than I had the last couple of years. I felt much stronger as well. It was as if I didn't know what I had lost until I started to get some of it back. All of this was coming from just the nutrition part of it, not the weight or circuit training, or cardio exercises.

In addition to Aponte, I connected with Jason Parillo, a boxing trainer from Orange County. I had met him years earlier, sometime before the Gomi fight, and we had worked out a little at the time. From everything I had heard, he could improve the boxing aspect of my game, which is exactly what I would need against Pulver. At the very least, he could analyze Pulver's game and help me break it down. Parillo came out to Hilo, and though he was a little shy at first, he soon fell right in with everyone else.

Between Aponte, Parillo, and the rest of my team, my training camp was great, and I really sensed everything coming together. This was especially true as I saw the weight coming off. I started to look like a guy who fought professionally, and I was counting the days until June 23, 2007, when Pulver and I would fight again.

When my team arrived in Las Vegas, we knew there was going to be a media circus, so instead of staying at the Palms Casino Hotel, where the event was taking place, we decided to find a place away from the action. I felt there were too many crazy elements that were out of my control and could mess up my head, and I didn't want to deal with them.

By the time fight night actually arrived, I was focused. There was a lot going on in my head before I ever entered the cage. With the words *Hawaiian Unity* on my shirt and my new entrance music, I was moments away from avenging what I believed was the biggest loss of my life.

Once the referee called us to fight, the jitters went away. I was no longer worried about what Pulver could do to me and just focused on hurting him. I came out and landed some punches, sending him into the fence with a big right hand to the face, followed with uppercuts. Soon after that, I shot on his legs, picked him up, and dumped him onto his back, where I landed in his half guard. He was unable to do much from the start of the fight, and I was really just trying to make him pay a little for past wrongs. While it is important to finish fights early because you never know what's going to happen, part of me really did want to work him over and land a lot of shots.

He was able to get off the mat, but again I put him on his butt. The second time I took him down, we were in the center of the cage, and I quickly transitioned into the mount position, attempting to secure an arm bar. It was no joke, I was going to get that arm of his, and what I did with it then we would have to wait and see.

I tried a couple of submissions, but he managed to escape, and the round ended with both of us on our feet with neither guy landing any serious blows. When I went to my corner, I knew I was dominating him, and for the first time in a while, I was not even remotely tired. Coming out for the second round, I was again able to do what I wanted. The first round had been almost like a cat playing with a ball of string, and I expected more of the same. Pulver came out swinging and missed with everything. I swept him off his feet for the third time, and was again in his half guard. His frustration was evident as I stayed in half guard and continued to hit him in the face and body. From the side, I worked my way to the mount one more time, flattened out his body with my legs, and forced him to turn over. Once on top, I started throwing punches repeatedly into his face, and at the same time I was telling myself this was for all the stuff he'd said about me over the years. He was in an awful position and had no choice but to roll over and give up his back. I continued dropping elbows and punches with the intent of making him pay.

Instead of finishing him immediately, I took some time to soak it in. Near the end of the second round, I did my signature move of trapping his arm with my leg as I formed a body triangle around his torso, and then choked him out just like I had done to so many other fighters before. I probably held on a second or two longer than I needed to just to send the message home that this was how it should have been years ago.

Once the fight was over, the two of us were on our knees, looking at each other, and then we just hugged. I know he was upset he had lost, and I was happy I had won, but it was more than that. It was about the years of us going back and forth, both having left the company, having come back around the same time, and just putting this whole saga to rest. Truth is, Pulver and I wanted to like each other; he even stated that he would love to train with me, which he's always welcome to do. But just like in Hilo, sometimes you fight a friend, but when it's over, it's over. You pick the guy up and help him walk away. With Jens and me, our feud was over. He got me once, and I got him back. There was nothing left between us.

UFC commentator Joe Rogan brought me to the center of the Octagon after the fight so I could walk him through what just happened and tell the fans how I was feeling. My mind was all over the place, having just avenged a loss and having this huge weight lifted off my shoulders. When Rogan asked me how I was feeling, I pretty much blew him off, and not because it was Rogan, but because in the moment I wanted to take something back from the UFC. Instead of announcing who I wanted to fight next and helping the UFC promote the division, I said, "If you want to know how BJ Penn is feeling right now, go to BJPenn.com."

The whole thing probably seemed weird to a lot of viewers and fans, but in my heightened emotional state, I decided to do it. Before the fight, I knew I was going to say something, and I'd even warned White to pay attention to my postfight interview. In retrospect, the only thing I regret is how I failed to thank the fans who came to the fight, watched on television, and supported me. I owe them everything I have achieved, but in that moment I was only thinking about taking something back from the UFC—for once.

White made this an issue after the fight. He approached me and said, "You fucked your fans! You should have told them who you wanted to fight!" He was right about one thing—I had not treated the fans the right way by not thanking them, but as for announcing who I wanted to fight, that was only about the UFC.

In all the time I've been around the UFC, I've noticed their assumption that fighters should be grateful to them for their opportunities. While I'm always thankful for the chances I have been given, I feel strongly I earned my way. I shouldn't have to view my opportunities as a favor I need to pay back, or something I constantly have to be thankful for. While a fighter has to be talented and successful to earn the opportunities he gets, the UFC's matchmaking is not based on rankings, statistics, or who deserves a title shot. It's based on how much money a match will generate for the UFC. Nothing more, and nothing less.

Who fights who is based on whether they can market the fight to a large audience, and generate cash flow, not on who really deserves a specific opportunity. I have no idea whether I was the best in the world when I entered the UFC. It is their company, and they can do with it what they want, but let's not act like there's some merit system in place which allows fighters to get to the top like there is in all of the other major sports.

The bottom line is there is no independent ranking system which clarifies who is the best and which fighters have earned the opportunity to fight the top guys. It should not be about your looks, what language you speak, where you live, the color of your skin, your personality, or any of these things. It should be about your abilities inside the cage, and within the world of mixed martial arts. For a lot of guys now, it seems the best shot they have at becoming a UFC champion is to join *The Ultimate Fighter* and work their way up the ranks. If the UFC can market you, build you, and have you play their game, you will get your shot faster. It doesn't matter if there are ten other guys in your weight class who can walk all over you. It's about you signing up with them and allowing them to think they're doing you a favor.

15

THE REAL
CHAMP

PRIOR TO MY SECOND FIGHT with Pulver, Sherk had
easily handled Kenny Florian to win the lightweight belt.
Sherk was definitely one of the top guys at the time, but
Florian was not yet ready to handle the big-time atmosphere of a
title fight. Ironically, this loss was probably the best thing that ever
happened to him since this loss would motivate him to become a
top guy.

It was a no-brainer I wanted a piece of Sherk and a chance to
get the belt. From my perspective, it was going to be one of two
things: three strikes and I'm out, or third time's a charm. I was
counting on the second scenario. Before I would have my chance,
Sherk was scheduled to defend his belt against the Brazilian jujitsu
fighter Hermes Franca, who was a very tough opponent for anyone

in the division. I was set up to face the winner of their fight, which took place in July of 2007.

The fight between the two of them was impressive, as Sherk was able to grind out the victory even after taking some vicious knees to the face. Anyone who watched the fight had to be impressed with Sherk's ability to overcome these big blows, over and over. There seemed to be a special reason for this, though.

As rules go, UFC fighters undergo drug testing after all fights, and in a championship bout they must do so before as well. After the fight, both Sherk, known as "The Muscle Shark," and Franca were caught using anabolic steroids by the California State Athletic Commission (CSAC). Franca's test revealed he'd used drostanolone, which is often used by runners and bodybuilders, while Sherk was caught using nandrolone, a steroid used by many well-known baseball and football players. Franca stepped up to the plate and admitted having turned to steroids to deal with a late training injury, claiming he needed the money from the fight and had no choice. His excuse may have been legitimate to himself, but he was still cheating. It is unfortunate some fighters feel pressured to cheat because they don't have enough money to sustain their training, or even put food on the table for their families. No one wants to hear it, but it's still cheating. No excuse is valid.

On the other hand, there was Sherk, who vehemently denied ever having used steriods. He went as far as hiring big-name lawyers, submitted to polygraph tests, and even had Dana White defend his honesty. Anything and everything to prove he did not knowingly take steroids. Unfortunately, there was little he could do to clear his name. This situation led to the UFC setting up an interim title fight between me and Joe Stevenson, the winner of season two of *The Ultimte Fighter,* until Sherk's case was decided.

Stevenson was a well-rounded and respected fighter, a guy who had been competing professionally since he was sixteen. In a lot of ways, his skill set was a near replica of mine, in that he was a jujitsu fighter first, who had a lot of power, but could also stand there and trade punches. The fight was scheduled to take place on January 19, 2008, in Newcastle, England, which was to be the first time I had competed in Europe.

I was excited to fight for the title again, even though Europe was a long way from Hawaii. Once I got there, though, I really came to love Newcastle. It was my kind of town on nearly every level. The people were incredibly nice, enthusiastic about MMA, many of them knew who I was, and of course, it was a party town, which I like. I am always in favor of a place that likes to have a good time and tries to make it welcoming for those who visit. Even though I was not going to be able to hang out and have fun, the vibe was right up my alley.

Getting to Newcastle took some time, though, and I'm referring to the days leading up to the fight. One would think a fighter would keep his mouth closed after being caught cheating, but not Sherk. From the day I was scheduled to fight Stevenson, he commented that our match was not a real title fight, and the only way to get the title was to beat him. Initially it was understandable to view the fight that way since it was set up as a fight for the "interim" belt, but later on, after Sherk lost his drug case, the *interim* was removed. The winner of this fight would be the only UFC lightweight champion.

Even though I thought Sherk was ridiculous to suggest he was still somehow the champion, it was understandable from his perspective. Putting aside his probable belief that he hadn't been cheating, or at least his ability to convince himself he had not, the UFC was publicly supporting him. White defended Sherk in the press countless times, even questioning how the California State Athletic Commission had handled the entire thing. However, I always looked at it as White defending the UFC from criticism, not necessarily Sherk or the sport.

As the fight neared, Stevenson and I did media for it; the UFC set up their media interviews via phone since I was basically training in Hilo. The whole steroid thing was not going away because our fight was so closely connected to it in time. I was trying to focus only on Stevenson, but even when the two of us spoke with the media, the question always came up about what we thought about Sherk and Franca being caught. On one particular occasion, I remember being asked my feelings on the matter, and then the reporter asked Stevenson too. I had no problem stating what I believed. I had been around, knew what went on, and believed the test results.

When it was time for Stevenn to respond, he didn't come right out and say, "Steroids are bad. If you do them you should pay a price." He hesitated and gave a roundabout answer, something about him being upset that people were questioning if our fight was a true title match. He probably didn't want to drag the UFC, or himself, through the steroid mud, especially knowing the UFC just wanted it to go away. It was more of a "politically correct" answer than anything else, but it surprised me he did not condemn steroid use outright, as any true athlete should. Again, I was seemingly alone in standing up for keeping drugs out of MMA.

By the time I made it over to England, I knew in my heart there was no way I was going to be denied again. Wearing the black belt RVCA shorts I'd designed with RVCA owner P. M. Tenore, I entered the Octagon prepared to be the second man to capture two different belts in the UFC.

Right from the opening bell, I attacked Stevenson the same way I'd attacked Uno when I KO'd him in the first few seconds of our fight. I immediately had him on the ground and was in control the entire fight. I figured if I came out and broke his will early, he would quit. I controlled Stevenson from top position, switching in and out of half guard and full mount for most of the first round. A lot of the time I had him pressed up against the cage, which actually prevented me from getting control of his back for a submission, but I was still able to inflict a lot of damage. He fought well from the bottom position, trying to slow me down by landing body shots, but it was not enough to turn the tide.

The most important moment of the first round, and quite possibly of the fight, was when I landed an elbow across his forehead with about one minute remaining. The blow cut him open in the dead center of his forehead, and he started bleeding like a fountain. From the moment the cut was opened, there was blood everywhere—on his head, my arms, all over the mat, and it didn't stop. Fortunately for Stevenson, he was able to escape the round and get checked by the doctors before the second round began.

The doctors gave Stevenson the green light to continue fighting, even though the blood was flowing even before we touched gloves to start the next round. The good thing for Stevenson was that because the cut was perfectly placed down the middle of his forehead, the blood was not going into his eyes too much, and mostly streamed down his nose. Knowing he was at risk of having the fight stopped, he came out like a raging bull, hoping to land a big punch that could swing the bout into his favor. I weathered the storm, brushing off a big elbow and following up with a few solid punches of my own. One or two landed cleanly, and I felt him buckle from a straight left. Eventually, I was able to take him down again, and this time I got control of him from the mount position and landed some shots to his face, which forced him to turn over and give up his back.

Throughout my career, this scenario has played out so many times for me, that it was just a matter of time before I secured the choke. Stevenson tapped out with little time remaining in the second round, and for the second time in my life, I had won a UFC championship belt with my signature move.

Oddly, even with all the new conditioning methods I had taken on, I still found myself tiring at the end of the round. Maybe it was the time difference, the weight cut, the mental pressure I had put on myself leading up to the fight, or just one of those days. I was able to push through and win the fight, but I was very surprised, and somewhat frustrated by the experience. As hard as I'd worked, I had still not perfected my training.

Regardless of what happened in the cage, I was extremely happy to have captured something that had evaded me for such a long time. For many years, I didn't think the UFC was ever going to bring the lightweight division back, and I'd really wondered if I'd missed my chance. Lucky for me, they brought it back at the prime of my career. I remember thinking to myself early on how I wanted to come in, win the belt, and leave. I envisioned a period of my life where I would be sitting back in Hilo inside my own school, teaching people how to fight, with the belt hanging on the wall. Maybe someone would walk in for a meeting, notice it, and say, "You won that?"

I would respond, "Oh, yeah, that thing. That was a long time ago. So, you want to learn martial arts?" What I thought would become a conversation piece had become the center of my life.

WINNING THE BELT MEANT IT WAS only a matter of time until I had to defend my title against Sherk. Him referring to himself as the true champion, and the UFC having him do commentary on the Stevenson fight, just made me sick. For months and months after he won the title, Sherk was in the news, with White promoting him as a guy who could take out world-class boxers like Floyd Mayweather and holding him up as an example of what a great MMA fighter looks like. Don't get me wrong, Sherk was certainly a really good fighter, but even after he'd been caught cheating, it seemed he was still being defended on all sides. With every passing day, I could find more ways to motivate myself for our impending fight.

As the fight approached, the two of us were scheduled to do media interviews, and on one occasion, I remember White was in on the call. The interviewer was asking us about the fight, and our expectations, but all I could think about was that this guy was caught cheating. It was eating away at me to think how this issue was not even part of the conversation, and everyone just wanted to talk about the fight itself. I didn't understand how everyone could ignore the elephant in the room.

I jumped all over Sherk and asked him flat out if he was using growth hormone, blood doping, or taking anabolic steroids. I wanted to keep the pressure on him just like I had planned to during our fight. All he could do was deny it, speak ahout how the CSAC reduced his suspension, and how he was the underdog. When he wasn't being pressed about steroids, he was comfortable saying he was the real champ, and it was his belt. But as soon as steroids came up, he would speak about how no one expected him to win, laughing a little and brushing aside my comments.

It would have been easy for me to just say nothing and go on training. Most of the other fighters didn't want to talk about the juicing, but if no one ever spoke about it, how would anything change? I'd been training every day for years, waking up in pain, sacrificing for this sport, and trying to set an example for others about how you should carry yourself as an athlete.

For years, I have had people approach me and tell me I should do this steroid and that steroid, but I've never even considered it. Yet you'd be surprised how many guys do think it is a legitimate choice—what with managers, trainers, fighters, and fans saying, "Everyone does it, it's no big deal," which is completely ridiculous. When I see Chuck Liddell, Nick Diaz, Nate Diaz, Kenny Florian, Anderson Silva, Kendall Grove, and a lot of other guys fight, I think to myself, *Now, these are people who have respect for themselves, and respect for the sport.*

Those who are in this business know what's up, but all we can do is focus on ourselves. It's not our job to start calling guys out, but let's not pretend steroid use exists in noncontact sports like golf but not in MMA. If I had to guess, I'd say a majority have cheated, or currently do. Throughout my career, though people have questioned my work ethic and stamina, few have implied I was an easy target for drug use. It has never been an option, and it will never be one.

There will always be cheaters, and most of them will continue not to get caught. As quickly as scientists, medical professionals, and governing bodies come up with ways to detect steroid use, performance-enhancing drugs (PED), blood doping, erythropoietin (EPO), and anything else fighters are using to excel, just as quickly will those who are supplying them find ways to get around it. The cheaters are always ahead of those who are trying to do the policing, and it will always be that way.

The UFC usually conducts drug tests before and after fighters step in the cage, usually on the day of a fight. I do not think it was a coincidence that two guys, Sherk and Franca, both tested by the state of California *the day before,* as opposed to the day of, ended up failing. Had the tests been administered the day of, which is normally the case, I would be willing to bet large sums of cash that they would both have passed. Their testosterone levels, like so many other guys', would be extremely high, but just short of crossing the line between legitimate and illegal. If Sherk had never cheated at all, then his testosterone levels would always be the same. If the levels are high naturally, then they should remain high. If they're low, then they'd always be low. They shouldn't fluctuate, and his seemed to. A fighter's particular level should always remain the same.

All I can do is show up and try to take the cheaters down one at a time, to show the purists, and those who believe in doing the right thing, that you don't have to cheat to win. If you're taking drugs to enhance your performance, I think you're a coward, a person of low moral character, and this is what went through my mind as I prepared for Sherk.

Over the years, there have been fighters who I have looked up to as champions, heroes, but then I would hear about suspected drug use, and it made me sick. These days, I may shake their hands and say hello, but the truth is, I don't respect them as fighters or as people. You might be a nice guy, someone who other people like to be around, but just because you are a kind and warm person with a smile on your face does not make you honest.

Sometimes it is not all about winning and losing, but about how you have conducted yourself in this sport. Liddell was a great champion, and even though he has recently taken his lumps as younger guys have come up, I know he wouldn't cheat just to maintain his legacy. He is one of the few guys I look at and think, *Now, there's a real champion.*

Needless to say, the fight with Sherk was huge. This would be the first time I was actually fighting to keep a belt I'd already won. It was also the biggest stage I had ever been on. In Japan, I'd fought in front of larger crowds, and in my return fights the crowds were just as large, but UFC 84 was to be my first headlined Las Vegas event after all the years I had been with the organization. There was as much hype and discord leading up to the fight as there had been for all of my other fights combined.

Even with all the excitement surrounding the fight, nothing seemed to faze me. I was in a really good place mentally and physically, which was a big thing for me at the time, after stumbling upon my return. I felt I was in the best shape of my life. I had worked for weeks on defending his takedowns, on wrestling, and on my ground-and-pound game, figuring this is where the fight was going to take place, but regardless of how it ended, I was confident that Sherk was not going to be able to stop me. After the St-Pierre and Hughes losses, I told myself I needed to take advantage of the opportunities that were right in front of me. I was dedicated to becoming and remaining a champion, and everything began again with this fight. I knew when this fight was over, questions about how hard I trained would finally be put to rest.

And so on May 24, 2008, I was back at the MGM Grand Garden Arena to prove to White, Cook, Sherk, and everyone else who questioned where I was in my life that I was not going away any time soon.

Walking out to the cage, I again had the music of my people behind me, and for the first time I was wearing the UFC belt around my waist. But the belt was not even relevant at this point, and I'm not sure if it ever is once you decide to fight someone. The belt represents something to the fans and the media, but to me it's just a symbol. Countless guys have held belts, some for a day, others for years, in the end it's only a symbol—that's something the UFC was actually right about. If Sherk and I had fought in the street that night, it would have had the same meaning as fighting inside the cage.

Right from the start, I came out throwing punches, utilizing my jab the entire time, and connecting easily. Throughout the first round I was a little bit hesitant, as I waited for Sherk to shoot at my legs and take me down, but for some reason this never happened. Once I realized he wanted to stand there and punch with me, I sat back, relaxed my shoulders, and worked on picking him apart.

Sherk remained content taking my jabs and trying to throw counterpunches, mostly a big left hook that never seemed to land. Having a couple inches in height and arm length on him allowed me to get in and out without him connecting with any big shots. From time to time, he would land some decent leg kicks, but they weren't effective in slowing me down. For the entire first round, I just kept up with the combinations, landing more than he did, and peppering his face a little. When the first round came to an end, I was feeling great, better than I had felt at the end of the Stevenson fight, and good enough to not need to sit down between rounds.

The second round was more of the same, with me landing jabs, hooks, and occasional uppercuts, and him infrequently landing some decent shots. I was surprised he was not going for the takedowns, even though he had said before the fight he was going to show people he knew how to box in addition to wrestle. As a fighter, you never believe that stuff. When a wrestler says he's going to box, it usually means he's going to wrestle, but Sherk had something to prove. I knew he had good boxing skills, but in no way did I believe that this was how he wanted the fight to go. I was not about to stop him, though; if he wanted to box and allow me to use my reach to hurt him, so be it. Round two was a near replica of the first, but now Sherk was bleeding on both sides of his face. I had landed my jab consistently on his right eye and started hitting his left as well. If things kept going this way, and he kept bleeding, there was always the chance that the referee, Yamasaki, would stop it.

Once again, I came out for round three feeling as good as I ever had this late in the fight, and things did not change at all. Sherk stuck with this plan of keeping the fight on the feet, sprinkling in a few good kicks, but again not landing any real good body or head shots. Throughout the round, I waited for him to try to take me down, but he only made one attempt, which I stopped. After he was unable to even get his hands on me too solidly, I stepped up the pressure. His effort to get me down was in some sense a way of him saying he no longer wanted to stand, but it was too late for that. I could sense he was getting weaker, slower, and more frustrated. But even though I was dominating, Sherk had a lot of weapons. A fight could end with one punch at any moment, and I continued to look for ways to finish him off. Once you stop attacking, that is when you get caught and lose.

With Sherk slowing down and the third round coming to a close, I was looking for a chance to finish him with one big shot. With ten seconds remaining, I heard the ringside official clap the two wood blocks together, signifying the final seconds. As soon as I heard that sound, I rushed into him, throwing a left cross and a right uppercut, both of which connected. The punches sent him backward into the fence, and I chased him down and followed up with a left knee that connected with his head as he was hunched over. Then I just threw as many punches as I could as the bell sounded.

I walked away thinking he'd been saved by the bell, but then I looked back at him sitting on the floor. I could see from the look in his eyes that there was no chance he was getting up from that, and he promptly collapsed onto his butt. That's when Yamasaki stepped in and officially called the fight. It was over in three rounds, and I had for the first time in my career defended the UFC title, leaving no doubt who the world's best lightweight really was. It had taken more than six years, but I finally felt I had proven myself.

FOR THE LONGEST TIME I WOULD have conversations with White about getting a chance to fight the best guys. Literally, every time we spoke I would tell him of my desire to fight champions, legends, the guys who were the best of the best, but his response was as predictable as my comments to him. "BJ, just stay at one fifty-five and clear out the lightweight division. Then we can talk about everything else."

Having defeated Pulver, Stevenson, and Sherk all in convincing fashion, I had done what he requested. Yes, there were more guys I *could* fight, but I had reached a point in my life where all I wanted was the opportunity to be a legend. The idea of padding my record did nothing for me. I did not want to be one of those guys who *could have been something*. I read the stuff being written about me in the media and by the fans, and realized that overall the perception of me had taken a turn for the worse. Even though some fans were making claims that I was "pound for pound" one of the best, those comments were based on what I had done in the past—not what I was doing right then and there. The only way to change the perception of me was to finish what had been started at UFC 58—to finish Georges St-Pierre.

Agreeing that I had accomplished what he asked of me, White finally made this fight happen, even if he didn't want me to ever leave my weight class. For all intents and purposes, it was going to be the first truly "superfight." At no time in the history of the UFC had two current champions faced each other, but that is what this fight would be. The two of us would be competing for St-Pierre's welterweight belt, but at the end of the day it would be "champion vs. champion."

I had more to prove than St-Pierre did, since he had already defeated me and had been cleaning out his own division as well. But he accepted the fight, and from that point forward the decent relationship the two of us had was history.

In a lot of ways, when you fight a guy you have to find a reason to want to inflict damage on him, even if you have no bad blood. Stevenson was a good example, since I had no reason to dislike him, but in order to hurt someone, inflict pain, and crush their spirit, you have to dig for something. With St-Pierre, it was not very hard.

From the day this fight was announced in mid-November of 2008, St-Pierre and I were filling media requests seemingly every day. The hype machine was in overdrive, as it was being called the biggest fight in UFC history, by fans, media, and White himself. I even remember White saying the fans would be lucky to see a fight like this two or three times in a lifetime, and there was no doubt I was happy to be a part of it.

It was all going to take place on January 31, 2009, at the MGM Grand Hotel in Las Vegas as part of UFC 94. It was the same weekend as the Superbowl, which was one of the biggest weekends of the year. There was a ton of excitement for this fight, and for the first time in my life it seemed everywhere I looked there was a reminder it was going to happen. This was officially big time.

The UFC set up media sessions for the two of us all across North America, and we both went to Toronto and Honolulu to promote the fight. It was the first time I had ever had to be around my opponent before a fight. Before, maybe I'd run into my next opponent at a UFC event, but now the two of us were flying with White on one of the Fertittas' private jets just to create buzz. We spent an entire day fielding questions from the media and fans, as well as signing autographs and taking photos for fans who spent hours waiting on line to see us. Everyone asking me the same questions over and over, talking about the last fight, and how this one would be different. "Are you going to train harder for this fight?" I was asked time and time again. The answer was yes, I would, that I was going to train harder than ever, and had already begun.

My preparation for this fight began five months out, well before I knew it was going to happen. I knew deep down it would soon be a reality and started working on my strength and conditioning, and then, about ten weeks out, I had most of my team in Hilo. Every type of guy you could think of, and it seemed there were more and more each week.

SINCE I HAD WANTED THIS FIGHT for such a long time, one would think it would be a very easy fight to focus on. As it turned out, nothing could have been further from the truth. I was distracted at nearly every turn during the last few months of 2008. Some things good, some things bad, but they all played a part in keeping my mind in many different places. One distraction, though, was better than anything that could have resulted from the fight.

In October, just weeks before the contract was signed, my girlfriend, Shea Uaiwa, gave birth to my daughter, Aeva Lili'u. She was the first child I had fathered and the most beautiful thing I had ever seen in my life (and still is). She looked just like Shea from the moment she was born, and just like her mother, she is absolutely beautiful. The birth of Aeva just before this fight really changed my perspective on life, the things I wanted for myself, but more importantly, what I had to give for my baby and her mother. For years it was really all just about me, being a champion, and doing what I could for anyone who looked up to me. Aeva changed all that in a moment. I had become a lot less important to myself, and I was reminded of it every time I laid eyes on her.

The only problem with the birth was the timing of it. Shea is quite a few years younger than me, and the two of us had just started living together when she became pregnant. Now we had a baby, but I was forced to go on the road and start promoting the fight. She understood all of this, and with my family close by and willing to help, she had all the support she could need. Plus members of her family could come to Hilo rather quickly since they lived close by on one of Hawaii's other islands. Still, that didn't make it easy.

The two of them were on my mind wherever I went, but they were a good distraction. The other distractions were not nearly as pleasant.

I imagine it is this way for most of their big-name fighters, but it seems every time I get involved with the UFC, there's always some type of drama. The bigger the stage, the bigger the drama. This was the biggest stage yet, so you can only imagine the size of the drama.

Over the next few months, the run-ins with White and the UFC seemed to come one on top of the next. The first was the new UFC video game, which was set to be launched sometime before UFC 100. In order for the UFC to use my likeness in the game in perpetuity, I had to sign a contract. Given my experiences with them, I was hesitant to allow them to have control over my likeness for the remainder of my life. Of course, this was what they wanted; they always do.

Now, one would think if the UFC has a video game, all the

fighters would be in it, they would sell the game, we would get some money, and that would be the end of it. This is how normal people think, but it's not how the UFC thinks. They want as much as they can get from you for as little as possible. Being in a video game is super exciting, especially for someone like me, who grew up playing them and still does to this day, but as much as I wanted to be in it, I told them I had no interest in giving away my likeness in its entirety. This started another drama.

The whole point was for Zuffa to make sure no fighter ever went off and established his own game with another distributor. They wanted to make sure the only game on the shelves was the game with the UFC stamp, forever. This is how they always operated. In the end, though, it was not a fight I cared too much about, so I relented.

AFTER I RETURNED FROM THE MEDIA tour, I prepared to focus and train, but since most people in Hilo know who I am, I could not go anywhere without having to talk about the fight, or at least be reminded of it. It was as if the entire town was with me every second, and in truth it became slightly difficult.

Until all this started, Hilo had been the one place where I could escape from the media and the craziness of people who wanted to talk about the fight. Now even there I had interview requests, on top of the fact I also had a newborn baby and a girlfriend who understandably had a need for privacy. At the same time I was hosting a local fighting show at my gym, broadcast on local television and on my Web site. To top it all off, there was soon to be a UFC camera crew in Hilo filming for the *Countdown* show. This program was to chronicle the lives St-Pierre and I lived leading up to January 31.

All of this became incredibly hectic for me. I needed more space. I wasn't fully prepared for all of the things I had on my plate. This environment created some tension, and the tension was felt by every person who was involved in this situation, except Reagan, of course. He never seems to change his pace, which is good because when I see him acting normal, it can help me reset myself.

At the end of the day, though, I probably had no one to blame but myself, at least on some level. Relinquishing responsibilities which are ultimately mine, and relying on other people to handle major aspects of my life, can cause more problems than are solved. Situations are never handled with a yes or no answer, and pushing things off to the side once wheels are already in motion does not cut it. The irony of it all was that the people around me were people who had my best interests at heart. Whether it was my mom, Parillo, my best friend Saul from childhood, Reagan, or any number of people, they were all trying to make my life easier. Just having them all around me all the time, though, made it difficult. I rarely had a moment alone, to sit down, relax, watch a movie, play with my baby, go surfing, or countless other things.

Then came the UFC's cameras, which raised everything up another notch. Now I had to sneak around everywhere.

The unfortunate aspect of the sport of MMA, to this day, is the fighters' struggle to make money. This is what the UFC's *Countdown* show was all about for both me and St-Pierre. As far as I knew, we were both getting a cut of the pay-per-view, so promoting the show was in our best interests. Some of the bigger-name fighters got this type of deal, and most of us were willing to do anything to earn a little more. In a sport where we put life and limb on the line, the window is small and the opportunities are few, so when an opportunity presents itself, you have to take it.

Before we even started filming, people from my camp communicated with St-Pierre's camp that I would say some things just to hype it up, and from what I gathered, they agreed to this. St-Pierre's manager had let us know they would do their part in hyping it up, but when the time came to do it, and I started making remarks about how I would win, and what would happen in this fight, St-Pierre said nothing. He basically left me on my own island, literally and figuratively, to look like the jerk. I was fine with the role, but it was one of those things, like when you and a buddy are going to jump off a cliff, both agreeing to jump, but only one of you does it. What do you think of the guy who doesn't jump?

I felt it was typical of his character, the type of person I always believed him to be. I view him as a guy who thinks if people think you are a good person, then you are a good person, even if deep down you are just the selfish type. While all the fans would see this show with BJ Penn being the villain and St-Pierre the hero, I was comfortable with it because I prefer to be judged by those who truly know me. While the public's perception of me matters, I cannot let it dictate who I am, and am comfortable in a villain's role as long as it's an honest role.

Despite all of this nonsense, my training had gone great. Right after the New Year I was already prepared to fight. I had been training for months, and it didn't matter when the fight was, I was ready to go on almost any day. I felt good about it, but there were concerns within my camp, and in my own head, that maybe I was peaking just a bit too early. It was more of a mental thing, and as Parillo would always say to me, "Don't mindfuck yourself." I did my best not to.

Still, having Aeva and Shea around just a few weeks out from the fight was proving too much. I decided to take the three of us on a long weekend to Kona, which is the coast of the Big Island, after which I would send them to Shea's family's place so I could really focus and prepare mentally. Having a little baby around, especially a girl, can bring out your softer side, and that was not what I needed at that juncture.

As it turned out, while I was away, the UFC's camera crew came to film me at home and the gym, and I was nowhere to be found. They contacted their superiors, and eventually this news got back to Dana White. White phoned Jay Dee to find out what was going on, and also had the camera crew go to Jay Dee's house to film him taking the call. White started asking Jay Dee where I was, what I was doing, whether I was training, and a host of other questions, that, frankly, were none of his business. White turned Jay Dee's effort to protect me into a situation that made Jay Dee look like a liar. He wasn't lying at all, but rather, he was dealing with a host of life problems in addition to mine, such as his pregnant wife, who was already past due. No matter to White, he used the footage of Jay Dee's phone call on television, making my brother look like an idiot, solely to promote the fight, and most importantly it seemed, himself.

The show was already making me look like the bad guy, and now here they were painting my brother as a liar. At a time of great tension, with pressure coming from every direction, I'd had enough with White's antics. When I got back from Kona, I told him I was done with the show, and I wanted nothing to do with him, or anyone else from the UFC, until the fight.

The television show aired on Spike TV, and White made comments on how I "better be training" and better not "be in Kona." Nothing could have been further from the truth , and to once again make me look like a lazy fighter was insulting.

Meanwhile, back in Montreal there were images of St-Pierre training relentlessly, but, of course, also hanging out in a strip club. It was hardly mentioned.

Every fighter takes a break, and every fighter needs time to heal, but the UFC took that one moment to paint me as a lazy island kid, once again not doing the right thing for a championship fight. Of course, after we called them out on it and told them we were done with the show, they used the next episode to reverse the image of me. Now it was BJ Penn, the guy training harder than ever, the family man, whose team was working toward a common goal, day after day. It was a little too late.

In the end, I did not *need* a story to hype this fight, since it was being billed by many as the biggest fight in the company's history. The truth was enough for me; the hype should have been left to pro wrestling. The real story was I trained harder and longer for this fight than I had any fight in my entire life. Harder than for Hughes, harder than for Sherk, harder than for anything I had ever tried to prepare for. After years of trying to perfect training, understanding my own body and how it works, I finally felt I was doing all of the right things. Whether I would look the part on fight night, if I would have six-pack abdominals, or neck muscles like Brock Lesnar, I had no idea. I just knew I would be ready.

WITH ONLY A COUPLE WEEKS to go before the fight, I was often stuck inside my house, thinking about everything related to it. Parillo was now living with me, and David Weintraub, my co-author, was down the street at my parents'. I had met Weintraub years earlier since he did some production work for the UFC and often interviewed me before my fights. We got along well, which was one of the main reasons we decided to work together.

There are two things about Weintraub that jump out at you within ten minutes of meeting him. The first thing is he has a mouth, and likes to use it. The second is what comes out of his mouth is the truth, at least from his perspective. I could always expect him to give it to me straight, even at the risk of making himself look bad. I respect that, and apparently a lot of the other fighters do as well, since he has formed a pretty solid bond with almost every well-known fighter in the UFC.

Weintraub was having a conversation with Kenny Florian, who was someone I had trained with and been pretty friendly with. Weintraub told Florian about how bothered I was regarding St-Pierre as a cheater. Eventually they started talking about "greasing," which is the act of applying lubricants to your body in order to avoid submissions, my best weapon. Their conversation ended, but soon after, Florian sent Weintraub a text message saying he hoped I would kick Georges St-Pierre's ass because he was a greaser just like Huerta (one of Florian's previous opponents, Roger Huerta, who had also used these tactics). As it turned out, St-Pierre had helped prepare Huerta for the fight against Florian.

Later on in the evening, I was pacing around the house while Parillo and Weintraub sat on the couch talking about the fight. At some point Weintraub said to me, "Your buddy Florian is on your side in this one. Thinks GSP is a greaser." He then showed me the text meassage, and I just stood there, thinking about this.

Truth is, I thought very little about the concept of greasing. Parillo had never heard a thing about it, and Weintraub told him he had seen guys doing it before. I never dreamed my upcoming fight would ever come down to that, or that any kind of grease could prevent me from doing what I wanted to do. Not Parillo, though; he kept digging, and asking Weintraub about what effect greasing could have. It stayed in his head from the moment he heard about it right up until the night of the fight. For me, it was in one ear and out the other.

THE WEEK OF THE FIGHT FINALLY arrived and I went out to Las Vegas the Tuesday before, with about fifteen others who were either training partners or working for me. I had a larger crew than ever before. If I thought the tension would die down once I left Hilo, I was wrong. On some level, the intensity only picked up for me.

The UFC press conference before the fight was the same as it always had been, with reporters wondering if we really did "hate each other." This time, though, there may have been a little more truth to the bad energy than usual, as seen on the *Primetime* show. Over time, my respect for St-Pierre had shrunk. The rumors of his cheating, his willingness to make me look bad on *Countdown,* and most other dealings I had with him just left me with a bad taste in my mouth.

The one question that stuck out for me was asked by a reporter: Was St-Pierre's size "going to be a problem" for me? Coincidentally, sitting up there on the podium at the press conference was Lyoto Machida, who was scheduled to face fellow Brazilian Thiago

Silva in a light-heavyweight fight. I wanted to say, *I fought this guy right here! Did you see it?* I suspected the reporter had not, since so often these new MMA journalists have little knowledge of the sport beyond the UFC. Instead I responded with my stock answer: "No, I don't think it's a problem."

The one thing I didn't have to worry about for this fight, something that was normally a concern, was cutting weight. This was my first fight in quite some time for which I didn't have to get down to 155 pounds, and that was a welcome relief. There is nothing fun about having to cut, and in the back of my mind I kept thinking about St-Pierre having to do so. Even though he fights in the welterweight division, in all likelihood he walks around when not fighting at around 185, at least. When weigh-ins finally arrived, I checked in at 168, two under the maximum, and St-Pierre was 170 on the dot. I knew this was going to be the last time I saw him before Saturday night, and looking into his eyes, I could tell that we were both ready.

WHEN I ARRIVED AT THE MGM GRAND on January 31, 2009, the atmosphere in the locker room was much calmer than any place I'd been during the previous few days because all the friends, family, and others who had been with me had had to go their own way. From that point on, it was only Jay Dee, Reagan, Rudy, Parillo, my wrestling coach Adam Disabato, and my physical therapist Gary Ohashi. Everyone else's job had ended, except for mine; mine was about to begin.

As I sat around the locker room, either resting on the mat or watching fights, I could feel the intensity in the building, and whenever something happened on the television screen, the walls shook softly, as fans inside the arena went crazy during the other matches.

At some point I did my standard warming up with Reagan and Parillo just to get loose, but unbeknownst to me, something else was going on, something I learned about only after the match. Still wondering about the whole concept of "greasing," Parillo had approached one of the commissioners of the Nevada State Athletic Commission (NSAC) to discuss his concerns about St-Pierre. He couldn't shake the idea that St-Pierre was going to use grease during this match, and he wanted the commission to be aware of it. He had been telling others, seemingly in jest, that he was going to say something to the commission, but no one had paid much attention.

Oddly enough, after the fact, Parillo said he hadn't planned on doing what he did, but once the commissioner had entered the dressing room, he said, "Hey, watch this guy . . . we have concerns he may put some things on his body, like some type of powder or balm, so that when he sweats, it will make him really slippery." The commissioner agreed to do his job, which was to watch the cornermen wrap the fighters' hands, ankles, or anything else related to taping, to monitor the drug tests, and to make sure neither fighter had any foreign objects on their person.

These commissioners usually have a boxing background, so you have to wonder if they know to look for things like greasing. When you get to the cage, the referee pats you down, but by that point it could well be too late.

As the earlier fights finished one by one, I could tell we were almost there, that it was time for me to fight what could be my last fight. The locker room had quieted down now that the other fighters had finished. All that remained was me and St-Pierre, somewhere beyond the walls around me. My team was around me and I could sense the energy flowing from them. I was not thinking about anything but St-Pierre, my training, and how prepared I was for this moment in time. It was to be the culmination of my entire career, on this night. In my mind I was going to be the first man in UFC history to hold two belts, in two divisions, at the same time. I had held each one, which put me in rare company, with Randy Couture, but now I had the chance to stand alone, holding both together. Quite possibly, the perfect ending to a career.

• • •

STANDING IN FRONT OF A BLACK CURTAIN, with my team behind me, I heard my music start to play inside a large arena. My song, "Hawaii '78," rang out, and as I had done many times before, I made the walk to the cage. Wading through the crowd, I could sense that the people were with me. The energy of the moment was unbelievable. Very few people have the opportunity to experience something like this, and I treasured every second of it.

As soon as Referee Herb Dean called us to fight, I raced right to the center, as did St-Pierre. Though the energy coming out was high for both of us, the first round was rather lackluster. Neither of us was able to connect with many hard shots. The one thing I realized immediately was that St-Pierre wanted to take me down. Any chance to tie me up, use leverage, and grab a hold of me, he was going to seize because he needed this fight to be on the ground. This was precisely what I had trained for with my team in Hawaii. I had spent a lot of time on my back, knowing he would try to take the fight there. Early on, when we were locked up, he was holding my arm real tight, so I backed myself to the fence to play it safe. He didn't feel extraordinarily strong, and his punches were not really hurting me physically. I could see his kicks coming and wasn't worried about them. With the adrenaline pumping, everything seemed to happen in slow motion.

As I often do, I brought my leg up to wedge it between him and me. Grabbing hold of that leg would have been an easy thing to do if he wanted to, but because I have a good base, and am well balanced, I was willing to put it out there as a defense, even at the risk that it might be used against me. However, instead of grabbing the leg, St-Pierre needed to take it a bit further immediately, going after my shorts and trying to use them as leverage to get me down.

I immediately signaled verbally that this was taking place to Referee Dean. He saw it, and he warned St-Pierre to stop. I had seen St-Pierre do it in other fights, so it wasn't surprising. To the average fan, or to any person who has never engaged in a mixed martial arts fight, grabbing someone's shorts may seem like a pretty small matter, but it's a big deal because it affects the fight. When a man can use leverage like that to get you down, it can definitely hurt you. Despite the warning, St-Pierre would try again.

The second round began, and I was in good shape. I still was not worried about the ground game, and not at all about standing up. I could tell that if St-Pierre could not get me down, he was going to hold me against the fence, use his size, and hope to tire me out. The fight did move to the fence pretty quickly, and again, to avoid the knees, I wedged my leg between our bodies. He got hold of my left leg, and was able to turn around and get me to the ground. Once I was down, he was in my guard, and immediately I started working my jujistu game. I was not constrained at all from getting my legs into position up over his shoulders, and since I'd spent so much time training from this position, this would be my equalizer that would eventually bring us back to our feet. Usually I would try to pop right back up to my feet when I'm on the bottom, but I wanted to bring my submission game into this fight to show him it was a bad idea to take me down, and there was no reason for him to try. It didn't go as planned.

I was unable to secure position on him from the bottom, but I thought nothing of it. Once a move failed, I just said to myself, *Okay, go onto the next one,* as I have always done in my career. I have been on my back in other fights, exhausted from fighting and unable to be aggressive, but this was not one of those times. The second round had just begun, and the first round hadn't taken a lot out of me. As St-Pierre stayed in my guard, I just kept working. It never came into my head that he was greasy, or sweatier than any other fighter. I've trained with hundreds of different people, and they all sweat differently. People slip all the time. It wasn't something that was on my mind. *He got out of there, what's my next move, he got out of that, what's my next move.* I was just trying to keep thinking ahead.

There did come a point, either in the second or third round, when he pushed my hands off his head pretty easily. He slipped right out and was able to get his posture back. This had not happened as easily when we fought last time, but I remember in that moment thinking, *He knows I can't hold on to him because he's slipping . . .* I was not thinking, *Oh, he must be greased up!* I just knew that he knew that I couldn't hold on, for whatever reason.

From this point on, it was a relatively one-sided fight. As Georges was able to keep me on my back, and use his extra size to tire me out, my greatest defense, considered by some to be as good as there is in MMA, was rendered nearly useless. Had I figured beforehand this would be the case, I probably would have spent a lot more time avoiding going to the ground. Instead, I had no fear of it. I figured *he* should have fear of it. I figured, when he realized that I could submit him, there was no way he was going to want to be here all night. I was wrong. It was the only place he wanted to be.

Soon thereafter he was able to get his legs out from my full guard, into half guard and side control, where he was able to tire me out and land a decent amount of shots. This would be the beginning of the end of this fight, and from this point forward I don't remember much of the action. Of course, once I was getting more and more tired, and he was still somewhat fresh, he was willing to show just what a great stand-up fighter he was, fearless of me being able to return fire.

Eventually, after the fourth round, I remember heading back to my corner toward cutman Leon Tabbs. He was saying something that I couldn't quite understand because I was just too tired. I was not going to quit on my own, I knew that. I would never quit inside the cage. You either have to knock me out, or have someone throw in the towel for me, which is inevitably what happened. Parillo, looking out for my best interests, and knowing me as well as almost anyone at this time, called the fight.

Once again, I lost to St-Pierre, and would be denied the chance to fulfill a dream. But it was certainly not the end of me since I still held my lightweight belt.

Little did I know that the end of this fight was only the beginning of another.

BACK IN THE LOCKER ROOM, THINGS were happening all around me. I was definitely hurt physically and emotionally. I couldn't believe I had just lost, and really couldn't understand why I'd been so ineffective.

All around me there seemed to be a lot of commotion. Once a fight ends, the UFC is a little looser about letting people into the locker room because they know you want to see your family and those who are there with you. My mother was now in the room, as was the rest of my camp. I took a seat in one of the chairs against the wall and waited for the doctor to come into the room to check on me.

The next thing I know, two of the commission guys came into the room and started saying things like "We caught him in the act . . . we caught him greasing . . . you have to file a complaint!" When I first heard this I thought nothing of it; I was so beaten up, worse than I had ever been. Then I started to hear other people in my camp, like Jay Dee and Parillo, talk about it. I remember someone else saying to me, "BJ, Raffi needs your shorts." I had no idea what anyone was talking about, especially why Raffi Nahabedian, my lawyer, wanted my shorts.

My response was "I'll punch that guy in the face if I see him." I really had no idea which way was up or down, or what I was thinking. I just felt beaten. As things began to settle down, Nahabedian had the opportunity to explain why he wanted my shorts—as evidence. Apparently, as I was walking into the locker room, I kept saying "He was so fucking slippery" over and over again. Since Nahabedian was right there, he immediately thought he needed my shorts to prove that Georges greased or had something on his body to make him so fucking slippery. Once this was explained to me, I no longer wanted to smack him—thinking he wanted to sell my shorts—I wanted to thank him for always having my back, even in the middle of such commotion.

There I sat, the guy who never makes excuses when he fights. Time and time again I have been in fights that I have won, and fights that I have lost, but other than blaming myself for mistakes, or for not having worked hard enough, I never make excuses. Here was my team making all this commotion about St-Pierre greasing, and being supported in their claims by the commission members themselves. All I could think about was the embarrassment, not about the possibility of my opponent having cheated.

In retrospect, maybe the commission members were more level-headed about the whole thing than anyone else. I really didn't have time to think about any of it. I was just hurt. Later on, I was able to put everything together and make sense of it all, how I had been so ineffective, and why St-Pierre had been so willing to fight me in my best position. Never in my career had I had a more difficult time controlling someone with my arms and legs, from my back, than I did on that night.

Outside the doors of my locker, Jay Dee was having words with the head of the commission, Keith Kizer. According to Kizer, they did catch St-Pierre's cornermen applying "some Vaseline on him, but we wiped it off." At the beginning of the second round, members of the commission were actually toweling him off. Now, I am no expert on grease since I have never applied any during a fight, but I know it takes a lot more to remove Vaseline from a sweating person than just a quick wipe with a towel. I have also never actually seen footage of St-Pierre being wiped down.

At the very least, the commission should have notified my corner. I don't know if it would have changed the outcome of the fight, but at least I'd have realized my opponent had a slippery substance on his body, and thus I'd have known being on my back was probably not as good a place to be as I had figured. Not to say I was having much success there in the first place, but I had trained to fight from there, figuring once he was ineffective from that position, like he had been in our first fight, he'd be forced to stand with me. It didn't happen this way.

That night it was me who went to the hospital, not St-Pierre, unlike our previous encounter. I had an incredible amount of pain in my jaw, and my four front teeth were also in a lot of pain. Even after I left the hospital, I had more pain in my jaw than I ever had in my life. My team and I went to an In-N-Out Burger afterward, and I could hardly even chew the food. I was swallowing big chunks of cheeseburger whole because it tasted so good. In spite of everything, I was going to eat whatever fast food was put in front of me.

Once I left Vegas for home, I still had this pain in my teeth and my nose. Every time I touched either, a shock would go through my body, and this lasted for nearly a week. I'd also suffered a slight concussion and intense vertigo, which were affecting my sleep. Sitting home, having all this time to think about the fight, having friends and others tell me about the possibility that St-Pierre had cheated really made me question his worth as a person. To think someone could cheat in the realm of martial arts, let alone a martial artist who bows upon entering the cage, was more than unsettling; it was disrespectful, and someone had to say something about it.

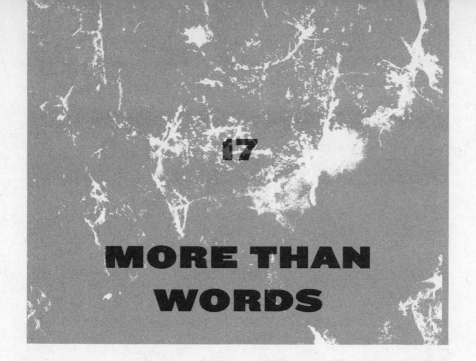

17

MORE THAN WORDS

N THE AFTERMATH OF THE St-Pierre fight, I dealt with a lot of new situations, none of which I had ever dealt with before. Almost as soon as it ended, a legal case was being contemplated with the NSAC, alleging that St-Pierre had cheated the night we fought. This was the first time I had ever been in the middle of a situation like this, and it was quickly becoming a big deal within MMA and the media. As if that wasn't enough, I was coping with the physical ramifications from the fight, such as dizziness, and other related ailments stemming from what was likely a concussion. I was seeing doctors, getting MRIs and CAT scans to make sure I was healthy. And then of course, I now had to focus on being a father to Aeva, which I couldn't do while training to fight, which I'd been doing from the moment she was born. This, however, was the easy part: every time I had to deal with something stressful, I could just pick her up and instantly feel better.

Among all of the things that were going on, the biggest issue was the accusation against St-Pierre. As a guy who rarely made excuses for losing a fight, this put me in a weird position. It was not about winning or losing, but about fair play, and respect for a sport I love as much as anyone ever has. Knowing the risks associated with being the "whistle-blower" in this situation, I still felt it was important to speak my mind, and what I believed to be the truth. It was no different than the time I called out Sherk for using steroids because I felt like everyone else was giving him a free pass. Fighters don't want to hear it because so many of them are cheating, and would rather it just get brushed under the rug. Not everyone cheats, though, and I had to speak out about what I believed was right, even in the face of mounting criticism.

This was not to say that I was the best I could have been on the night of January 31, or that I would have defeated St-Pierre if greasing hadn't entered the picture. Looking back on it, I'd say my game plan was flawed, and I had allowed him to gain positions advantageous to him which I had not expected to be in. Without the grease, the fight would have been different and the injuries I sustained would have been minimized, but that doesn't mean I believe I would have won or lost either way.

With the fight weeks behind me, my team and my lawyers were discussing the steps we needed to take to make a case with the Nevada State Athletic Commission against St-Pierre. The legal case we were going to present basically stated our belief that St-Pierre had not only applied grease during the fight, which he was caught doing, but also that he had done so beforehand as well. Additionally, we were bothered by the fact the commission did not tell us during the fight that they caught St-Pierre applying Vaseline. Had I known this, at the very least I would have been aware of what not to do and adjusted my game plan—that is, I would not have allowed him to take me down as easily as I had as a means to get him into my submission position. And I would not have lifted my leg across my body and welcomed takedown attempts in the same fashion.

After my attorney, Raffi Nahabedian, filed a formal complaint with the NSAC, they scheduled a hearing. The complaint had many formal allegations against St-Pierre and cited various regulations governing MMA that were violated by St-Pierre, in particular the greasing. These were not made-up rules created to serve my purpose; these were actual regulations enacted to protect MMA athletes from exactly what I had experienced during the bout. Because these rules were already on the books, the commission had the power to void the results of the fight and strip St-Pierre of his purse (an action similar to what would occur if an athlete were caught using steroids).

In March of 2009, I attended the hearing before the NSAC in Las Vegas, where I had the chance to speak, as well as hear from the commission members. Nahabedian, Parillo, and my mother were all with me as my side of the story was told. I explained to the commission plainly how I felt about the matter based on the facts: that we warned the commission before the bout, that St-Pierre was caught during the bout, and that no one told me or my corner of the greasing. I also explained why I had filed the complaint: to ensure the sport was clean and free of cheaters, and to help prevent it from being compromised by scandalous behavior. From a personal perspective, I felt and still feel no one should ever want to win a championship, or any fight, by cheating.

We explained why we'd mentioned greasing to the commission before the fight, and repeated the conversations we had back in Hilo and comments we'd heard from other fighters about St-Pierre's history and of slipperiness. At the same time there were other UFC fighters stepping up and making similar accusations, which we told the commission. However, none of this seemed to matter to them and, unfortunately, to the fans, as all I ever read or heard about in the media was how I was "crying" and should just "shut up already." The most disturbing thing about the NSAC is they never interviewed any of the other fighters who made public statements about St-Pierre—even in an effort to improve the sport, or safeguard fighters. It seemed the media and many of the fans didn't care either.

Ultimately, I was cast as the villain for speaking up. I started reading about how absurd it was that my mother accompanied me to the hearing, as if this somehow made me weak. My mother is one of the brightest and, more importantly, toughest people anyone is going to come across. I viewed the jokes about her as childish, simplistic, and sexist. Had it been my father, or any number of men, no one would have said a word. The whole thing was a circus, and the coverage about it seemed to be no better than what you'd find in a tabloid.

Truth is, I knew I would come out on the wrong side of all this just because I know how the MMA media treats these things. And as for my mother, she asked me if she could read a statement on my behalf, and out of my desire to not hurt her feelings, I said she could do so. I knew full well what the ramifications would be, but public perception is less important to me than my family and doing what I believe is right.

What the fans and many fighters may not know is that there was/is a clearly written rule stating that there cannot be excessive grease or a foreign substance on the face or body of a fighter and that a fighter cannot act in a manner that would result in an unfair advantage. In fact, as long as I've been in the UFC, they've wiped us down before we enter the Octagon in acknowledgment of this rule. These rules and my clear purpose for bringing the complaint notwithstanding, the rebuttals from the NSAC left a truly bad taste in my mouth, specifically those made by the head of the commission, Keith Kizer.

Right from the get-go, there was a sense that even with the facts on our side, it was not going to matter. In the end, the commission did nothing. St-Pierre kept his title and purse. No investigation was conducted to confirm the evidence that we provided from other fighters that St-Pierre had cheated in the past. Our recommendation that all fighters shower before a match to prevent greasing was ignored.

For an organization that was formed to protect the integrity of a sport and the safety of its athletes, the commission appeared to have no interest in performing its duties. But given the controversy and media attention, the commission apparently decided something had to be done to at least give the appearance of action, so a "new" rule against "excessive" greasing was issued, even though the current rules already prohibited it.

The irony of it all is that they named the rule the BJ Penn Rule as opposed to the St-Pierre Rule, which means I have the stigma of being attached to it whenever it's mentioned, as if I did something wrong. I figured they would at least name it after the guy who was caught greasing during a fight. I guess even that was too much to ask.

WEEKS HAD PASSED WHEN I LEARNED that my next opponent was going to be Kenny Florian, but this time it would be for my lightweight title. It was almost too perfect a coincidence, since Florian's name had come up over and over again throughout the dealings with the NSAC, since it was Florian who initially tipped me off about St-Pierre's greasing. Nevertheless, in the media coverage about St-Pierre and me, Florian denied everything he'd said, trying to make me look like an idiot.

It didn't take much, but I went from respecting Florian as a solid fighter and a seemingly good person, to seeing him as someone who would do anything to help himself. He appeared all too happy to watch me hang myself and act like he had no idea how he became involved.

So it was too perfect that he was going to be my next opponent, and I certainly didn't need any motivation. What I did need, though, was a change in my training, and on some level, in my surroundings. In early March 2009, one of the people who worked with my sponsors had suggested I try out this new training method going in San Diego. There were a few different people involved with the training, but the primary trainer was a man named Marv Marinovich. Marinovich was better known for having coached his son Todd, who went on to play football at the University of Southern California and later on professionally with the Los Angeles Raiders, than as a trainer. However, at this point in his career, he was working with Troy Polamalu, one of the best defensive players in the National Football League. Polamalu had sworn "Marv's" methods were second to none, and it was hard to argue with the success Polamalu was having.

Initially I had been skeptical because time and time again I have heard people say "this guy is the best in the business," only to find out the new and improved method is just a repackaged version of the old one. As it turned out, this was not the case with Marv. From the moment I met him in San Diego, I knew this was totally different. He and his brother Gary were working on training the body to "explode," and on pushing yourself as hard as you could in bursts, recovering quickly, and exploding again. Through different types of machines, exercises, and water-based workouts, all focused on improving the responsiveness of the nervous system, they promised to transform me.

It was hard to really consider them as coaches at first because MMA is such a young sport, relatively speaking, and Marv and Gary were much older than the usual trainers I came across. At the same time, though, Marv had already been successful, and had seen everything in the world of training. Built like a truck, about six three, 250 pounds, with wavy gray hair, Marv cut an imposing figure. His brother Gary, one year younger, also a hard-core fitness trainer, brought us into the pool for the first time to test out the methods.

Unlike everyone else who tries to sell me a method, the two of them had nothing to prove, and they didn't care if I stayed or went.

This fact alone made me trust them. It didn't hurt that I loved their methods. After one day of training with them, being put to their tests, I could already feel the difference in my body. After some deliberating, Jay Dee and I decided that going forward with the Marinoviches was a step in the right direction, especially since I had most likely overtrained for St-Pierre, and I never wanted to experience a poor training camp again. I was confident that in a short time I would never have to.

Truth is, I could not have met Marv and Gary at a better time in my life, and not just because of my desire to find a better way to train. The loss to St-Pierre and the ensuing drama had really taken a toll on me emotionally. One of the hardest things a championship fighter has to deal with is getting amped up again to compete in another huge fight, and in my case the situation was unique. Normally, if a champion loses, he will face an easier opponent in the next fight, but because I was still the lightweight champion, I would again be defending my belt. It is rare for a champion to lose the way I had, remain champ, and then have to start all over again. This was why I was so fortunate to meet these new trainers; they motivated me to become an even better fighter, using techniques and methods that were different from anything I'd ever tried.

After spending a bit more than a week with them in May, I realized if I was really going to commit to this, it would mean moving the entirety of my training camp to San Clemente, California. I would be away from my family for at least six weeks. A year earlier this would not have been a big deal, but with Jay Dee and me both having newborns, it was no longer easy to pick up and leave for long periods of time. While I knew it would be hard on Shea having to be with Aeva alone for such a long period of time, it was something I really needed.

Now the only thing which had to be ironed out was where I would do all my training. Back in Hilo I could train at my own gym, but in California we didn't have such a luxury. This problem was solved by P. M. Tenore, the owner of the apparel company

RVCA, my longtime sponsor. Tenore had been a friend of mine for years, going all the way back to my early BJJ days, and I was the first person he ever sponsored. The growth of his company had coincided with the growth of MMA, and my own success. He told me if I came to Costa Mesa to train, he would build an MMA gym in his warehouse, and even help us find a place to live. True to his word, he literally built an RVCA/BJ Penn training center in the rear of the building, complete with a cage, mats, and workout equipment catering to the Marinoviches' methods.

The gym really is unbelievable, and for Tenore to build it was an amazing gesture. It's not as if RVCA sponsors many fighters, or was going to make any money by building it. In fact, in all likelihood the gym would usually be empty, and it would be a financial loss. Tenore didn't care because he was committed to helping me succeed, and it is one of the reasons I've always remained with him. Together, the two of us designed my unique "black belt"–style shorts, and have worked together to be mindful of who I am, and what RVCA is. It is not "just a sponsor."

Over the years, many other sponsors and companies have made me huge financial offers to endorse their products and wear their merchandise. I have always been very selective about the ones I have chosen to work with because it's not about the money, it's about what I am endorsing and how it reflects upon me. The people Tenore surrounds himself with are people I like. I do not wear the products because I am paid to, but because I really like them. There is a symbiotic relationship between RVCA and me, and I think it's a great thing when a fighter and a sponsor can have not only a business relationship, but a friendship.

THE FLORIAN FIGHT WAS SCHEDULED for August 8, 2009, in Philadelphia, as part of UFC 101: Declaration. There were so many reasons I wanted this fight to happen I couldn't even list them all, but the one most important to me was the chance to put a beating on Florian. As the days passed, it seemed I could not escape the drama surrounding the greasing incident, and Florian was a huge part of why this was so. Putting aside the fact that he'd planted the seed about St-Pierre's cheating, he was now training with the guy. On top of it all, Florian's attitude toward me, and the way he carried himself, just seemed so different from how he was when he first came to Hawaii to train at my school. He was once a nice, friendly, outgoing guy, who didn't have a chip on his shoulder. From the moment he became my next opponent, all I could see was the chip.

Because of all this, Florian was the perfect opponent for me to get revenge on. My goal was to make him pay for everything I was dealing with. But even with the motivation, my confidence remained shaken from the previous fight, and I was concerned about the skills Florian brought to the table. While I knew he hadn't been ready for a title shot when he fought Sherk a couple years before, I considered him a top opponent who was deserving of one now.

My training had begun well before the summer, but it was not until I made it to Costa Mesa that things really got under way. It was going to be a great camp; not only was I training for a fight, but my training partner Shane Nelson was as well, on the same card. The two of us would be going through the entire camp together, which was not very common for me. Along with Jay Dee, Reagan, Parillo, and the Marinoviches, we worked together nearly every day, transforming me back from a welterweight fighter to a lightweight. We also had with us a cook from Hawaii named Evan Ida, who was incredibly valuable. I could see my body changing right before my eyes, and I could see the same in Shane's and my other training partners'.

I had never felt better about fight preparation in my entire career. At over 165 pounds, I had muscle definition, which I am not sure I ever really had. When I'm not 155 pounds, I just look like I'm in good shape, but somewhat soft around the edges. Now I not only looked better, but I felt faster and stronger than I had in years. The training for the St-Pierre fight had nearly broken me down; now Marv and Gary were erasing what had been done and building me back up from square one.

It also didn't hurt being in Costa Mesa because I could leave the house without really being noticed, affording me a freedom I don't really have back home. On "Cheat Day," the one day I don't train and I can eat almost anything I want, I had new places to go and new restaurants to choose from. While this may seem simplistic to a regular person, Cheat Day is the best day in the world when you are training for a fight. We would drive around Orange County just looking for new places to eat.

The whole experience felt like I had a new lease on my career, and my mind started to release the tension that had been building up for months. Outside of missing Shea, Aeva, my new nephew, and the rest of my family, I was putting behind me a lot of the lingering doubts I had about my career. I've now come to believe the doubts actually helped me to push harder than ever before, and this entirely new experience was helping to reinvigorate me.

By the time August came around and I was heading out to Philadelphia, I had completed a tremendous camp. Physically I was in the best shape I had ever been in, especially considering the years of wear and tear on my body. My mind was clear, as I was finally putting all of the drama I'd been living with since February behind me. Even the differences between myself and Florian—I no longer even cared about any of that stuff. It had all been played out for months during interviews, the UFC's *Countdown* show, and among the fans.

At the same time I sensed from comments made by Florian that he was less at ease than I was. He was saying outlandish things, like the student was going to "kill the master," and had expectations of being able to beat me in every round. He wanted to "kill" me. It was more proof to me Kenny was a much different person from the guy I'd known a few years earlier. I even heard rumors about his camp fracturing the entire time; how he was choosing St-Pierre and his trainers over his longtime coach, Mark Dellagrotte. Casting aside the guy who had taken him from a nobody to a top fighter said everything about his character and where his head was at coming into this fight.

Once again my camp decided to avoid being stuck inside a hotel for five days and we got a house outside of Philadelphia in Mullica Hill, New Jersey. This area of New Jersey was really in the countryside, or so it seemed, with nothing but farms surrounding us and no one around to bother us. In the days leading up to the fight, we just relaxed around the house, trained in the garage, barbecued on the patio, and enjoyed each other's company. It was as perfect a situation as I could have asked for.

The Thursday night before the fight I went through my final training session in the garage. Jay Dee and our friend Rich Chou had gone out and purchased these children's play mats to line the cement floor, and then we took the carpets from inside the house to create a makeshift training area. I trained for five hard rounds, working on my ground game with Reagan, my stand-up with Rob Emerson (another UFC fighter who was a former teammate on *The Ultimate Fighter*), and the rest with Rudy—each of them rotating every minute. At the end of the five rounds I felt great, like I could keep going endlessly. It was one of the best prefight workouts I'd ever had.

WHEN I WOKE UP ON SATURDAY morning, the day of the fight, I had an awakening of another sort. After all of the drama I had put up with for over half of the year, and the evident tension and stress that existed among my entire team, I had a major realization: I no longer wanted fighting to be a job.

For years, the day of the fight had been the worst day. It had always been hard to carry all the tension and pressure around all day. Suddenly I had reached the point of just letting go. I went downstairs to the living room, to Rudy and Parillo, so I could tell them what was on my mind.

"I've been doing this for nine years already," I began, "and what am I doing to myself? Why do I keep putting myself through this? I make myself feel so bad in this moment, over and over, and for what?" I went on to tell them how I wanted to just go out there have fun, to get into a scrap, to be a kid again. "For all I know, this could be the last time I ever do this!

"You guys should just kick back, relax, and enjoy the show. You don't have to do anything tonight. Just watch." They must have thought I was crazy, but when you know you know. In that moment I knew exactly what was going to happen.

By the time we arrived at the Wachovia Center, I was at complete peace with myself as I entered the small locker room I was sharing with Shane Nelson and Kendall Grove, who were both fighting on the card. I had high hopes for "Nelly" since the two of us had been going through the same things for the last couple of months, but he unfortunately lost his rematch with Aaron Riley, whom he had defeated earlier in the year. Kendall also had a very tough match with Ricardo Almeida, a fighter I had known for years through BJJ.

There was a feeling in the air that things were not going well for the Hawaiians, and I could sense some of my training partners were worried. I was not concerned. I'd wanted Shane and Kendall to win, but their results would have no effect on my fight.

Finally, my time had come, and I heard the voice of the UFC's Bert Watson calling us both out of our locker rooms. I was hard to contain and came flying out, not even wanting to wait for my song to begin. From the moment I was allowed to walk, I started racing to the cage, almost possessed by the moment, as ready as I had ever been for a fight. I knew this time would come, and that I had to be patient, always knowing the only way I could ever feel good again was to get back to this moment and do better than I ever had before.

As soon as referee Dan Miragliotta called us to fight, I came across the cage right after Florian. Florian has very good side-to-side movement, but I was prepared for it, assuming he wanted to strike quick and get out as fast as possible. He was engaging me somewhat, but more moving backward than anything else. He threw a kick, which I blocked, and then another into my midsection, but I caught it and landed a punch, sending him backward into the cage.

We danced around the cage for a while, and then clinched up. I threw him aside, and realized I was not going to have much trouble moving him around, since I felt much stronger than I had felt for some time. He continued to move around the cage, trying to throw some weak punches and kicks, but most were missing, or were too sporadic to have any real effect. I was getting the feeling early on that he didn't want to stand in the middle and fight.

Toward the end of the round he shot in on my leg and tried to go for a takedown. When he was unable to do so, we separated again and moved toward the center of the Octagon. Florian attempted a right hand that missed, and I countered with a right hook that landed on the side of his head. It wobbled him good, and as he was falling back toward the cage, I went in for the kill. I threw a knee that just missed, and in that moment he was able to get back to his feet, just as time expired.

When round two began, Florian came out and landed an inside leg kick, and I assumed there would be more. The second one missed, and I tried to land a punch. Florian again shot in on my legs and pushed me against the cage. I was fighting off any efforts he had to "dirty-box" on the inside, which is the art of throwing short elbows, uppercuts, and punches in tight quarters. Even with my back against the cage, I was landing as many shots as he was, and his knees and punches were doing little damage. When he saw that his approach was ineffective, he dropped down again, grabbed a leg, and continued to push my body into the cage. This was doing nothing to me.

With much less success, Florian was trying to employ the strategy St-Pierre and, to some extent, Lyoto Machida had used. Its ineffectiveness came from the fact that Florian was not stronger than me, as those other two had been, and he did not weigh more than I did, as the others had. He had been training with St-Pierre, so maybe he figured he could pull off the same strategy, but it was pointless. If he thought he was tiring me out he was mistaken, and in all likelihood was only tiring out himself. There was only one person wasting energy here, and it was not me.

Round two came to a somewhat boring close, but at least I knew his plan. As I looked across the ring, I saw him sitting in his chair getting toweled off, while I stood in my corner, talking to my trainers. It seemed to me only one of us had become tired, and it was probably not the guy who was standing up between rounds.

When I came out for round three, I continued to be patient. In all likelihood, I had won the first two rounds, so I had no problem letting him do whatever it was he was attempting. He continued to stay far on the outside, but then went back to the strategy of pushing me against the cage. His attempts at knees and elbows were having no effect, but I could still hear his corner screaming at him, telling him he was doing the right thing.

When Florian saw another opportunity to grab my leg, shoving me back into the cage, he took it, repeating the same mistakes he had made the first two rounds. With about one minute remaining in the round, I was almost getting bored with his strategy, which Marv Marinovich referred to as "junior varsity," since it was such a complete joke. I almost laughed during the fight.

I decided to end the boredom. With his arms wrapped around my left leg, I pushed his head down as far as I could, reached across his body for his left leg, and then swept him down to the ground. After I attempted a shot to his head, he escaped back to his feet. With just seconds remaining in the round, he tried to hit me with a surprise right hand, but I landed a stiff jab that almost knocked him down.

Back in my corner we were very calm, not even thinking about his strategy. It just seemed he wanted to avoid punching in the middle of the cage, and had hoped I would tire late so he could take advantage. We all realized his game plan was only about making me tired, which for us was fine because I felt like the fight had yet to begin.

When round four began, he seemed like he wanted to trade some punches and kicks, maybe out of desperation. He had to know his strategy had gotten him nowhere, so now it was time to shake it up. Or maybe this was all part of the plan from the beginning. Either way, from the start of the round I was landing the bigger punches, which knocked him back. Seemingly fearful of the punches, he took one last shot at my legs and pushed me into the cage.

After a few seconds with my back against the cage, I could hear the fans starting to boo, becoming restless with this strategy. I too had tired of it, and maybe he had as well. He tried to throw a big left hand but missed, and I stepped off the cage, countering with a big right hand to his face, which knocked him back along the cage. As he tried to move along the fence away from me, I stalked him and landed another punch. I then shot in, grabbed his legs, picked him up with relative ease, and slammed him into the mat. It was only a matter of time.

I landed on top of him in his half guard, and kept the pressure on with elbows into his head and short punches. I did my best to get my leg out from between his legs so I could mount him fully. He was able to fight me off for a moment, so I continued to press my forearm across his neck and throw elbows into his head. Eventually I was able to get the full mount, but he turned over quickly to avoid taking strikes to the face. As had happened in so many of my other fights, I was able to fully control his body, forcing him to give up his back. I wrapped my legs around his body and pulled him on top of me, with my back to the mat. I began kicking him in the stomach and ribs with my right heel while trying to untangle his arms. Eventually he tried to stop this from happening with his hands, and when he did, I sank my left arm under his neck and choked him out with my signature rear naked choke. Within a second he tapped out.

As I always do, I helped him up, making sure he was okay, and said, "We're friends again . . ." He did not respond in the moment, or afterward.

Moments later, ring announcer Bruce Buffer called out, "And still the undisputed UFC lightweight champion of the world . . ." I must admit, hearing him say that never gets old.

AFTERWORD

EVEN THOUGH EVERYONE HAS HEARD the expression "what a difference a year makes," I am not sure if a whole book could really explain how much those words apply to me. As I finish this book, I am thinking back a year ago, and how different everything was from what it is today. I was not yet a father, but was soon going to be. I had not yet fought the biggest fight of my life. The media was not yet fixated on my every word regarding the rules of MMA. My new training partners had never heard my name, nor I theirs. I was in my twenties, but now I'm in my thirties. The thought of retirement was on my mind. Nearly everything I have to think about today is very different from just a year ago. Though I live in the same town, work out at the same gym, hang out with many of the same friends, and do a lot of the same things, so much has changed.

It may sound surprising that I view the last year as a positive one. Without question, there were some negative moments, and I may have more critics now than I had a year ago, but that is not important. I've discovered a lot about myself, and I would rather be judged as the person I am today than the person I was before my last few fights.

Fighting has afforded me the opportunity to see and do so much that it almost makes me uneasy when I think about how the pressure of it all had me thinking about giving it up. Now all I think about is moving forward. The prospect of fighting the next three, four, five, or six guys excites me. I am looking forward to the challenge as much as I did when I fought Joey Gilbert. Yet only a year ago I considered never fighting again. In so many ways I have embraced this sport once more, and look at every opportunity as a chance to grow and become not just a better fighter, but a better person.

One of the most unique opportunities I have had the last couple of years was an offer to go to Afghanistan to visit members of the U.S. military. For years I have been involved with the military, helping to train elite combat units in the martial arts. Reagan and I have spent countless hours with soldiers, practicing hand-to-hand combat, submission techniques, and ways to get back on your feet quickly to avoid losing your life. We have received awards which I cherish, and the opportunity to see what it's like to fight in a different sense has been eye-opening, to say the least. I respect every single person who chooses to defend peaceful societies around the world, and I have been deeply honored to support the military's efforts abroad as much as I can. Trust me when I say, there are a lot of skilled fighters protecting you around the world who could be very successful in MMA.

At the same time, though, I do not mind speaking out about my feelings about war, why we fight them, and whether or not one is more justified than another. I do not disapprove of soldiers fighting for their country, but sometimes I question whether those who direct them to fight are acting in the soldiers' best interests. Oddly enough, just a year ago I was less willing to talk about things like this, but after what I have been through the last 365 days, I feel less worried about how I will be received as long as I know I am being honest with myself. Speaking my mind over the last couple of years has really helped me become comfortable with myself, rather than being a person who just says nothing. Whether it was the steroid controversy, the whole greasing episode, battling with Dana and the UFC over a number of things, all of it has made me more comfortable with who I am. I have nothing to hide from anyone. I think if more people took this approach, especially within the sport of MMA, things would be better for everyone.

Like most professional athletes, fighters are afforded a little more time than others when it comes to "growing up." I think the reason is obvious: professional athletes have the luxury of continuing to play games that kids love. Putting aside the raw desire to win, this is probably one of the reasons you see guys like Randy Couture, Chuck Liddell, and Dan Henderson still fighting. Why stop if you don't have to? Who doesn't want to stay young forever? Ironically, though, we are all forced to take on larger responsibilities because we get to play these games. I now own a gym, as do these other fighters. Running a gym, training for fights, and traveling the world are no small tasks, especially when you have a family. But our jobs don't last forever. Most people can do what they do in life for much longer than we can, so I had to start planning ahead. It's not like this sport is paying us the type of money you see elsewhere, and for many fighters a career is not very lucrative. And it can be over in a second.

In many ways, I've grown up along with the UFC. I've come of age watching the organization turn from a small business into a national phenomenon. Part of that coming-of-age has involved realizing that the UFC doesn't always have my best interests at heart. It's been a hard but valuable education. At the end of all my fights, I give thanks to the fans for supporting me, and then I say, "If you want to know more . . . go to BJPenn.com!" My Web site is something I do for myself and for my fans that's outside of the constraints of the UFC. My Web site has become a place where people who really want to know how I feel, who really want to support me, and ultimately the things I support, can come and be a part of my life. This is why I do it. If I do not control the image of who I am, in this day and age, someone else will create that image for me. And for a kid who was always raised to represent his name in the best way possible, it's important to me to have that control.

Even with all of this, though, I am still a kid—at least for the moments when I'm fighting. There was a point when fighting became only a job, which is why I felt myself pushing it away. Now I realize that despite all of these outside factors forcing me to grow up, there inside the cage, whether it's a second, a minute, or a few rounds, I can still be a kid. Likewise, fans of mine get to have fun when they watch me, and if I'm doing my job right, then maybe I can give a few of them the feeling of being a kid too.

As I go forward in my fighting career, my goals are a bit different than they were. While I still want to win, to compete against the best fighters, and test myself in news ways, I also want to have as much fun as possible in doing it. I never dreamed I would make it this far, and I didn't start down this road with the goal of becoming a world champion.

From the time I was a child, I have been fighting in one form or another, not because it was going to make me wealthy, or famous, but because it is something I love. This is why I lace my gloves and get into the ring.

This is why I fight.